For Dustin, Hannah, and John Paul.
You're my people.
I love you bigger than the entire universe.

CONTENTS

moth·er·hood

/ˈməTHərˌho͝od/

noun

the state of being a mother. "she juggles motherhood
with a demanding career"

strip

/strip/

verb

PAST TENSE: **STRIPPED**; PAST PARTICIPLE: **STRIPPED**

remove all coverings from

THE ANXIETY ATTACK

IT WAS AN EARLY MARCH DAY. I don't remember the date exactly, but I honestly don't remember all that much from that time in my life. I was simply surviving, so the details are fuzzy and innocuous. I know that it had been warm enough that the day prior I had taken my 17-month-old little boy to a playground to meet a friend. While so many details are blurry and out of focus for that day, too, I remember exactly what he was wearing and how in love I was in that moment looking at him. He was wearing a sweat suit. It was heather gray and navy with a number patch sewn on the left breast of the zip-up sweat jacket and a little hood on the back. It was in that moment I realized my baby was becoming a toddler. I remember him standing there with his small, yet powerful stature, wearing sunglasses and smiling at me with a mouth not quite yet full of teeth. I felt a flood of joy and gratitude for motherhood. I wasn't meant to be or do anything else but stand beside my beautiful boy on that early spring day in the crisp, fresh air.

Not every day was bad, you see. That's what makes it so hard to navigate. It's a little bit (or a lot) like riding a roller coaster of emotion and confidence. It's a relentless tug of war, convincing yourself one day that you're doing just fine, maybe even succeeding in motherhood, but the next day, you can hardly function. This was that day for me. It hit me like a ton of bricks that I never saw coming.

The next day began like any other. I had a photo shoot and another feeling of unease. This part still confuses me. Photography is my love and passion and continues to be, but I regularly felt massive anxiety when I left my house to go to photo shoots. At this point, all I can conclude is that I was overworked and my body was trying to communicate this. And when you don't listen to what your body is saying, it gets louder.

Anyway, on this day, my body was communicating by beating the shit out of me. In the moments that I felt knocked down, I couldn't quite put my finger on the feeling that sat inside me. It felt like pins and needles, dread, or fear. I had been experiencing that feeling for a few months now, on and off, but it was even heavier on this day. I really don't know what it was, but it made me feel like I wanted to climb out of my own skin.

I remember when I was a young, bright-eyed, new school counselor talking to a friend who had already embarked on the journey of motherhood, and she shared her story of postpartum anxiety. She explained, "I constantly felt like there was a tiger in the room." Back then, I didn't get it. What did that mean? Well, I'm pretty sure this is what it meant: Imagine needing to defend yourself from death at a moment's notice. Just imagine that?! The adrenaline, fear, and feeling like you're walking on eggshells. THIS is what it felt like.

In hindsight, I thank this friend for talking about her postpartum anxiety openly with me. I didn't realize the magnitude of her experience or how many women have had and will have an experience similar to hers—and mine.

On my way to my photography session, I decided to stop at my best friend's house. She had a baby a few weeks earlier. Any time I had photo sessions in my hometown, which is a few towns south of where I live now, I always piggy-backed them with visits to family and friends.

I pulled into my best friend's townhouse neighborhood. The houses all looked the same—new construction townhouses that stood three stories tall, one next to the other, as if they were linking arms. The townhouses had only subtle differences, so subtle I can't even tell you what they were. The road was not yet fully paved, and the sewer caps swelled a bit higher than the rest of the road. Curbs stood taller than the average, and mounds of dirt and land lined the background, patiently waiting for more identical townhomes to stand.

Because the townhouses were so similar, it was hard for me to tell which house I was looking for, even on a day that I was alert and felt good. But that day, I felt completely lost. I stopped at the curb, knowing my best friend's home was one of the two outside my passenger window.

I've been here so many freaking times. Why the hell am I so beat that I have no idea which house I need to walk into? I asked myself. My self-talk was a bitch. *Think, think, think.* I had a little grin as I pictured Winnie the Pooh saying those words. I spotted a Sixers garden flag at the bottom of the steps and thanked God for the clue. My friend's husband is an avid Sixers fan, and his enthusiasm saved me from knocking on the wrong door and spiraling into even more shame and self-judgement.

As I got out of my car, my breathing was labored, I was light-headed and out of breath. It felt like an elephant was sitting on my chest. *Great, so there are tigers and elephants. What next?* I began to focus on my physical symptoms, which naturally made them worse. I felt like I was going to vomit everywhere. *Oh, God. Am I sick?* Stomach ailments had become a phobia at that point in my life. The dreaded stomach bug. *Oh, God. That's what it is. I'm gonna be sick,* I thought. And then my phone rang to signal an incoming text message.

"Ugh. Billy has the stomach bug," said my friend on the other line.

I immediately felt even more nauseous. The friend who I met with yesterday at the playground? Yeah, that was her, and Billy is her son—the son I was in contact with. The words rung in my ears over and over again, and with each ring I felt worse. Maybe I got it, too?

I slowly walked up the stairs to my friend's house as if I were gliding. It was four, maybe five stairs—run-of-the mill cement stairs. I imagine there was a hand rail, too, but you can guess that there's no way I'd remember this detail if I couldn't even remember what house my best friend lived in. If there was a rail, I'm positive my hand was white knuckling that thing. Somehow, I got myself up those stairs without falling or fainting. That was a win. I remember so little at this point. My thoughts were snowballing around my physical symptoms, trying to investigate every single thing. I was desperate to figure out what the heck was happening to me and what I should do. I had to work for Pete's sake! How on earth was I going to show up to a photo shoot and pretend I was fine? I'm strong and I'm stubborn, but this was bigger than me. I was looking for the white flag.

My best friend greeted me as if it were any other day, and so did her puggle, a little guy who was ecstatic to greet any visitor with snorting hellos and jumping around on short little legs. I bent down to pet him, and, for a brief moment, I could breathe. Any moment that I can connect with an animal, I can breathe. After greeting the sweet puggle, I carefully raised myself back up on my shaking legs, and I smiled with my lips but not my eyes. I couldn't. I didn't have the strength. The couch was about two steps away from the front door, thank God, and the bathroom about two steps away from the door in the other direction. I needed to know where the toilet was in case I felt the urge to throw up.

I walked to the L-shaped couch and sat down as my friend sat across from me on the other side. I think she started talking at this point, but I don't know for sure. I do know that I was coming up with quite the plan for when I was going to throw up. My mind was in full-on panic mode, trying to figure out how I would explain *that* to my friend. *She had a brand-new baby in the house. I can't bring these germs into a house with a brand-new baby. Oh, God, what am I doing? And this photo shoot! It's for a six-month-old baby. This is irresponsible. But what if I'm not sick? Maybe I'm overreacting. Overreacting to what, though? WHAT IS GOING ON?!* My mind raced.

I sank further and further into the plush, beige couch with each repeat of "stomach bug" in my head. I remember my friend was talking, but I couldn't make out the words. She sounded eerily similar to Charlie Brown's teacher.

I looked at my friend, and it felt like the face I had on wasn't even my own.

"I don't feel well." Oh, God. I said it out loud.

"Yeah. Um. You kinda look like shit. Are you okay?"

"I don't know. I don't think so."

Instantly, I was declining faster. I felt like I had no blood pumping through me. My heart was racing, and my hands were clammy. Reluctantly, I called my client and told her I was unwell and needed to cancel our session. This part was really hard for me. My client was a friend of my best friend, and she had also become a friend of mine through the years. I felt mixed emotions: Because I knew her, I felt that it was okay to cancel, but at the same time I felt guilty for disappointing her. (While this won't be a part of what I share in this book, it's profound that this beautiful mother, years later, also suffered from anxiety. I have been able to be a coach for her, and we've become even closer friends. It's really quite poetic.)

After a complete flop of a visit with my best friend, I slowly made my way back to my car, promising her I'd come back another day, while secretly wishing I could go home and never leave again. I wondered, *Why though? Why is today so hard?*

Driving home, I sat in a dirty bath of guilt and shame. I felt so out of control, but I didn't even know what I was losing control of! Then my hands went numb. And then my face. I remember smacking my lips together, trying to see if I felt anything, but nothing. It reminded me of the first time I drank whiskey and lost the feeling in my lips, except this time, instead of being paired with giggles, flirtation, and laughter, the numbness was combined with fear of losing my life.

I called my mother-in-law, who was watching my kids. "Hey, I'm on my way back home. I think I need to go to urgent care. I don't feel well."

I was incredibly embarrassed to make this phone call. But my mother-in-law, concerned on the other end of the line, assured me that she'd be able to stay with my kids until I got home.

I arrived at urgent care and immediately second-guessed my decision. *Do I belong here? Is it worth going into a sauna of germs?* I pulled one door open, leading me to another set. I carefully grabbed the handles of the doors in the places that I hoped the fewest amount of people probably touched them. I slowly made my way down the aisle of outdated chairs to the front desk.

She doesn't give a shit, was the first thing that crossed my mind as I looked at the receptionist. *She's probably thinking about her lunch break, and I feel like I'm standing here in front of her fighting for my life.* The contrast between the two different worlds the receptionist and I stood in while looking at each other across the Formica countertop was nearly comical. Yet it created a lump of grief in my throat. I hardly recognized who I was.

I signed in, then I was told to take a seat. The fabric on the disgusting seats reminded me of one of Zack Morris's sweaters from *Saved by the Bell*—straight out of the 90s. Why does it take decades for doctors to update the decor in their offices? I'll never understand this.

I carefully placed my hands in my lap. I clutched my cell phone in hand as a buffer to my thoughts and texted my husband, Dustin, to let him know where I was. I secretly wanted someone to save me—to literally scoop me up and wash away the dread and fear that filled the space of me that used to be unshakable joy and love. But instead I sat alone. Oh, I was so alone—both physically in the waiting room and within the core of my being. I felt a quiet and darkness that is unfathomable and full of intense confusion. For me—a mother, happily married wife, and photographer who is around so many people all of the time—I had never felt so alone in my life. As I sat with my swirling, compulsive thoughts, I realized something. My symptoms were dissipating. My hands weren't as clammy, my heart rate was maybe under 100 beats per minute by now, and I think I felt a pang of hunger. Wasn't I sick? And then I was slapped in the face. Hard. No, not by another waiting patient, but by this realization.

I had just had an anxiety attack.

I laughed. I actually sat in that stiff waiting room chair and laughed. Me! A certified counselor, trained to support others who deal with anxiety, had an anxiety attack and didn't even know it. Holy shit, do they suck. No wonder people think they're dying!

I stayed to see the doctor, figuring it couldn't hurt. The nurse took me back and asked why I was in. I reluctantly and shamefully explained why I *thought* I was there. She took my vitals and handed me the classic line, "The doctor will be right in."

When the doctor walked in, he asked me the same questions. Again, I shamefully reiterated and relived one of the worst experiences of my life that happened approximately 15 minutes prior.

"Do you have kids?" the doctor asked

"Yes. 17 months and almost 3 years old," I answered. *What does this have to do with anything?*

He responded, "How is your relationship with your husband?"

This caught me off-guard. I thought, *Okay, seriously? What the hell is this?* I became defensive, so I replied with a snarky tone, "It's great. He's my favorite person on the planet, and I adore him," which is all true, despite my defensiveness, by the way.

"Do you feel safe in your relationship?" the doctor asked.

I thought, *Okay, listen. First, I am very grateful that these questions are asked because so many women are in abusive relationships and knowing that a doctor is concerned for you and there to help is critically validating.* But intuitively I knew that this wasn't going to lead to a solution to why I just had an anxiety attack, or more importantly, it wasn't going to get to the root, so I gave him my honest answer and said, "I feel very safe in my relationship."

The doctor then wrote a prescription for daily anti-anxiety medication. The nurse walked me to the counter, assuring me that anxiety was super common and then shared all about her college-aged daughter's fight with anxiety and how she has to take medication, too. The nurse was so compassionate, yet it felt belittling.

Is this a joke? This is it? Just a script? No investigation as to why this happened? No questions of what I eat or if I take care of myself? Not even a question of if I drink enough water in a day? I kept thinking, *This isn't ME. Something is WRONG.* I smiled and checked out. After all, I had no idea how to advocate for myself because I had no idea what the hell happened to me. I just wanted to sleep.

After my seven-minute drive home, I pulled up to our house. Dustin had just gotten home from work. He stood out front of our house with my mother-in-law, watching our kids run around, all bundled up in their winter gear while the spring weather continued to tease us.

"So, you're okay?" Dustin asked.

There it was again. That shame. Oh, God, it grew so big. With each passing moment, it grew bigger, weighing on my chest, making it hard to breath. And then there was that lump in my throat. I fought with myself for what felt like several minutes—but was likely only five seconds. I wondered if I should lie about how I was feeling or if I should be completely honest. Honesty is the best policy, right? But I felt like lying would be filled with a little less shame—maybe. I looked up at Dustin with tear-filled eyes. Honesty won. I said, "I think it was an anxiety attack, and the doctor gave me a script." It felt like a weight was lifted off me when I said it out loud, but it was accompanied with earth shattering vulnerability.

"Oh. Are you gonna get the script filled?" Dustin asked. I think he hugged me, too. In fact, I'm positive he did. And like so many times before, even though I don't have a clear memory of it from that day, I'm sure I curled my head into the nook of his chest, balled my fists up under my chin, and quietly let a few tears fall down my face. And just when I let some walls down is likely when I wiped my tears and pushed him away. It was my pattern.

"I don't know." My intense shame was met with his benign ignorance mixed with discomfort. "I guess I'll head in to make dinner."

And so I did. That was it. Aside from my wedding day and having my children, I had just experienced the most profound, life-altering event in my life, and it was summed up with, "I guess I'll head in to make dinner."

The evening was spent like any other, except I was profoundly more exhausted than I was most other nights. Naturally, I ignored my fatigue because I didn't know what to do except to keep doing what I always did: live with overwhelm and exhaustion by keeping busy and ignoring what was really going on.

In hindsight, I'm angry. I'm angry that my husband and mother-in-law didn't know how to respond. I'm angry that they didn't say, "Let's figure this out together. Let's get to the root of what's going on here." I'm angry that they didn't say, "Go take a bath and go to bed. We will take care of everything tonight." I'm angry that they didn't know how to help me.

But I didn't know how to help me either, so how on earth could I have expected them to know?

INTRODUCTION

AFTER MY INITIAL ANXIETY ATTACK, I was determined to fight for my health by figuring out what was happening to me and why. So many women are handed a script, take the medication, and silently move through life in their loneliness and shame—now possibly with some side effects. It's important to note that I won't be discussing medication in this book. I encourage women to determine if medication is necessary (because sometimes it is), and I also encourage you to dig deep to heal the root of your anxiety. While medication might help the symptoms, it doesn't necessarily treat the cause.

Throughout the course of my journey, I found I wasn't the only one who struggled with anxiety. I also learned an incredible amount of valuable tools that pulled me out of my lowest low, and those assets continue to catapult me forward into a beautiful life I never imagined I could have designed for myself. I am writing this book to describe my journey and share my tools.

In the thick of my low, I had a strong desire to be open about my anxiety. No, not "scream it from the rooftop" open, but to share it where I felt safe and could connect with other women. One of the first times I felt safe to share was at a Barre3 class that I had been attending. One day, I was talking to some of the ladies as we slipped our shoes back on before heading back out into the big, scary world. I explained that I had been dealing with some anxiety and that sometimes I couldn't make it to class because of it.

I was shocked. No, I was befuddled when all of the women responded with a variation of, "Me, too."

Wait. Was this a coincidence? As I continued to share, I was met with more "me, too's." While you'd expect me to feel a camaraderie and sense of belonging, instead I felt angry. Not just angry, but livid. How on earth are this many women dealing with anxiety, and so few people are talking about it?! Why is there nowhere to go for support? Why are we all dealing with anxiety by ourselves, in isolated shame? If we as a society talked about this, Dustin and my mother-in-law would have greeted me with acceptance and support because they would have known HOW to do that and because I would have felt comfortable saying, "Oh, hey! Just had an anxiety attack!" If we talked about it, I wouldn't have spent the entire day in my self-imposed darkness, wondering what was wrong with me because I would have been understood. If we had talked about it, I likely would not have ended up in darkness in the first place. I would have understood how to care for myself and not reach the depths of an illness that I didn't even know I had invited myself into.

My fire was lit. This had to change. It's a disservice to women out there that we are not creating a space to talk about this, normalize it, and know that we're not alone in experiencing it.

According to the Anxiety and Depression Association of America, around 264 million people worldwide have an anxiety disorder, and women are nearly twice as likely as men to be diagnosed with an anxiety disorder in their lifetime. In the past year, the prevalence of anxiety disorders was significantly higher for females (23.4 percent) than for males (14.3 percent), with women being almost 10 percent more likely to suffer from anxiety than men.

But why? In the conversations I've had with women both locally and in my online community, I've found a very large percentage of women self-report that their anxiety began after having children. Myself included. That got me thinking.

An article on theconversation.com reported that, "[Anxiety] could be because of differences in brain chemistry and hormone fluctuations. Reproductive events across a woman's life are associated with hormonal changes, which have been linked to anxiety." This makes sense to me. It got me thinking about postpartum anxiety. My anxiety didn't hit until my youngest was 14 months old. (Yup, you did your math right. Three months of having anxiety and not a clue I had until I suffered my anxiety attack) Many of the women I have spoken to describe anxiety as an uninvited guest that shows up and never leaves. How do we define this trend of women experiencing anxiety outside of the threshold of what's considered "postpartum anxiety"? In our current culture, there seems to be a trend: If you have a baby, you are likely to experience anxiety.

Awesome. Glad people omitted this fun fact at my baby shower or when they were teaching me how my baby should latch onto my breast. Seems like an important detail, right?

However! I have good news. The goals of this book are to change the trajectory and storyline around motherhood, anxiety, and overwhelm. For that, I'm excited.

Throughout this book, I hope to share my personal story with you. Think of the nursery rhyme, "First comes love, then comes marriage, then comes baby in a baby carriage." Notice there's a period after the baby? This left the picture of life as a mother up to our imagination. I painted one hell of a gorgeous picture. In that picture, my hair was done, my makeup was on, and I was smiling a lot. And I was a REALLY good mom. I slept. I felt even-keeled. I lost the baby weight right away, and my husband and I were blissfully in love and always on the same page. And my kids? They were also perfect. They never misbehaved, they never got sick, and we spent every day enjoying life together.

I imagine many women have painted this same picture in their minds. Most of us are creative and amazingly talented in the arts, aren't we? It's no wonder we are completely blindsided once reality sets in. The truth is: Motherhood is messy. It's demanding. There's an unbelievable amount of sleep deprivation, germs, challenges, and noise. Mothering takes a level of patience that I don't even think exists. When you're blind-sided by the reality of motherhood, it's because you're unprepared. You're "attacked" from an unexpected position. So how can we be more prepared going into motherhood?

By having honest conversations.

I want to have a very honest conversation with you, stripping away all of the facades, fantasies, and false romanticizations of motherhood. But I also want to strip away the images, memes, and GIFs that show motherhood to be impossible, ugly, and draining. I want you to read the last page of this book and feel *empowered* in motherhood because it can be the most beautiful and mighty role that you could ever add to your life.

This book comes from the depths of my soul to help anxious mamas and also to prepare expectant mamas embarking on the journey of motherhood. I want them to be prepared and to be able to live some of their painted picture as their reality. When we look at our lives in hindsight, everything is crystal clear; we see the entire story. While you can't live your life with hindsight vision, you CAN use foresight to be better prepared for what lies ahead. The best way to get foresight on motherhood is to have an honest conversation with a woman who's been through it—a raw, authentic conversation that strips motherhood from any exterior or anything it hides behind.

If you're a mom-to-be, it's important to me that you hear my story so you know what motherhood anxiety looks like. My story isn't profound, it's not even all that unique.

That's why it's so important to share it with you. When stories or events are unique, it's easy for us to say, "That will never happen to me." When we all know there is a small likelihood that a traumatic life-altering event could happen to us, we feel safe in that small percentage of "not me." Here's the thing with my experience: Motherhood anxiety happens to a lot of women. A lot.

Our society talks a lot about postpartum *depression*—not postpartum *anxiety*. The Cleveland Clinic reports that "Postpartum blues—Better known as the "baby blues . . ." affects between 50 and 75 percent of women after delivery." However, in this book, we won't be talking about the well-known baby blues or postpartum depression. This book is about anxiety, a very different condition than depression. Despite this, I think a lot of what I share here will support you if you experience depression along with anxiety, so keep on reading, Mama.

According to drsarahallen.com, 10 percent of new mothers report having anxiety. (Statistics on this are very hard to find. I find it validating that this isn't researched enough. There is a lot of research on depression in mothers, but very little on anxiety.) I believe the actual number is much, much higher. You know why this is a problem? It directly reflects the lack of normalcy of experiencing anxiety. That little number "10" is a safety net for the woman who doesn't want to admit that she may have it. Can you imagine finding this statistic if you're dealing with anxiety and seeing that only 10 percent of women experience it? Immediately, I would be filled with shame of thinking, *Something must be wrong with me.* There is no way that I would fit into that measly 10 percent. There's no way that I could fit into a box and know that I can be fixed. I must be an outlier, a broken woman who can't handle being a mom. While the alternative of this statistic feels worse, it feels safer because no one wants to fall into that small statistic of "that will never happen to me."

Even though I experienced anxiety after having children, coach women on how to overcome it, and am writing a book on it, I wouldn't have believed I was part of that 10 percent of new moms with anxiety. Why? Because I never took medication for it. I even passed my postpartum depression screenings with flying colors at my OB's office because I was dressed with makeup and a smile. And you know why? Because I wasn't suffering from depression! I was suffering from anxiety, and those are two very different things. Even though I had seen a therapist and my primary physician as a new mom, I wasn't diagnosed with anxiety. This is huge.

So many mothers suffer with debilitating anxiety and don't seek help—or even if they seek help, don't receive the correct diagnosis of anxiety. That's why I feel that sharing this information is so very important. Mothers need to be educated and learn how to support ourselves and live healthy lives. We need to learn the signs of anxiety. I fear that so many people, our friends and family, brush off this disorder by saying, "It's mother's worry. It's normal."

No, this is not normal. This is *not* what parenting should feel like.

In Part One of this book, I will share how sneaky this anxiety can be, how gradual your health can decline without you realizing it, yet how things shift and change in the blink of an eye, and how our lives don't always play out as we had imagined in our heads. If you're already a mama suffering from anxiety, I want you to read my story so that you can see you're not alone. I want you to see yourself in my story. I want you to take comfort in knowing that what you're experiencing is not different. My story is powerful because it could very well be your story, too.

In Part Two of this book, I'm going to share the gold: the tools I used to climb out of an ugly, dark, low point in my life, using my Layered Growth Method. It takes work, consistency, action, communication, resiliency, experimentation, and time. And it's worth it.

I climbed out of my low, and four years after my first anxiety attack, I am at a place in my life I never expected to be. I'm living my best life.

My mission is to help you realize you can live your best life, too. I am not different than you. I wasn't dealt different cards. I AM you, and you can be me, too—living *your* best life.

My biggest takeaway from my motherhood experience thus far is that so many mothers—with burp cloths on their shoulders, crying babies in their arms, and bags under their eyes—desperately miss the women we used to be. We miss the carefree woman who had no worries in the world and had all of her ducks in a row. We question how we got to this space, which in turn can lead us to resent motherhood. Certainly, this isn't true for every mother, but I bet that many of us have reached this moment at some point or another. If we're not careful, it can lead us down a spiraling path of no return.

Today, I love the woman I used to be, but boy do I love the woman I have become. It's taken work for me to find her, truly see her, and appreciate her. Motherhood is a gift, and I'm eternally grateful to be on this journey. Our power as mothers lies in our ability to embrace who we are today while also looking forward to the women we want to become.

How do you want to FEEL as a mother? What's the first word that comes to mind? Write that here. Hang onto that word. We'll get to it later. For now, let's start at the beginning.

The way I want to feel as a mother is _____.

PART ONE

In Hindsight

hind·sight

/ˈhīn(d)ˌsīt/

noun

understanding of a situation or event
only after it has happened or developed.

FIRST COMES LOVE

College Grad and Self-Proclaimed Single Lady

WHEN I GRADUATED FROM COLLEGE IN 2005, I never, ever expected to be a woman at home with her beautiful children, lying on a floor, trying to get enough air into her lungs so that she didn't pass out. But it happened. To me. The woman who used to have it all together.

My story is not unusual. It's actually quite common, but that's why it's so important. Anxiety is not a tragedy that happens to outliers. It's a normalcy that happens to a significant amount of people. It happens quite gradually. I want to illustrate the gradual decline so that you can catch it before you completely fall. I want you to see yourself in me and see how susceptible you are to the same stuff. But even more, I want you to see how capable you are at not becoming a victim to it and, even better, to create the life of your dreams.

For four years, I lived it up at West Virginia University. After a rocky start my freshmen year, my pride and stubbornness persevered, and I learned to come out of my shell. I put my empathic qualities and highly sensitive person characteristics aside and fully contributed to the college that was recognized as the number-one party school. In hindsight, my binge drinking probably helped numb the overwhelming sensitivity I typically experience as an empath and highly sensitive person and allowed me to feel comfortable in jam-packed clubs and house parties.

Despite being a party girl in college, I never let go of my Type A personality. I'm the kind of person who labels everything, has everything in order, and would never miss a class. Ever. Even when I was hung over, my rear end sat in all of those classes and took every single test. I loved school, and I graduated cum laude with a big fat smile on my face.

I smiled right up until I realized now I had to be a grown up.

The transition from high school, to college, to back home as a graduate is disorienting. In four short years, you go from being a kid in high school, to complete collegiate freedom, to likely living back at home yet work-wise being spit out into the "real world." After college, I felt like I had been whirled in a blender but was then poured out and asked to stand upright without fumbling a single step.

After college graduation, I moved back into my parents' home, like many graduates do. I found myself struggling over letting go of being a college student and being a grown woman earning a salary. Slowly, but surely, over about six months, I ditched my club shirts and jean skirts for blouses and slacks as I proudly found myself in an entry level job as a case manager.

Also at this time, I declared myself finished with dating—dating non-committal boys in particular. I was done playing the non-committal games. Done. Finished. I swear I nearly announced it to the world by standing outside, arms open, face to the sky, proclaiming, "I'm done! No more dating!" I felt free and alive! A weight had been lifted from my beautiful 22-year-old body that was now dressed in important work clothes fresh off the rack from Old Navy.

One day in 2006, as I stood in my metaphorical freedom stance, arms open, face up to the cold January sky, my neighbor from across the street walked over to say hi. It was fun being the older "kid" in the neighborhood. I was in this funny in-between role in life. When I was a kid in the early 1990s, my family was one of the OG families that moved into our new construction, cookie-cutter Bucks County, Pennsylvania, neighborhood. As other houses turned over and younger families moved in, my family remained. I was no longer the little kid "running the streets," but instead I was the go-to babysitter, although I still got to hold onto my "kid" status because I lived with my parents. I got to know the new kids in the neighborhood as their babysitter. At the same time, I got to create a relationship with all of their parents, too. I loved that new role in my life.

That day, my neighbor came over with his Northeast Philly energy asking how things were going. (If you're from NE Philly, you know exactly what I'm talking about. If not, imagine someone downing a couple energy drinks and then talking a mile a minute with a lot of laughing, quick wit, and a few f-bombs). I filled him in on the accident that totaled my sea-foam green Toyota Tercel lovingly named Millie that had left me driving my step-dad's GMC pickup truck. (Side note: If you want to feel bad-ass as a woman, drive a truck. It's the most liberating combination of feeling strong and sexy at the same time.)

After I told my neighbor about my car accident, he unapologetically asked me if I was dating anyone. I responded with a crooked, cynical smile as I wondered if he had heard my proclamation to freedom a few minutes earlier.

"No way! I'm DONE," I said. "Finished. I just dumped this last guy two days ago, and I need a break from the BS." I was serious. Done.

If you know the personality type of my neighbor, his response was certainly no surprise. "That's great! Cause I work with this kid who has an ass like this and shoulders like this, and I really wanna give him your number." His hand gestures along with his description left everything to my imagination.

My response was a blank face and no words, so my neighbor filled the silence with more words of his own, and to be honest, I don't even remember what else he said. No wait, I lie. I asked how old his friend was. When he told me he was only 20 years old, I was like, no way. Nope! Not dating a kid who can't have a drink with me. Clearly I had my priorities straight.

As my neighbor continued to share how adamant he was about giving this kid my number, I finally obliged. What would it hurt to tell this neighbor to go ahead and give the kid my number? It'd make him feel happy and get him off my back, and then I'd never have to speak to the 20-year-old friend again.

"Fine!" I replied, completely succumbing to the pressure.

THE CALL + THE BLIND DATE

I screened the call. Hey, listen, I always screen my calls. I'm an introvert and an empath. I need to be in the right mindspace to take your call. I will not apologize for this boundary. Don't like it? Don't call me.

I listened to his voicemail. I smiled because he sounded so professional and nervous.

"Hi, Erin. This is Dustin Miller. I got your number from [your neighbor] and wanted to give you a call. You can give me a call back at [my number]. Look forward to talking with you."

Awwww how cute! Little did I know, I'd save that voicemail and listen to it over and over until the day it accidentally, tragically got erased a few years later. I opened my brand-new silver flip phone, punched in his number, and held my breath when he answered.

It was the kind of moment that takes your breath away. Making that call was a seemingly simple decision; I had no clue that it was about to change the entire trajectory of my life. I sat at my childhood desk, in front of my college laptop, and talked to this stranger, a young man, two years my junior. I didn't realize then that I was speaking to my soulmate—the man who would be the father of my children.

Tears roll down my face as I type this. In hindsight, that night on the phone with Dustin was one of the most magical moments of my life. But I think I knew it in the moment, too. The conversation was effortless; it led right into deciding to go out on a date that Friday night. As soon as we decided to meet, I had to know how tall he was. Yup, again, my priorities were on point back then. I'm not a short woman and, back when my priorities were about vanity instead of emotions, I wasn't thrilled with the idea of possibly being taller than my date if I was wearing heels. Fortunately, Dustin's 6-foot stature just made my cut-off to my 5'8" long-legged body. I could wear heels. Pro. He's too young for a beer. Con.

As that Friday rolled around, I felt a complicated mix of excitement and irritation. I honestly didn't want to waste my time on another date. Although our conversation flowed, we got along great, and he seemed really excited, I was just over guys. My proclamation a week earlier wasn't fair-weathered. I really was tired of the energetic output required to date these silly guys! I needed to get my own head together and figure out how I wanted to show up in life as a grownup. My next step in doing that was buying a brand-new car.

After my sweet Millie was totaled, I had to figure out what to do next. With a grownup job, it was time to do it on my own. On that Friday, date night, my stepdad and I were heading to the car dealership after work to buy a car. I was really freaking excited. I think it's important to note that I had never bought a car in my life and had no idea how long it was going to take. Dustin was going to meet me at my neighbor's house that evening, and then he was going to take me to dinner from there. I don't remember the exact time, but let's say it was 6 pm. As I sat at the car dealership, 35 minutes away from my house, and we crept into the 5 o'clock hour and weren't even close to being finished, I knew I wasn't going to make the date. New to texting (yes, we are that old), I opened my phone and painstakingly used the numbers to punch in every single letter to type out a long-winded text, telling Dustin I was going to be late, but that I was still coming. Phew! Done. I closed my phone with a click, threw it back in my purse, and continued the exciting milestone into adulthood of buying my fancy new car.

I painfully watched the clock as time ticked away. I was officially missing my date, but dammit, I was getting a new car with heated leather seats! I was nailing this single, independent adult woman thing.

I didn't hear back from Dustin, so I figured he either didn't want to wait for me or, well, I didn't know what he might be thinking. I was so fixated on buying that new car that I hadn't really thought about the date. I just planned to address it after I got home. As I pulled into the driveway at close to 8 pm, I saw an unfamiliar car at my neighbor's curb. I was shocked to see that it looked like Dustin was still waiting at my neighbor's house. Ah, I still have to do this!

I parked my new shining beauty, lovingly named Audrey, in the driveway and looked at her adoringly before slowly making my way to my neighbor's house. I felt a mix of emotions. I was flattered that Dustin had waited for me, not even knowing if I was going to show up. Turns out, he never got my text! I felt ashamed that I disrespected him by being late. I felt embarrassed that my neighbors sat with my date for two hours without knowing if I was going to show up. The excitement of my new car was replaced by nerves about my date.

My neighbor let me in, excited to see I finally showed up. He walked me through the front foyer, then through the open kitchen, and finally into the family room that was a later addition to the house. It had high vaulted ceilings, surrounded by windows and a plush, shaggy rug that I always enjoyed sinking my feet into. All of my experience in this back room was playing with their kids, taking in all of their toys and the TV. I instantly remembered the show I watched with them the last time I was in there. It took me a minute to shake out the distractions of the environment and to look Dustin in the face. He immediately stood and extended his hand to introduce himself. I was taken aback by his presence, like a blow to my chest. He didn't seem 20. He was different.

Through our entire date, Dustin continued to strike me with his presence. Because of his line of work, he had been up for more than

24 hours, he was fighting a cold, and he still waited for me. He made dinner reservations at an amazing restaurant 45 minutes from my house that we missed. Instead, we went to a local chain and had a so-so meal, but it didn't seem to faze him. He was just happy to take me out on a date. *He was different.*

After our dinner, Dustin drove me back home in his tripped out, shiny red Jeep Grand Cherokee. I found fate lying in the 10 CDs that were held in his visor. The four albums that I had rotating on repeat were Joss Stone: *Mind Body & Soul*, John Legend: *Get Lifted*, Kanye West: *Late Registration*, and Common: *Be*. That eclectic mix of music defined that time in my life and was so specific to me, yet here I was next to a person who had the same eclectic mix on the same rotation. It immediately made me put my guard up. How was this happening? *I'm fooling myself. I'm believing something that's not true.* The latest round of men I had dated unequivocally proved that there was no point. They were all playing games, and I was better off single. This blind date of mine had to fall into that category, too. *Don't be fooled, Erin. Don't be fooled!* I thought as we sat in my driveway.

And then he didn't kiss me. *He was different.*

We spoke the next night, and the next, and the next. The conversation never waned. The more I spoke to him, the more I wanted to get to know him, and I even began missing him. He lived nearly an hour away from me; we liked to say 45 minutes because it felt easier and more feasible. So, for our second date, just a few days later, we met at a coffee shop at a middle point between our houses. Little did I know that for the next two years, almost every single Wednesday, we'd meet at that coffee shop for a mid-week date. When I saw him on this second date, I tried to find anything I could to throw myself off the course of falling in love. My guard was still up. It felt too good to be true to have this connection and chemistry with someone so unassuming and who showed up promptly after I decided I was finished dating. But here he stood.

It was on this date, this second date approximately one week after our first phone call, that I sat across from Dustin and immediately knew I was going to marry him. And it scared the ever-loving shit out of me. We sat at a little, round, wooden table, hardly big enough for two people and their coffees, pushed up against the bathroom wall. It was one of those seats that no matter how close in you pulled your chair, you felt like you were in the aisle or in someone's way. I remember Dustin sat confidently with his left elbow slung over the back of his chair and his forearm and hand hanging forward. His right hand held his paper coffee cup on the table, and as he talked, his left wrist bobbed up and down so his hand could assist in telling his story. It was a moment I'll never forget. I don't remember what he talked about. It was like all of the noise shut off. I could see his mouth moving, but I couldn't hear the words, and then I saw a flash of him wearing a wedding ring on his story-telling left hand. It was in that moment that I knew. I knew this man was going to be my husband.

As suddenly as the moment came, it was just as quickly dismissed. I told my intuition to take a hike. Who needs it, anyway? (Ha! We'll delve deep into this later!) I sat there scared, but also strangely excited. I wanted to protect myself and my heart. I didn't want to be played with and to fall hard only to have him change his mind about me. I didn't want to play the dismissive, casual dating games with which I had become so familiar. But I couldn't help myself. This was my guy. At 22 years old, I knew I found my guy, but I needed to be proven I was right, and so the dating commenced.

After our coffee, Dustin walked me out to our cars, my shiny new Mazda 3 next to his beloved Jeep. My coyness and nervousness confirmed how much I liked him as I stood terrified for him to lean in for a kiss. And then he did. His perfect 6 feet leaned down to meet my 5'8" and planted the sweetest, softest kiss on my lips. A single peck and then he stood back up. *He was different.* He wasn't overzealous or sex-crazed. He was reserved, respectful, and mature at his ripe old age of 20. I hardly knew what to do with it, so instead, I fell. I just let myself fall.

We continued dating at the same speed and frequency for the next few months. In late March, only two months after meeting, we sat at that coffee shop, and he said, "We're going to New York City on Saturday." We live only a couple hours from NYC, so it's an easy day trip, but it had been forever since I had been there. And I was shocked. Never in my young life had I been with a guy who took so much initiative and care in a relationship. Time and time again over a few short weeks, Dustin showed me his thoughtfulness and desire to truly get to know me and respect me. With each moment, my trust grew a little bit more and my cautious walls slowly came down, one brick at a time.

That trip to New York will forever be one of my favorite day trips. I wore a coral long-sleeved top matched with one of my favorite jean skirts. (Okay, I didn't get RID of my jean skirts, but I saved them for the weekends.) I matched that with my fake UGGs and little Dooney & Bourke purse. It was a warm, early spring day, the calendar having just turned over into April. Dustin and I made our way throughout the entire city. I was madly in love with him. My chest felt like it was going to explode with joy that I found the person who I had dreamt of my entire life.

Many little girls dream of their wedding day, but I had only ever dreamt of the guy. I had always envisioned a man who was honest, brave, compassionate, thoughtful, sensitive, strong, and courageous. A man who respected me and made me feel empowered in who I was. A man I felt madly in love with, yet still felt strong on my own. *This* was my fairytale, and he was right in front of me. It was on this day that I knew he felt the same way.

In Central Park, horses and carriages were lined up awaiting passengers. Dustin led me to one of them and helped me into the horse-drawn carriage. Seriously? I found a guy who takes me to New York City on a whim and puts me in a horse-drawn carriage? Pro. As we rode through Central Park and kissed in the carriage under a shared blanket, my heart was in my throat. Dustin held my face, our noses still touching as we pulled apart ever so slightly, our eyes still closed. I heard him say, "I love you." It was immediately met with the biggest smile as I replied with my full heart, "I love you, too."

Our romance felt like a whirlwind as we swept each other off our feet. We spent every Wednesday evening and weekend together. Before that first date, we both carried on in a life that didn't include each other. After that date, our lives completely changed. Our courtship wasn't an easy transition for me, my family, or my friends. I went from being single and available with my attention and time to being madly in love, regularly out of town, and being much less available for my other friends and family. Unquestionably, I wanted to spend every moment I could with Dustin, but I think the change was really hard for my friends and even harder for my parents. I don't think it was easy for my Catholic parents to see me leaving every Friday after work to go bunk with my boyfriend at his parents' house, whom they hardly knew. My friends, who I used to spend every Friday happy hour with, all of a sudden had a missing friend. My absence wasn't met with, "I'm so happy for you!" It was met with pettiness, exclusion, gossip, and pushing me out.

I grieved as I lost my friends, as I began to shift into a different person—a person who chose spending a night in with her boyfriend over going out to clubs. I was even shifting where I was physically, now spending my free time an hour north of where I lived, where I grew up, and where all of my friends were. I was in muddy waters of trying to find my own independence as an adult woman and still be present in all my childhood relationships.

Despite the grief and messiness in the transition, this was easily one of the happiest parts of my life. I had a secure job as an Intellectual Disabilities Coordinator at a mental health agency where I adored my co-workers. I had been accepted into a graduate program at Holy Family University to earn a master's degree in counseling psychology, and I was madly in love with the man I wanted to marry. Things were really, really good. I lived each day on a cloud filled with joy, excitement, and happiness. Every morning, I woke up excited.

While dating our future spouse, we have our whole life ahead of us, don't we? We are constantly daydreaming about the next big thing, and everything that waits ahead. Everything feels new and exciting. It's such a special, magical time in life, and we assume this feeling of excitement for new things will continue into all of the other stages of our life. Spoiler alert: It doesn't. Just a heads-up.

MOVING IN

About 11 months after our meeting, my 21-year-old boyfriend was in the place in life to buy a house together. Pro. He found a Realtor, and we started spending our weekends house hunting. I found myself in the middle of another messy transition. Not even a year earlier, I was fresh out of college, swearing off guys, and living with my parents. And here I stood with this young man who I knew was "it," looking for a house, and terrified to let people know we were taking this step. I wanted so badly to live a life that would make my family and friends proud. I sought their approval of my decisions. I was terrified that my family and friends, who weren't enthusiastic about my dating Dustin, would give me the same lackadaisical, passively unsupportive response to the idea of us moving in together. Talk about contrasting emotions.

The stakes were even higher because I knew moving in with Dustin would be my permanent move away from home. It's not like I was moving out of state, but I was moving out of the area, and I needed to give up that part of my identity. The real estate market in my hometown couldn't compete with what we could buy for our money just a few towns north of Bucks County.

One day in the winter of 2007, Dustin and I walked into a beautiful farmhouse, close to where Dustin grew up. Everything about it was perfect—the size, condition, location, and even detached garage. We knew we had to act fast to get the house, so we put in a full-price offer right away. And it was accepted.

Holy shit, this is actually happening, I thought to myself. I knew I couldn't put it off any longer. I had to tell my parents.

I was a child who lived to please my parents. We had a lot of stress growing up in a blended family household, between custody and finances. I am one of four children. While all of us are seriously awesome people (I'm not biased or anything), growing up, two of us required more emotional attention and needs. I refused to take attention away from my siblings who needed it or put more stress on my parents. So, the result? I tried to be the perfect kid—do the chores, make the right choices, get good grades, do what I was told, take initiative, you name it. When you grow up that way, that parent-pleasing switch doesn't ever get turned off. Cue therapy.

So, at 23 years old, I was terrified to tell my parents of my future plans—for no reason other than the fact that I was afraid it wasn't what they expected of me. Even today, at 36 years old, I can't say that I knew what they expected of me. Do we *ever*? We project our parents' expectations onto ourselves. I wish so badly that I had understood that at a much younger age. I could have navigated my life with more confidence and certainty—without the constant cloud of worry of others' judgements of me.

I let my parents know I needed to speak to them. We sat in their notoriously dark living room with the new, stiff blue carpet that replaced the old blue carpet from the original 1992 construction. I sat on one of the maroon wingback chairs that sat catty-corner flanking the bay window adorned by my mother's lace doilies and tchotchkes. My stepdad sat in the other. He lifted one leg to rest his ankle over his other knee and looked at me, waiting. My mom sat on the floral loveseat across from the seat I was sitting in, with a square glass-top coffee table separating us. The silence and the darkness were killing me. Those moments of anticipation before doing something scary are easily some of the hardest for me to work through, but that was exactly the point. The only way out of it was *through* it. So, naturally, I started to ball my eyes out.

Well, crap, this was not going as I expected, but I couldn't hold in all of the feelings anymore! The tears flew out of my eyeballs, as if from a five year old who just let go of her balloon. My mom and stepdad exchanged looks, then brought their eyes back to me, waiting. I knew I had to jump, so I did.

"Dustin and I are planning to move in together. We want to buy a house, and we found one that we put an offer in on, and it was accepted," I said. It fell out of my mouth in one breath.

They quietly looked at me as I shared the news, and they responded by asking me if it was what I really wanted to do. Oh, gosh. That question was like a dagger to my heart. It validated every single fear that they didn't approve of my relationship and what I was choosing to do with my life. It killed every part of the child left inside of me. I was 23 years old, graduated cum laude with a dual minor, secured a good job right out of college, was dating a *good man* who respected me, and we were buying a house at 23 and 21 years old. Yet, somehow, I still felt like I wasn't doing the right thing.

"Of course, it's what I want to do! Why would you ask that?" I cried.

"Well, you seem to be having a big emotional response. If you really wanted to do this, wouldn't you be excited to tell us and not crying?" my mom asked.

"I'm crying because I'm terrified to tell you that we want to live together and that you won't support the decision. THAT is why I'm crying," I replied back as the truth fell out of my uncensored mouth.

I don't remember the rest of the conversation because I sat in a state of calming relief. I felt relieved that I opened up to my parents. Even though I didn't feel fully supported, I was incredibly confident in my decision and choice to move forward in my relationship. I was unshakeable in the choices I was making in my life—despite the part of me that was grieving the loss of friendships and lack of support from the people who mattered most to me. Although the confidence that I felt in that moment was fleeting, a seed was planted. I spent the next decade looking for validation in everything I did. But the seed that had been planted that day would eventually grow, lead me into the roots of my healing, and essentially save my life. I was relieved that our conversation ended with my mom and stepdad both showing interest and excitement as I shared the pictures and stats on the house that Dustin and I were about to buy.

Then a few days later, we backed out of the sale. I thank that house. It was one of those amazing things in life that we expect to go a certain way only to learn that it had a different purpose. That house prompted a very timely conversation with my parents, and even with myself, and that in turn made the rest of our house-hunting journey feel lighter and more aligned.

In February, shortly after backing out of the first house, Dustin and I walked into a home that was preserved in its 1950s glory, boasting textured green wall-to-wall carpets, tiny broken-up rooms, and heavy wood trim. It was perfect. There was character in this beautiful Craftsman home, and we knew we could make it ours— after we made a few cosmetic updates.

The "few cosmetic updates" took much longer than I anticipated. Thirteen months later, still living in our parents' homes, I called it. It was time. Finished or not, we *had* to move into the darn house. That house was the first of many renovations-requiring houses we'd end up owning over the years. Dustin and I have done so many renovations that our friends and family joke we should have our own HGTV show, but I digress.

Our move-in day was in April 2008. I felt similar butterflies as I had felt when I'd move back to college each year. I could easily have become addicted to the heady feeling of anticipation, thinking about how I'd decorate and set up the house to make it our home. Perhaps my addiction to that feeling is why we've moved three times since our first house. I was excited to move. It was a huge milestone and transition in my young adult life. I was leaving the nest for good, and I was moving in with my best friend.

At this point, Dustin and I had been together for two amazing years. For much of those two years, I spent almost every single weekend up at his parents' house, soaking up as much of our two days a week together as we could. Our weekends were filled with sleeping in, eating out, shopping, camping, and renovating. We were two kids making salaries—with no mortgage or utility payments. Gosh, I wish we had understood back then how lucky we were! Like clockwork, on Sundays after watching the popular primetime show *Desperate Housewives*, I would tearfully get into my car, hugging him in the driveway, feeling an ache in my chest that I had to separate from him for another few days. I would always listen to The Fray's self-titled album on the way home. To this day, when I listen to that album, I feel the grief build in my chest and up into my throat.

The realization that we were taking the next step in our relationship was an indescribable excitement. My life was moving along so beautifully. I couldn't have written out my own love story any better. The idea of coming home to Dustin every evening, eating dinner with him every night, and then having a sleepover was something I could hardly wrap my head around.

On move-in day in April, we closed the door behind our friends and family who had helped us move in. And then there were three— Dustin, me, and Riley. Yes, we got a dog before we moved in together, and he was one of the biggest loves of our lives.

2

THEN COMES MARRIAGE

The Proposal

AS OUR LOVE STORY PROGRESSED into the fall of 2008, I fell more and more in love with this man of mine, now at the ripe old age of 23. We had settled into the most beautiful life and routine together. We added a blue-point Siamese cat, Grayson, to the family, who is still with us today. I continued to work in my case management position while taking graduate courses for my master's degree in counseling psychology. Dustin was excelling in his career as a lineman.

Dustin woke religiously every morning at 5 am to walk the dog a few miles before leaving for work at 6:15. We'd share a kiss with our coffee breath and smiles, and he'd head into work as I got myself together for my workday ahead. On days that I didn't have a late class, I'd come home and work out. Then we'd eat dinner together, watch a show, and be in bed by 9 pm. I read novels I loved, got great sleep, and woke each day excited to do the routine all over again. On Fridays, we'd drive down to the local watering hole for happy hour.

It was a ritual that we still talk about regularly and remember fondly. We'd get in there early enough that it wasn't jam-packed with the local university students. Dustin would always order a new craft beer, way before craft beers were cool, and I would have two Sam Adams Cherry Wheat beers with a side of broccoli bites. I lived for Fridays, to eat the fried goodness of those bites, washed down with my light, sweet beer, and chat with my man about our weekend plans ahead.

On Saturdays, I cleaned our house top to bottom—religiously and literally. I'd start in the master bedroom with dusting, making my way through the entire house, followed by vacuuming the hardwood floors and area rugs in each room upstairs. I'd then scrub our upstairs bathroom, and I mean *scrub*. I was not a person who wiped things down once a week. I cleaned every bit of that house—every single week. I'd make my way downstairs, cleaning our second full bath, scrubbing the kitchen, and wrapping things up with a wet mopping of the hardwoods both upstairs and down. I cleaned every part of that 2,000-square-foot house on Saturdays. For the rest of the weekend, according to my app that brings up past social media memories, I spent a lot of time studying, writing papers, reading any books I felt like reading, watching TV, and having one more glass of wine.

I share this to paint a picture of our days. Dustin and I were happy, aligned, full of energy, and excited about life. I thrived in our daily and weekly routines. I felt myself eager for each part of the day and week. Certainly, we had our fair share of bad days, stressful times, illnesses, and other typical human experiences, but overall, we were both genuinely happy.

That time in my life didn't require hindsight to know how much I loved it and how blessed I felt. Our life was stunning and felt perfect. I was doing everything I wanted to do and pursuing my career goals with flying colors. All I wanted at that point was to get married. I was more than ready.

And then I reached a point of impatience with Dustin. I wasn't mad or frustrated, but I was ready to *officially* spend the rest of my life with him. We had been creeping toward being together for three years. I had known I wanted to marry him on our second date, so, at this point, I was more than ready. I would hold out my left hand with my fingers spread and look at my naked ring finger, imagining what it would look like to have an engagement ring. Up until that point, I hadn't been someone to daydream about my wedding. I was now. I began picturing all of the details of the day and planning it in my head. Now all I needed was for Dustin to ask.

One late October weekend, Saturday October 25th to be exact, we planned a camping weekend away in Jim Thorpe, a beautiful, historic town in Pennsylvania. One of my graduate classes was held on Saturday mornings, and I had an exam that Saturday. I bunked at Dustin's brother's place, who lived about four miles from my university, so I could get more sleep, wake up, and have a shorter drive to my exam. After my exam, I drove solo to the campground to meet Dustin.

I had a gut feeling it was the weekend he'd propose. I held out my left hand more than normal the week leading up to this trip. I had convinced myself my finger would have a ring on it by Monday.

It was a gorgeous fall weekend—full of crisp autumn air, stunning foliage, pumpkin carving, ghost tours, and fun. With each passing moment, I waited for Dustin to take a knee, but it didn't happen. On Sunday, we packed up our things, planning on a bike ride and lunch before we left town. I was agitated and disappointed—not so much in Dustin or the fact that he hadn't proposed, but in myself for allowing the anticipation of it to seep into my weekend and prevent me from fully enjoying our time together. I knew that we were meant to be together, and I knew that Dustin felt the same way. But each passing day, week, and month without a proposal eroded my confidence that he really did feel the same way.

As we geared up for our bike ride, I was grumpy. I will absolutely pretend that I put it behind me and came to my senses. Nope, I was disappointed, grumpy, and ready to go home. Also, I hated "riding bike." I put this in quotes because this is how the Pennsylvania Dutch people refer to riding a bike. I remember when I first started dating Dustin, he used this phrase, and to this day, I don't understand it. We began to move through the switchback trails of Mauch Chunk Lake. It had rained most of the weekend. So, it required a tremendous effort to move through the muddy trails whilst having mud slung up my back from the thick mountain bike tires. Dustin was adamant about climbing the mountain, and I was annoyed. I didn't think Dustin recognized the conditions of the trail or the fact that I was miserable.

After a bit, Dustin finally conceded to my grumbling, whining, and complaining. Even *he* could only take so much of it, and we moved to a flatter trail around the lake, which confused me. I was done. I could feel my sugar level dropping, my legs were numb and tired, and I just wanted to go home. Dustin was being weird, and I hadn't picked up on it in the moment, which is unusual for me, but I was so caught up in the disappointment of my marital status and the fact that I hated biking so much. Dustin was determined to continue on with biking, and my stubbornness met his. I actually got off of my bike, dropped it to the ground, and said, "I'm done." I pulled a protein bar out of my under-seat bag, stared off at the lake, and begrudgingly ate my bland protein bar that filled zero of the current voids in my life, most of which revolved around the fact that I wasn't engaged yet.

Then, Dustin insisted that I at least move my crabby butt over to the middle of the lake because the foliage looked so much more beautiful. As he asked this, I was terribly confused because I could look at the center of the lake right where I was, so naturally I said no. He persisted. "Hey, come over here and look at this thing," he said, pointing at some type of drain for the lake. I thought, *Ohmygosh, what the heck is his deal?* I made my way over to look at the drain, finding absolutely no interest in it and continuing to be terribly confused as to why he was so insistent on me moving a few feet to the center of the lake. As I stood in my confusion, he commented that he heard his phone ring. At this point, he was acting so weird, I didn't even consider the fact that *I* didn't hear his phone ring. As I stood there, looking off at the beautiful lake, allowing the protein bar to settle my hanger, I realized I didn't hear him talking on the phone. I turned around to see him on one knee.

Holy crap. It's actually happening, I thought. Suddenly, the entire day began to make sense to me. He wanted to get to the top of the mountain for the perfect proposal spot and, when this failed, he counted on the lake to be our backdrop. My mood shifted immediately. My perspective changed from him being ignorant to my mood to realizing that he was leading the whole day with romance and finding the courage to ask me the biggest question of his life. I realized that the phone he pretended to hear was a sneaky decoy for him to get the ring out of his bag—the ring that sat in that seat bag the entire weekend.

The moment that I had been dreaming about since our second date was actually happening. *This man is on one knee and wants me to be his wife. This is the man I'm going to commit my life to, have children with, and dance with for the rest of my life.* So, naturally I responded with, "Are you kidding?" My question was followed by tears and falling to my knees in his embrace. Despite how eager and impatient I was for this to actually happen, it was one of the most surreal moments I had ever experienced. My daydream met reality.

Our story continued to be written beautifully. With each milestone of our relationship, I couldn't wait for the next.

THE WEDDING

As a wedding photographer, I love that, 10 years later, I continue to feel the magic of the wedding planning process. I also feel a bit sad for my photo client couples because I think society does a disservice to the human experience in not having an honest discussion of what comes after the wedding. The couples I photograph are so beautiful, in love, bright-eyed, and excited for their future. I was the same way.

While everyone's story is different, and we don't all anticipate the same milestones in the same order, most of us do anticipate these milestones with excitement. Each new milestone is often felt with

even more happiness and more excitement. This was my story:
A blind date, followed by an amazing courtship, having the perfect
dog and cat, buying a house, and then the proposal. It was all unfold-
ing exactly as it was "supposed" to. And like everything that came
before this, the next beautiful piece of our story was our wedding.

Planning our wedding was a truly amazing process. We matched
up our church's availability with our venue's schedule to give us a
wedding date of November 20, 2009, a short 13 months after our
engagement when we solidified this date, it was incredibly surreal. I
hadn't spent time imagining the details of my wedding. It had been
an amorphous dream with no boundaries or concrete idea of what it
would look or feel like. But now, with a date, it was becoming real.
My heart was filled with gratitude and excitement.

For the next year, I diligently planned our wedding with joy and
enthusiasm. I paid attention to the details, as I always did as an
accomplished type A personality. Planning was a beautiful bonding
experience with my mom, my mother-in-law, and my best friend—
sharing e-mails, choosing dresses, running errands, designing
invitations, and picking out songs, readings, and decor. Pulling it all
together made it one of my favorite years of my life. As our wedding
approached and the nitty gritty details were all coming together, they
no longer mattered to me. I just wanted to marry this man of mine
and start my life with him. I didn't care how the napkins were folded!

On November 20, 2009, I woke up with butterflies in my belly
matched with a grounding in my feet. I was ready. The day was good,
everything from getting our hair done, to getting dressed, and finally
pulling up to the church. I had imagined walking down that very
aisle for 13 months. Every Sunday at Mass, I sat in church and tears

would well up in my eyes as I imagined walking down the aisle toward Dustin. Funny enough, I was so nervous, I hardly even remember walking down the aisle at all, but I do remember the moment I stood next to Dustin, ready to be wed. And we were to be married not by just anyone, but by my childhood priest. I had dreamt of this priest marrying me to my husband for as long as I can remember. So, I guess I lied about not dreaming at all of my wedding day. That was the only piece I dreamt about. I was struck with so much emotion as I stood at that alter with Monsignor Ricci officiating my wedding to a man I could have only created in my dreams. Dreams really do come true.

Following our ceremony, we had an amazing party at our venue, a local ski resort where Dustin and I and many of our guests stayed the night. Waking up, I was still on cloud nine. We got to see so many of our guests again at our private breakfast—a buffet of the most delicious mounds of the best hangover food anyone could dream, including buttery eggs, greasy bacon, and piles of donuts and baked goods. We all sat and mingled with our fuzzy tongues, churning bellies, smiles, and high vibes. Post-weddings are of some of the best hangovers, aren't they?

Our guests began to leave slowly, one by one. I stood there, holding Dustin's hand, and I felt the whirlwind of the past year drop me carelessly into reality. I couldn't quite comprehend the feeling. I had such peace, joy, and gratitude moving through my body, but there was an unfamiliar, unexpected sadness in my heart. Dustin and I decided to walk around the resort, which was gorgeously set at the bottom of a mountain lined with snowless ski trails and trees losing their last bit of leaves. It was Saturday, November 21st, and I remember walking with Dustin around the property, thinking about how still everything felt. It wasn't just the grounds that felt still, nor the trees or the wind, but the energy. Everything over the past year had been so busy and noisy, filled with an energy of excitement and anticipation, but overnight it dissipated into a small, still, quiet feeling. On that walk, I started to harness the emotion I had been feeling that I couldn't quite understand.

Dustin and I continued to walk around the back of the resort, and I looked up into the distance to see a bride. I immediately smiled in excitement for her. But, just as quickly as I felt the smile come to my face, I felt it fade, replaced by a frown and slightly furrowed brows. I was completely unprepared for the unintentional shift in my emotions. It was a blow to my very core.

For my entire life, *my entire life*, I dreamt of finding a dream man. I found him and then spent the past three years envisioning our next step together, which was getting married. And for the past 13 months, I had spent *every single day* imagining our wedding day. For, essentially, 26 years of my life, I lived with a daydream that came closer and closer to a reality. But what I never considered was the reality of it being over. The sadness.

That's the part that no one told me about—the part where in the matter of one sleep, you go from being a bride to being a wife. You go from the excitement of daydreaming of your wedding day, that culmination of your love and beginning of your life together, to waking up and no longer having that daydream. It's no longer a part of you. That loss brought a grief that I never knew existed. I know I may sound dramatic in sharing this, but this moment hurt me. It felt incredibly confusing to feel this grief combined with just as much eagerness to move into married life together. Maybe that's why no one talks about it? I wonder if people are afraid that sharing the grief after your wedding day would be judged and viewed as taking away or interfering with a woman's excitement to be a wife. But in my experience, these two emotions aren't mutually exclusive. They sat next to each other in their own isolated existence.

Everyone tells you about the exciting parts of dating and planning a wedding. All of that panned out better than I could have ever imagined. Yet there I stood, one day after my wedding, feeling betrayed. I don't know by whom, maybe by society as a whole? I knew that this feeling wasn't unique to me, and I was positive that other married women have felt this way, too. It made me mad. Why didn't anyone tell me about this? People took the time to advise me on which undergarments are best to wear with my dress. Why didn't someone share with me that the day after your wedding is going to feel a little sad, and that's okay?

Little did I know this was a foreshadowing for the entire next phase of my life. It turns out my response to it was a foreshadowing as well. I observed what I was feeling, felt confused by it, and put it away. I tucked the grief and sadness under the rug, like society teaches us to do, and I chose to focus on the positive. And it really was positive. To say that I was happy to be married to Dustin and start my life with him was a huge understatement. Living the next chapter of our life was one that I could hardly wait to do, and I thanked God every day for the past 26 years of my life and the opportunities that were ahead. I was and am forever grateful to live life next to my husband.

3

THEN COMES BABY

Trying

DUSTIN AND I MARRIED AT 26 AND 24 years old. We both
were excited to start a family, but not right away. I wanted to be sure
that I finished my master's degree first, secured a full-time job, and
could earn some vacation time to use for my maternity leave. The
first hit as a mother is being forced to go back to work too early
because we have such abysmal maternity and paternity leave options,
but I'll avoid that tangent.

In our first two years of marriage, Dustin and I went on a lot of
adventures with our camper in tow, continued our beautiful daily
routine that gave me life, and then we began our next transition as a
couple. In May 2011, I walked to receive my master's degree in school
counseling psychology, graduating magna cum laude, and felt a
well-deserved sense of pride and accomplishment. I beamed in that
huge auditorium, hip to hip with my beautiful girlfriends, a degree in
one hand and several bouquets of flowers in the other. I love looking

back at my graduation pictures, seeing a smile so big it was nearly unattractive.

That summer, we also found a new house. While our first home was one that laid a beautiful foundation for our life and opened the doors to our renovation hobby, we knew we'd want to move to a different school district for our future children and find a house that suited us even better. After another lengthy house hunt, we walked into a house on Wood Lane. Walking through that house, I knew deep down in the pit of my stomach it was our house. I felt a sense of urgency—an urgency to secure this house to make it our home. To this day, even though we've moved a few more times since then, the house on Wood Lane holds a special place in my heart. It stood lonely with its grey siding and faded blue shudders. It had a colonial floor plan that looked like so many others, covered in beautiful hardwood flooring and fresh carpet. The house had been foreclosed, and it sat, patiently waiting for its new family. The moment I saw it, I knew it was ours.

Dustin and I stood in the backyard, its perimeter adorned with blooming raspberry bushes and singing birds. We are never quick to make decisions, especially with houses, but I said, "This is our house. We can't risk losing it. I want to put in an offer right now." So, we did.

After a speedy and stunning six-week kitchen remodel, we moved in August 2011, a few weeks before I started my new position as an elementary school counselor at a school that I simply adored. It was a few miles north of my parents' house where I grew up. I daydreamed about having a child and meeting my mom in my work parking lot to pass off the baby for the day while I worked at the job I loved. Everything was falling perfectly in place. In this time, I began to feel truly ready to have a baby.

By December, my desire to have a baby was no longer just a little feeling. It had grown into a huge desire, one that I couldn't ignore because it was on my mind regularly. I noticed babies everywhere in stores, saw my friends have babies, and listened to the teachers' stories of their own babies. I became envious. I craved having a baby of my own so badly.

One day over lunch break, I visited a friend while she was on leave with her new daughter. I felt a bit of jealousy seeing her at home in the middle of the day with her baby. So many people dream of what they'll be when they grow up, and, while I have many aspirations, the one thing I always wanted to be was a mom—specifically a stay-at-home mom. Seeing moms grocery shop with their babies as I ran into the store for a salad on my short lunch break, imagining them sitting on the floor watching *Sesame Street* with their babies, and picturing them waking up and drinking coffee as their babies played with their toys—the whole idea of it was such a romanticized fantasy for me that I wanted to live. As I sat with my friend, I asked her questions to feed my fantasy, and maybe even paint me a little more green with envy. I asked what her day looked like at home. She described her slow mornings, taking a walk with the stroller around the neighborhood, eating lunch, and playing, I practically resented having to work. However, after landing my dream job at a school that I adored, I was at a point in my life that I no longer wanted to be a stay-at-home mom permanently. I simply fantasized about the 12 weeks I'd get to stay home with my baby on my maternity leave.

My baby fever became more than I could handle. Yet with each passing day, I couldn't find the nerve to talk to Dustin about how I was feeling. I constantly found reasons to convince myself, "not yet"— until one day I had had an epiphany. I usually loved sleeping in and running errands by myself. But one day, I reached the point of wanting a baby *more* than I wanted to sleep in or do errands solo. In that moment, I realized it was time.

A part of me was hoping Dustin would bring it up first, but I don't know that men ever feel the craving to become a parent the way women do, though I could certainly be wrong. I decided that I'd have to face the music and find the courage to have the conversation that lead us into the next transition together and take the next beautiful step in our beautiful life.

One Friday night, we decided to go out for dinner like we often did, because we didn't need a sitter or to plan ahead. As we sat at the table, I was obviously distracted in my thoughts and nervousness to talk about having a baby. Over Italian appetizers at our high-top table in the middle of a busy bar, I looked at my husband and said, "I think I'm ready to have kids." Or it was at least something to that effect. I held my breath, waiting for him to say that he wasn't and that he wanted to wait a little longer. While I'm only two years older, in that moment I was a 28-year-old woman with 30 right around the corner, talking to my husband who was still in his mid-twenties. He smiled at me and said, "I think I am, too." I realized that I had been holding my breath when my audible exhale filled the space around us. I smiled and dropped my shoulders as the weight had been lifted. Dustin's rational mind helped ground me as he brought up timing. We decided to wait until summer to start trying. That would allow me to use my maternity leave for the last part of the school year and extend it right into my summer break, offering me a leave that could be twice as long. Good thinking on my husband's part!

For a few months, I counted down to when we'd get to start

trying for a baby. Trying for a baby was the most exciting, exhausting, and emotional experience I've ever been through. Anyone who has gone through this process knows the "two week wait" window, the time between ovulation and your period, otherwise known as the time you can frantically start peeing on tests that can give you a response six full days before a missed period.

In May, when we started trying, I became fixated on baby forums, checking them daily and reading about everyone's journey to get pregnant. I quickly became familiar with all of the acronyms and lingo associated with trying to get pregnant. It was a world I never knew existed, and I quickly became obsessed with it.

When I got my period in May, I was so disappointed. It was a no go. While it was only one month, it prompted me to do a ridiculous amount of research on how long it typically takes a couple to conceive, learning that the average length was six months. Six months? On average! I feel selfish saying it out loud, but I wasn't sure that I could emotionally handle it taking more than six months to get pregnant. I feel selfish sharing this because I know so many women who have struggled with fertility, and their story and perspective would be that they'd do anything to get pregnant within six months. What I can say is that both of these are our truths and, while I live in mine, I still honor, see, and hold space for people who have a different reality.

A POSITIVE TEST

In June, six days before my missed period, I took a test. At this point, I was buying them in bulk, and I had developed a hobby out of failing these tests. On this day in June, I took another test, and I waited the crucial three minutes, staring at it the whole time anyway because who has the self-discipline to not look at it constantly. I impatiently stared at the test sitting on the bathroom windowsill, and I was shocked to see two faint pink lines. There were two lines—the control line and the "yes, you are pregnant" line! My mind couldn't comprehend what I was looking at, but I knew that a line was a line. You can't be a little bit pregnant. You are or you aren't. The pregnancy line was so faint, and I hadn't technically missed my period, so I stayed cautiously optimistic. In my optimism, I decided to wait for my missed period and a stronger pregnancy line on my test to confirm a true pregnancy before sharing the exciting news with Dustin.

The next day, a Friday, I took another test, and got an even fainter line, but still a line. I had such mixed feelings about what I was experiencing. I felt hope and excitement but also confusion and fear.

On that same day, we left for a camping trip, and Sunday was Father's Day. I knew that by Sunday I'd have missed my period, and a test should have a strong line. I was hopeful and praying for a pregnancy, because what better time to tell Dustin that he was going to be a dad than on Father's Day? That whole weekend, I drank white grape juice out of my wine glass while I moved around the campground, visiting all of our camping friends, many of whom were my coworkers, holding in a huge secret—the secret that we wanted to start a family and that by the start of next school year, I'd hopefully be pregnant. As the weekend progressed, I walked around with a smile on my face and hope in my heart. All the while, I nursed my insanely sore breasts and pretended to drink wine.

On Sunday morning, as I nervously took another pregnancy test, I imagined what it would be like to get a positive test and to share that with Dustin. My eyes filled with tears when I looked down to find only one line. I couldn't find any hint of a second pink line, and I looked *hard*. I didn't understand. There was a line there a few days ago. Why wasn't there one now?

My hope and excitement were immediately replaced with a grief that I couldn't fully understand. I anticipated that we'd decide to have a baby and get pregnant right away—our story would continue to be written perfectly. But the past two months didn't align with my dream. I again felt betrayed and confused.

Later that week, on day 35 of my cycle, I got my period. It was heavy and clotted for one day before it ended. When I got it, I laid in my bed in the fetal position, and my entire body was wracked by sobs. Dustin knelt by my side, assuring me that we would get pregnant, that it was only two months. He was so compassionate and encouraging. I laid there explaining to him that I knew that. I couldn't even fully comprehend the grief that was pouring out of me in that moment, but it was, and so I let it.

About a year later, I fully realized what had happened. I had a chemical pregnancy, which is a really shitty way to say that I had suffered a miscarriage. A chemical pregnancy is when you get a positive pregnancy test, but it "doesn't stick," and you end up getting your period. My "period" was about 10 days late. But it wasn't technically a late period; it was a loss. I had gotten pregnant, but it wasn't a viable pregnancy. The pregnancy turned into a loss, and that's why my perceived period was only one day long.

While, at the time, I hadn't understood what happened, that

experience completely exasperated me. In hindsight, I realized that, while my brain didn't understand what had happened, my body absolutely did. My fixation with the pregnancy forums, counting the days of my cycle, and obsessively taking pregnancy tests was destroying me from the inside out. I had to let go of the process and surrender to what our destiny was going to be. At the end of that June, I made the decision to let go and enjoy the rest of the summer.

DON'T HAVE KIDS

Making the decision to surrender my pregnancy journey to God and fate was the most freeing thing I could have done for myself. I had been white-knuckling the entire time, and it was depleting all of my energy and ability to truly enjoy life as it was.

That summer, I had been nannying for a local family—a successful mother and father who chose to adopt a little later in life. The mom and I talked a lot about life and kids. One day, we were chatting, and she flat-out said to me, "Don't have kids." I stood there shocked because I was holding the secret that we were, in fact, trying to have children. I responded with a nervous laugh, to which she replied, "Seriously. It's so hard. I adore these kids so much and love them with all of my heart, but my life will never be what it was. We would come home from work, pour a glass of wine, eat dinner, talk about our day, and have a lovely evening before going to bed and getting good sleep."

I was shocked by her honesty. If I had any type of verbal reply at this point, I have no idea what it was. I don't know that I had ever heard anyone be so honest about parenthood. She continued, "It's so physically, emotionally, and mentally draining raising other people.

They have their own emotions and feelings. Every day requires more than I usually have. Don't have kids."

I left that day feeling really confused. I could tell how honest her statements were, which scared me. It created a cognitive dissonance I wasn't prepared for. I lived my life dreaming of nothing else but to be a mom. How could I possibly consider not being one? I couldn't, and I wouldn't. I decided that while there was truth to that woman's feelings, they didn't have to be *my* truth. On my short drive back home, I opened my windows, turned up the radio, and relished in the warmth and freedom of the summer air, continuing my surrender to allow God to bless us with a baby when it was our turn.

HAPPY BIRTHDAY

The end of July approached far too quickly, as it always does. My days were filled with swimming in the pool, camping, sweating, enjoying open windows, listening to good music, planting flowers, walking with our dog, shooting photography, and loving the freedom of a summer off with no schoolwork for the first time in what felt like forever. Naturally, I had to fill that space with something productive. I started taking online photography courses to learn how to shoot a DSLR (digital single-lens reflex camera) also known as a "big girl camera." This is a camera that has interchangeable lenses, and you can manually adjust the settings for exposure. I had put my photography passion off for so long that my knowledge of shooting was all film and dark rooms. With the freedom of extra time, it was fun to have the space to take on this new hobby.

A few days after my mid-week birthday, Dustin and I went to one of our favorite restaurants. It's a small restaurant that we personally think is the best-kept secret in our area—a renovated old farm house with creaky, wide-planked wood floors, low ceilings, and candlelight. The food is beautifully presented, the menu is curated by a brilliant chef, and the food melts in your mouth, making your taste buds dance. It's always a treat to eat there.

As Dustin and I sat at a table against a front window, we waited for our food and chatted. I had gotten a whiff of someone's seafood dish and was taken aback by how pungent the smell was. "Wow! That is one potent smelling crab cake, huh?" I asked Dustin.

He looked at me confused. "What are you talking about?" he asked.

Men. How could he not smell that? I thought. *Anyway.*

We enjoyed our beautiful dinner as I celebrated another rotation around the sun, welcoming 29. Twenty-nine. Wow. That was really close to 30. And there I was, still not a mom. "Can I have another glass of wine please? Thanks," I said to the waiter.

Another sweltering summer week flew by with Dustin's birthday approaching that Thursday, the day we'd be leaving for our next camping trip to the shore. On Wednesday, I realized my cycle had been very long. Since giving up on white knuckling, I hadn't been paying much attention to my cycle. So, when I realized how long it had been, I fell apart. Something was wrong. My cycle the month before was nearly 35 days, and it was happening again. My mind spiraled. *Of course. Right when we decide we want to have children, this happens. I'm broken. I'm unable to give us a family because something's wrong.* I called my OB/GYN office to schedule an appointment.

"Hi. I'm on my second month of having an abnormally long cycle.

My husband and I are hoping to get pregnant, and I think something is wrong, so I'd like to come in to get some testing and figure out what's going on," I unapologetically shared with the nurse on the other line.

She responded with silence, followed by, "Sweetie, have you taken a pregnancy test?"

Irritated, I replied, "Um, no."

While she didn't laugh, I could hear her smile as she replied, "Okay. Why don't you go do that, and then give us a call back."

I hung up, feeling defeated. I just wanted to have a baby. I had daydreamed about this baby, like my husband, for my entire life, and I felt like I had come to a roadblock that I never saw a sign for.

That evening, Dustin was working late. I sat on the couch watching TV and wallowing in my sorrows. I began to spiral in my sadness, convincing myself that Dustin and I were about to start a long journey ahead with a difficult time getting pregnant. I ended my wallowing by dragging my butt to bed and ending the day.

The next morning, I rose and quickly began to get myself together for my nannying gig, excited that when I got home we'd be getting ready to leave for our weekend away. I knew a weekend away with my guy would help. As I was quickly putting on my face, I remembered that I should take a pregnancy test so the doctor's office would see me. To speed things along, I peed in a disposable cup, opened one of my several tests, stuck it in the cup, put the cap back on, and threw it on the counter. I was amazed at my ability to detach from this whole process after having an incredibly difficult start to it all. As I scurried around, I glanced at the test and saw two pink lines—not a faded almost-pink line, but two *very* pink lines. I froze. I felt pins and needles move throughout my whole body as I stared at the test sitting on the counter. I was in a complete state of shock.

Wait. That says I'm pregnant. I'm pregnant? I thought as I began to process that my body was actually holding and growing a baby. A rush of dots connected as I remembered how I had been falling asleep a lot during the day, my ability to smell could have beaten a trained dog (*that's* why Dustin couldn't smell those crab cakes!), I was uncomfortably bloated, and my breasts were insanely sore. It all started to make sense. Shaking, I quickly opened two other tests, both digital because seeing the words "YES" and "PREGNANT" were absolutely going to validate what I just saw on the other test. Sure enough, a few minutes later, both tests confirmed that I was in fact pregnant—and also running late for work.

How on earth was I going to concentrate today? How was I going to tell Dustin? My brain spun in circles the entire day as I balanced caring for someone else's children while processing that I would soon be having a baby of my own. As I watched the kids I nannied that day, I couldn't wait to get home and begin my even newer hobby of suffocating my brain by researching everything I could about pregnancy.

As soon as I got home, I wrapped the positive tests and a cigar in some leftover wrapping paper. I was too excited to make it look pretty and besides, have you ever tried wrapping pregnancy tests? It's absolutely easy. It was Dustin's birthday, so the timing couldn't have been any more perfect. We were back on track with our perfect story. Dustin arrived home from work and quickly began packing the camper so we could get on the road. When he packs for a trip away, he becomes so focused and fast that it's almost impossible to interfere with his speed and mission to get us out of the house in record time. I somehow needed to get him to stop moving and sit down to open his birthday gift. Interrupting his packing marathon wasn't an easy task, but I somehow convinced him. He slowly opened it, staring at the tests and taking a moment to process what he was looking at. These few seconds felt like an eternity to me as I realized I was witnessing the moment that Dustin shifted from just being Dustin to realizing he was going to be a dad. As soon as it registered, we embraced in the biggest hug and maybe shed some tears. We were going to be parents.

BACK TO WORK

As I entered into a new school year, I naively imagined another happy one—one that felt aligned, exciting, and fulfilling as I moved through my pregnancy with the plan to leave in March to have my beautiful baby. In August, my co-workers and I greeted one another with fresh summer glows, rested bodies, and an energy that we were convinced would carry us through the school year, but inevitably, as all educators know, it usually diminished by November—just in time for the holiday breaks. My smile hid my secret, safely growing under my looser clothes as friends likely assumed my new body was accounted for by summer indulgences. While my secret was safe, on many days I thought I'd give myself up by a face that was surely green all day every day. Almost every smell made me want to vomit, and I picked at my sad breakfast, usually just bread, from the time I left my house at 7 am all the way through to 11 am. Eating was unbelievably difficult. That was the hardest part for me to hide, but I somehow did it successfully.

As October rolled around and I safely made it to 12 weeks, I let my principal know that I was expecting—with shaking kneecaps, sweaty palms, and breaking voice. He greeted my news with surprise and congratulations while I breathed in a sigh of relief and excitement. That same week, I began to share the news with my staff and students. The students read the announcements over the loud speaker each morning. One morning, a beautiful fifth grade student excitedly shared, "Mrs. Miller is having a baby."

The staff members who hadn't yet known came running into my office with the biggest hugs and smiles. When you're pregnant, it's in this moment that it becomes real. People around you know that you're going to become a mother; those who are already mothers offer their unasked, but genuine advice and stories. It's incredibly comforting and validating to hear how amazing motherhood is. (No one shares the lows of motherhood with moms-to-be because that would be cruel to do to an expectant mother, wouldn't it?) I was showered with advice, but only positive-slanted advice, such as keep a notebook by the rocking chair so you can write moments down that you don't want to forget, swaddle your baby to help her sleep, sleep when the baby sleeps, and eat extra oatmeal and flax to bring your milk supply up.

No one told me how to eat to balance my hormones, that sleeping when the baby sleeps isn't only a good idea but vital for your mental health, that there are days that you feel trapped, isolated, and alone, and that it's really important to connect with other women to curb this feeling, or to schedule date nights with your husband, not for a break, but because in the blink of an eye you can drift apart without realizing it and then it's harder to get your closeness back. No one gave me this advice. I had to figure it out for myself. I know so many other mothers did, too.

Regardless, the moment in pregnancy when you no longer have to keep a secret, and everyone around you can celebrate you and the life inside you is one of the best.

The school year continued with high vibes and happy times. I felt connected to my work, staff, and students. I truly couldn't have dreamt of better dynamics, and it's something that my principal, secretary, and I would mention all the time. Our connection and relationship made us a dream team and a once-in-a lifetime bond. We always recognized and appreciated this with a lot of gratitude— which is why we were blindsided when it was ripped apart.

What happened at this point in my career was a nail in a coffin I didn't even know I was lying in. Perhaps it was a blessing in disguise because the coffin was the career I would soon realize I didn't want. I was completely unprepared for the grief that I was about to experience.

Of the three elementary schools in our district, we lost one principal and one school counselor due to moves and resignations. Instead of hiring new people for the positions, they moved my principal to another school. Instead of giving us a replacement principal, they rotated the other principals to our school. And they made me counselor to an additional school. Some days, we didn't have a principal at all, and guess who was the acting principal? Me. Seven months pregnant, the elementary school counselor to two schools, serving two student bodies, and supporting two schools' staff. And now also playing principal some days. My career world completely imploded on itself.

For the first time in my life, I felt a stress that I didn't know existed. It was the kind of stress that your parents dismissed by saying, "It's a grown-up problem," and you didn't fully understand what that actually meant. Well, now I understood. I felt a tug of war and fear that the high levels of stress were going to hurt my beautiful daughter growing inside of me. At the end of the day, I got into my car and broke down crying. At the dinner table with my husband I fell into tears and anger, not even wanting to eat. I felt so angry. I felt taken advantage of and unseen. I felt anger for my students, who I feared weren't receiving the support they deserved. I felt out of alignment. I felt trapped, like I was in a cage, and all I could focus on was getting out.

At one of my OB appointments in late February, I asked my doctor if there was any way to get a note to allow me to start my leave early due to the stress, pleading with him that the stress was unsafe for my baby. Going into that appointment, I had convinced myself that he would write this note, and it was my ticket out. I'd get my "get out of work free" card. After I pled my case to the doctor, he told me that the type of stress I was dealing with was normal, that the body could handle it and so could my baby. You know that feeling when you have a weight lifted? That feeling like when I told my principal I was expecting; how I had breathed in that sigh of relief and literally felt lighter? Well, in the moment talking with my doctor and hearing him say this, I felt the complete opposite. It was my last ditch effort to get out of a toxic situation, and it didn't work. I was absolutely heartbroken.

After that appointment, I mustered up the strength to continue forward. I had about a month left of work before I could take 12 blissful weeks off to be home with my beautiful baby. At the end of one long day as acting principal, a student had missed her bus. I was required to stay until she got picked up. I wanted to fall into a puddle. I knew this child well; while I cared for her, in the back of my mind,

I felt a nagging guilt at the fact that I didn't want to wait with her. It honestly didn't even have anything to do with her; I was just exhausted and had my mind set on leaving on time that day. I was angry that I was being put into a position by my district to be taking on these roles—almost carelessly and without compensation.

As I waited with the second grader, her explosive behaviors began to manifest. I wasn't alone; another teacher was with me, one I'm so grateful stayed and supported me in my exhaustion and overwhelm. In this child's behavioral outburst (which was often sudden and explosive), she began to physically attack me, and one of her flying limbs hit my stomach—my swelling, eight-month pregnant stomach. My child. She kicked my unborn child. And that was my last straw. I wasn't upset with this little girl. Her soul needed healing, and I was truly grateful to be an adult in her life who cared about her and could be there for her. And of course it was upsetting that she ended up hitting me, but my final straw was in the fact that I felt alone and unsupported in my position. I was increasingly concerned that I would find myself in a situation that could be much worse.

We'll talk about boundaries later, but in this moment I chose my boundary. I had no idea I was doing it, but this was where I had to draw a line between what I was okay with doing and what I was not okay with doing. In hindsight, I realize this moment would solidify the career choice I'd make a few months later. But at the time, I knew only that I had to start my maternity leave as soon as possible.

In sharing this part of my life, I think it's really important to make a note that I loved that district, and I support the decisions that were made—even though it felt really hard for me and a lot of others, too. Public education is under a lot of pressure to figure out how to make things work with the funding (or lack thereof) that they receive. Schools work as a team to make decisions that are in the best interests of the district and the children—and that are approved by the school board. It's a massive juggling act. I don't hold the district accountable for anything I went through. It's "how the cookie crumbled." I believe that every single administrator and staff person showed up (and continue to) as their best and in the best way they knew how, including me. I knew in that particular stretch of my time as a counselor, the best way for me to show up was to start my maternity leave early. No one was responsible for my physical, mental, and emotional well-being but me.

The stress continued for a few more weeks, accompanied by physiological responses that validated that I was fully in fight-or-flight mode. I had my first ocular migraine at the end of my pregnancy, which freaked everyone out. To reduce my stress level, I had to request my maternity leave to start a week earlier. I didn't want to take a week away from my time with my daughter, but I had to. I had to catch my breath and prepare for her arrival. I refused to bring her into the world while I was in a state of such high stress.

When the decision was made, I felt relief. The weight had lifted, and I could breathe again. My stress was replaced with anticipation. I could once again focus 100 percent on how my life was going to change any day. I prepped by grocery shopping, cleaning, and preparing freezer meals for after my baby arrived. Multiple times a day, I stood in her nursery and lost a sense of time as I imagined what she would look and smell like and who she would grow up to be. I stared at every part of her perfectly decorated room—the white crib and floral sheets, the light gray walls and framed word art, the closet full of the tiniest clothes hanging in size order, the changing table impeccably organized and ready for her with a basket full of diapers and diaper cream, and the pink-covered changing pad. I sat in the gilder, looking out the window, rocking and holding my belly in full surrender as I tried to grasp the realization that I had no control over when she'd show up. By that Friday morning, three days before she was due, she was ready to join us. And it happened in a way I never could have predicted.

FIRST MOM FAIL: DELIVERY

My entire life I took care of children. Truly. I started babysitting at age 11, and I didn't stop babysitting until the summer I became pregnant with my daughter at age 29. Becoming a mother didn't scare me because I knew how to take care of babies and kids. I had dealt with the puke and snot and refusal to sleep, the bedtime games and the not-eating games, defiant behavior and talking back. My 18 years of watching kids gave me a beautiful head start to motherhood—well, kind of.

The two things I didn't have experience with were delivering and nursing a baby. Of the two, the one that I was terrified to do was breastfeeding, because it was so foreign to me. I was caught up in my head about it, and I lacked confidence in my body's ability to do it. Yet, I was confident and convinced I could deliver my baby. I am a strong woman, and I had no concern or worry about getting that kid out. I was up for the challenge.

My mom is easily motherhood's number one fan. At least once a year, she retold my siblings and me details of our labor and delivery stories. She'd share the details of how she had to hold me in on the drive to the hospital, how she pushed, how fast I came out, and even the noises I made as I nursed. I felt like I had been mentally prepping my entire life to have a successful natural childbirth. My mom delivered three babies naturally—with her small and mighty body. I had always shown similar physical strength as her, so I believed I'd have the same experience: that I'd be able to forgo the epidural, buckle down, and surprise the doctors at my success in delivery even as a first-time mom. I was actually excited for the experience.

I'm going to share my daughter's delivery story because I think it's powerful in teaching the importance of surrender, that not everything goes as planned. It's an example of how even when we experience joy in life, there is sometimes also grief, and that's okay. My daughter's birth story is one of my proudest stories, and one that I am eternally grateful to have. It completely changed who I am as a woman, how I view my body, and how I choose to raise my daughter.

Our children's birth stories define who we are in the most remarkably profound way. However, I feel that our society does a "not so great" job at preparing women for childbirth and everything that comes after. I believe this happens for two reasons: First, I believe that many people are hesitant to share anything negative about motherhood due to fear of being judged and assumed to not love motherhood. Second, I believe that people are scared to share the frightening parts of motherhood because they don't want to evoke fear in an expectant mother. What kind of help is that?

My disclaimer to my story and motherhood in general is that it's the most extraordinary experience you'll ever have as a woman. Every moment that feels bad, scary, unexpected, or exhausting is likely offset by another moment that is beautiful, deep, awe-inspiring, and full of the biggest love. Just as we may not be prepared for some of the hard stuff, we often aren't prepared for how much we are going to feel our hearts expand, either. I share this part of my journey with love and honesty in hopes to support you to experience motherhood the way I've learned how—without fear, resentment, or anger, but instead with joy, surrender, an open heart, and understanding. I believe the best way to get to this point is through honesty. Here is how my journey started.

On Thursday, March 21, 2013, I went to bed with lower back pain. In my gut, I knew labor was starting, and I knew going to sleep would put it off. Keeping the possibility of labor to myself, I knew that it was important to sleep and rest. If my body was truly ready, it'd wake me up. So, with that, I allowed myself to sleep and happily found that I slept through the night. Dustin had gone off to work in the morning while I rested. When I got up, I felt the contractions beginning again. I was familiar with the feeling because I had Braxton Hicks contractions every day of my pregnancy from 12 weeks on. But these were a little different. A pain in my lower back would come and then it would go, and then come and then go. It was sharp and uncomfortable, and I was confused that I felt the pain in my back. My belly would tighten, similar to Braxton Hicks, but it wouldn't hurt the way my back did.

Even though labor felt a little different than I thought it would, I knew very well what it was, so I took a shower and got ready for the day. My mother had taught me that labor and delivery are hard, physical work.

"You're going to sweat and feel dirty and you usually can't shower for some time after that, so be sure you shower every day leading up to delivery so that you feel as clean as you can when it happens," she told me.

I knew it was D day, so I sure as heck took a nice long shower. The nerves really started to settle in. I moved around the house after my shower without focus, unsure of what to do, so I just kinda kept my mind busy. I took pictures. I cleaned a little more. I made sure my hospital bag was packed. As the pain continued to increase, I called my mom, crying.

"Mom?" I said her name as if I was a little girl scared to go to the first day of school. I continued, "I think I'm in labor."

"Ohmygod! You are?" she answered and then spattered a million more questions, including asking if I needed her to come up to my house.

"No, no! It's okay. I don't need you to come up," I responded, even though I sort of wanted her to. But I knew Dustin's workday would be done soon, and he'd be on his way home. My mom gave me her love and support through the phone as she guided me in being sure to labor as much as I could at home and to not stop moving. You'd probably think that I'd call my husband to let him know, too, but I didn't. He is a lineman and works on high voltage lines. I didn't need him to be home with me in that moment and didn't want him to know I was in labor for fear that he'd be distracted working on lines. It was too dangerous to risk.

"You need to walk," she said. "The contractions will slow down if you stop moving."

I walked up and down our little cul-de-sac all bundled up in the raw March air. My walking was slow and painful, and I feared what my neighbors would think if they saw me out their windows. I continued to breathe and work through my labor alone, which now thinking back feels sad. I could have easily had people around me, supporting me and guiding me, but instead I chose to be alone in my pride to prove that I could do this.

At 3:30 pm, the time Dustin left work, I called him because I knew that he planned to go to someone's house to check out a renovation job, but I knew that I couldn't wait to go to the hospital until he made that stop. I finally shared with him that I was in full-blown labor. By the time he made it home after 4 pm, I was beginning to need to breathe through my contractions. They were getting harder and closer together, so we made our way to the hospital.

In triage, I was measured at 4 centimeters, which felt incredibly discouraging, considering how much my labor hurt. The contractions continued to be in my back, and with each one the pain was worse and worse, like a knife twisting. With each contraction, my faith that I could do this naturally began to diminish—along with my pride and self-confidence. I walked the halls of the hospital, still not admitted, until the nurses finally flagged me, convinced that I was in active labor and was there to have a baby. The first test of being a mother, before actually being a mother, is knowing instinctively that you are in labor and needing to prove it to a bunch of people who don't believe you. The foreshadowing of motherhood here is not lost on me.

When Dustin and I were admitted into a room, our parents and my brother came to the hospital and sat in the waiting room, anxious, I'm sure. In my room, my confidence diminished more. I looked anywhere for support through my contractions. The only way poor Dustin could support me was to sit next to me and hold my hand. In my tears of pain, my angel of a nurse became the person who got me through everything. I don't remember her name, and, at this point, I don't even remember her face, but I cry as I type this because she gave me the strength I needed to get through a very scary labor and delivery. As I approached 7 centimeters in excruciating pain, I knew I'd never get through the last 3 centimeters and delivery without an epidural. I needed something to take the edge off. The pain that I was feeling was not normal, and I later found out why.

As I finally succumbed to my pain, I resignedly accepted the epidural because I was told it was my last chance to get one before I was too far along for one to work at all. I held a pillow in my lap, tightly against my chest with my chin pressed into it. I rounded my back and held the nurse's hands in front of me. Dustin sat next to me. The anesthesiologist did his thing, and it seemed like it took forever. I learned later that it took three tries to get the needle into my back. Three. The amount of physical and mental strength it took me to keep my body still through those contractions was one of the most demanding things I've ever felt in my life. After the epidural was administered, I vulnerably opened my legs for the nurse to insert a catheter—another thing I knew nothing about and had no time to process.

I continued to feel the contractions, but now I had a bit of relief from the pain. I finally got a bit settled into my luxurious hospital bed. It felt like the chaos settled even though I had gone through serious trauma to get there. From the hospital bed, I looked at the newborn baby incubator and found the gratitude and peace I needed in that moment, knowing my baby would be lying there in just a couple hours.

The doctor came in to check on me, giving me a thumbs up and the news that I'd likely have baby on March 22nd. Looking at the clock, I saw it was just about 10 pm. The realization that I'd have a baby in my arms before midnight was getting me through. I reminded Dustin of my birth plan, that I wanted skin-to-skin contact as soon as my baby came out, to nurse her immediately, and to have the nurse put her footprints in her baby book. I laid there with a renewed sense of determination.

Let's do this! I thought.

Once I was settled, my mom and stepdad came in to see me. When I told my mom I had gotten an epidural, I felt like I let her down, like I was weak and had given up. I felt it was my first failure as a mother that I wasn't able to get my daughter here without drugs. Did my mom actually think these things? Probably not, but it's what I projected onto her.

As my mom and stepdad stood at the foot of my bed, looking uncomfortable, I felt another contraction come. The pain was slightly muted from the epidural, but the tightness from my back around to the front of my belly took my breath away. I had to breathe through it, which made me feel embarrassed. The fact that I had to breathe through painful contractions even with an epidural was like pouring salt into the wound. My stepdad looked even more uncomfortable. He moved his body around like a voice with a stutter and finally gave his love, explaining that he wanted to give me space and quiet to labor. Then they left the room.

I know that it was hard for them to see me in such a vulnerable position, laboring. But in those vulnerable moments, a person needs the feelings of belongingness and acceptance even more. I felt so lonely lying in that bed. My husband was there, but unsure of how to support me. I knew our parents were out in the waiting room, and yet I somehow felt alone.

That's when the shift happened. During labor, there's a shift where everyone who used to be focused on the mom and her health is now focused on the baby. Suddenly, I realized that everyone who I thought was there for me was really there for the baby. Certainly, everyone was there for me, too, but, essentially, they had to be sure I was okay because I was the vessel to deliver the baby. The attention that I almost didn't even realize I was getting immediately shifted away from me with a snap of the fingers. It didn't matter that I was sitting in the most vulnerable position I'd ever experienced, literally and figuratively, that I was dealing with physical and emotional trauma, and that I was mentally unraveling—so long as I delivered our baby safely.

It was ironic to me that everyone was so laser focused on our baby, and they didn't even know her name. Dustin and I had kept her name secret. Everyone wanted to know her darn name, including the nurse who relentlessly begged us to give it up. We wouldn't budge. This was our first parenting decision that was met with unvoiced judgement. Who knew that every other parenting decision we'd make would also be judged? That's another thing no one tells you about.

The time continued to tick by as I managed my contractions. A short while later, I was incredibly excited to find out that I was at 9.5 centimeters. It was happening! It was almost time! Our one barrier was that my water hadn't broken yet. I was surprised to learn that this is common, and the doctor needed to break it.

The hospital I delivered at is a teaching hospital. I had to sign a waiver to allow residents to assist the doctor, and a resident was given the job to break my water. As she sat at the foot of my bed, my vagina out there for all to see, she checked to see where the bag was to pop it. I saw her face change. Something was wrong. The resident consulted with the doctor, who quickly called for an ultrasound machine. As we waited a brief second for the machine, the resident told me that they thought the baby was breech. She was a position called "frank breech," which she said tricks a lot of people. The physical sinking feeling I felt in my body was incomprehensible, like I was on the initial drop of a roller coaster, but, instead of exhilaration, it was filled with intense fear. I knew what it meant. If my baby was breech, I'd need a c-section.

Never in my life did I even consider having a c-section. I suppose I had the impression that they were a choice: that women would choose a date for a c-section and simply opt out of a vaginal delivery. Or that they just couldn't push anymore or that the baby's head wasn't dropping. I assumed a c-section would never happen to me, but even more than that, I never thought to consider that it could. Because of that, I had no ability to even process what this meant for me.

The ancient Greeks broke time into two experiences: chronos and kairos. Chronos time is the time we are all very familiar with—the chronological order of time. It's 60 seconds equaling 1 minute, and 24 hours equaling 1 day. Kairos time is when we experience the same amount of time differently. For example, when my kids are in school, those six hours fly by. It actually blows my mind how fast the school days go as a mother. But if I need to sit in a plane for six hours, it will feel more like 12.

The kairos time I experienced as they pulled in the ultrasound machine was like slow motion. Even as I play back the memory in my head, my visual of the scene moves at half the rate that it probably actually did. In those two minutes, I'd either find relief in hearing that the resident was wrong and my baby was positioned perfectly, and I could continue to deliver vaginally. Or I'd find sadness in hearing confirmation that she was breech, and I'd need to have a c-section.

My modesty continued to be disregarded as they ripped my gown away to put the sticky ultrasound gel on my stomach. During the ultrasound, I felt full of fear and rushed, a stark difference from all of my other ultrasounds, which had been slow paced and happy as we got to see our baby's face and hear to her heartbeat. The ultrasound I got on that hospital bed was the one that confirmed, "Yup, she's breech. Let's go."

In the moments that followed, I could hardly process what was happening. I think this was the hardest part. I already felt like I was failing at childbirth. Now I couldn't even deliver my baby vaginally, but instead I needed to have surgery. I stared off into space as a whirlwind of people scurried around me, looking almost as if they danced and moved to the beat of *Flight of the Bumblebee*. I laid there, unblinking with a single tear falling down my right cheek. My nurse stopped and saw me, not just the tear, not just me, but really *saw* me.

"What's wrong?" she asked.

I turned to look at her and quietly responded in my fear, with a dry mouth, "I never expected to need a c-section."

She rested her hand on my shoulder and said, "I know, but they do it all the time. You're going to be okay and so is the baby. That's what matters."

While I appreciated her sentiments, I didn't quite feel the same, but I had no choice. I was rushed through the halls, with the double doors opening for us as they raced me to the operating room, needing to beat my body's natural inclination to begin pushing. They rolled me into a cold, sterile room. The single operating table sat in the middle of the large, bright room. My medical team worked quickly as they counted together to shift me over to the table from my bed. The table felt like it was 30 degrees Fahrenheit. I laid there, staring at the cold ceiling. I felt all alone—even with all of the people around me.

I'd never had surgery before, and I hadn't had any mental or emotional preparation for what I was about to go through. At some point, Dustin came beside my head as I laid staring at the ceiling, using every ounce of energy I had left in me to stop shaking. No one tells you about the labor shakes, but they are common during and after delivery. My body still thought it was trying to deliver a baby as I laid there, nearly convulsing and trying to find warmth in such a cold room. They laid blankets over the top half of my body, a gesture that you'd expect to be comforting. But it was done in desperation, an attempt to make my body be still. Remember, it was all about the baby now.

The anesthesiologist, another saint that day, saw me, too. She really *saw* me—just like the nurse. She assured me that the surgery would only be about 20 minutes, and in no time I'd be in a room holding my baby.

The fact that this doctor took the time to explain what was about to happen eased my mind and brought me the slightest bit of comfort. Here's the thing: The nurses and doctors deliver babies every single day. But this was the first time I had experienced any of these things.

I laid on that table a woman, and in a moment I was going to become a mother.

As I laid on the table, my husband on one side of my head, the anesthesiologist on the other, and who knows on the other side of the drape, I began to feel tugging and pulling at my stomach. I was grateful that the medicine was working, and I didn't feel the pain. I analyzed every tug and move. All of a sudden, I tuned in to every emotion and energy in the room, all with the motherly instincts I didn't know I had. I was relieved to feel a calm in the air. The doctors moved through my surgery with a flow, even having a normal conversation. Some people might perceive that as a lack of care, but I found it incredibly comforting that my surgery was going so smoothly that they were able to have a regular conversation.

As I felt my baby tugged from my midsection, I heard them move her over to the bassinet. I held my breath, waiting to hear a cry. And then I heard it. The wind was knocked out of my chest as I heard my baby cry. It's something you see in movies and on TV throughout your whole life, but hearing my baby's first cry was one of the most remarkable sounds I had ever heard. As the entire room got to see my daughter, I laid behind a sheet, my face pointed up toward the ceiling. I was the only one who hadn't gotten to see her yet. It's painful, this knowing. As I laid there, the anesthesiologist whispered in my ear, "She's perfect. She has a head of black, curly hair." Again I thanked God for the angels he gave to me that day. A moment later, I heard my nurse yell from across the room, "What's her name?!"

"Hannah Gray!" my husband replied with the biggest smile on his face. The nurse shared so much happiness with us and genuine approval of a name "that sounded like a famous author," as she described it.

I did it. I gave birth to our daughter. I made it. She arrived just past midnight. She was perfectly healthy, and I would get to hold her in just a few minutes. As soon as Hannah was born, Dustin left the room. I laugh as I write this because I actually have no idea where he went. A lot of the details at this point are fuzzy to me, and my sense of time was completely lost. While time was lost, I could feel that I was laying on that table too long. There was actually an anesthesiologist shift change! I had to ask my new anesthesiologist for another pump of pain medication because I was beginning to feel them sewing me back up. I didn't understand what was taking so long. That time, on that table, were some of the longest and most painful minutes of my life. My body continued to shake uncontrollably, and the only way I could get it to stop was to clench my teeth together, which eventually resulted in tremendous jaw pain. In time, the doctors finished. I believe I was in the operating room for nearly two hours, which was much longer than the 20 minutes the doctor had originally told me. There were no complications. It took so long because the resident who found that my baby was breech was given the opportunity to perform her very first c-section on me. I regularly fight with how I feel about this. Part of me feels gratitude that I was able to help a doctor learn. Another part of me feels angry, like I was taken advantage of and not treated like a human with emotions and fears.

In the recovery room, as I sat slightly inclined in my bed, a nurse brought Hannah to me. I looked down to find my breasts were completely exposed. When the nurse brought Hannah to me, Hannah's mouth was open like a hungry bird. The nurse aimed her at my nipple, and she latched on immediately.

Hey, look at that! I thought. *I'm doing it! I'm breastfeeding!*

After nursing, all of our family came in. Can you believe that I don't remember if Hannah was in the room at this point? I was so drugged up, I hardly knew where I was. Do you know why? Because no one considered telling me anything. The one thing I remember from my time in that room was when we announced Hannah's name to the family. I suppose it's good that I was under the influence because I don't remember anyone's reactions. I remember feeling really happy and light—and incredibly exhausted. Suddenly, I had a wave of nausea come over me.

I heard my mom say, "I was worried you'd feel sick."

Why? I thought.

Around 3 am, our families sleepily said their goodbyes, congratulations, and promises that they'd be back the next day. After they left, I was rolled into a mother-baby room, the entire ride there inflicting more and more nausea.

The next part of having a baby that they don't prepare you for is that you don't just have the baby and get to have a peaceful night's sleep. You get wheeled into a bright room. Ours happened to be directly across from the nursery and nurse's station, and no one seemed to care that it was 4 am or that I just actively labored for nine hours and delivered a baby through an emergency c-section. Oh, and that I began to vomit all over myself. Nope. No one talks about this stuff.

The next 24 hours were atrocious for Dustin and me. We were both sleep deprived, and I couldn't stop throwing up. Moving my head in the slightest brought on such intense nausea that I grabbed the shameful plastic puke bin, and my husband or a nurse grabbed Hannah before she could fall out of my arms. Nurses were coming in every few minutes to check my vitals and the pumping wraps around my ankles. Did you know that you have a risk of having a blood clot after surgery? Because of this, your legs need constant massaging to keep the blood moving. I will say, those things were absolutely not the worst part of the whole experience.

Later the next afternoon, another amazing nurse encouraged me to get up. I looked at her and told her I wasn't sure if I could do it.

"I don't know why you're so sick," she said. "Women usually don't stay this sick for so long."

Great, thanks, I thought.

"We need to get you up," the nurse continued. "We don't want to leave the catheter in for too long. Can you try to get up?"

With her persistence, I slowly and painfully began to move my legs off the side of the bed. With the nurse's assistance, I got to a seated position.

"I'm gonna throw up!" I yelled.

I had given getting up a good old college try, but I wasn't ready yet. Later that evening, or maybe not until the next day, I finally was able to sit up without vomiting. The nurse took out my bloody catheter and then told me to go pee—with the bathroom door open, while she watched. It would have been really, really helpful if *someone* told me about all of what happens when having a baby. This was an unbelievable experience so far! Even though my mom prepared me so well for how contractions would feel and how to "bear down" the right way, who knew how ill prepared I actually was. She shared *her* experiences, but it turned out mine were completely different.

Once I could stand on my own and pee (what accomplishments!), everything began to slowly but surely feel better. I was beginning to get hungry, Hannah was nursing like a champ, and I was able to take a shower. I felt like a new woman. I was back. I had made it to the other side of a birthing experience I was totally unprepared for, one that caused trauma and brought so many issues and insecurities to the surface. But as my nausea and grogginess fell away, I fell madly in love with my new family.

Although my birthing experience brought some issues to the surface, it also brought a new self-confidence and adoration of my body. My precious Hannah Gray was here and loved by so many already. Over the next couple days, we welcomed many guests, who came to meet this new person who I could no longer remember not being here on this earth. It's amazing how quickly your mind, life, and heart calibrate and bond with the soul of your child. I couldn't wait to start our life with her.

Because I was doing so well and Hannah was born just past midnight, we got the okay to leave a day earlier than we were supposed to. Despite the challenges with the entire experience, Hannah's birth is actually one of my very favorite experiences in my life. I was a little sad to leave the hospital, although we were ready to be home. We live right by this hospital, and every single time I drive by it I get a flash of nostalgia. It was a time that my husband, our baby, and I got to cozy up in a room, just us three as a new family. Dustin and I fell in love all over again in that room, and it's a time I will cherish forever.

My birthing experience was not all bad. I share all of it because I know that if I had any understanding of these untold pieces of childbirth, I would have felt a lot more ease and trust in all of it—

instead of feeling forced and pushed through it all, processing the most I could in those quick moments.

FAMILY OF THREE

Our transition into becoming a new family was overall quite easy for us. Being a mother is the one thing I've always known that I wanted, without any question. I was blessed to have made the decision of when I wanted to become a mother, have it happen, and experience it in a really beautiful way.

As the winter shifted quickly into spring, my baby girl and I created a new routine together. Those days off during my maternity leave are some of the best memories of my life, just Hannah and me. She always slept well and woke for her first nursing at about 7 am. I would get her, nurse her in my bed, and hold her tiny little body against my chest as she fell back to sleep. I would hold her and simply be. I relished in those slow, still mornings, with the sun steadily filling my bedroom with light and warmth.

Something shifted for me in those 11 weeks home with her. I can't describe the shift in a concrete way, but it was a feeling—a knowing. It was a new understanding of life and purpose. In hindsight, I'm not sure that I actually understood how profound this new perspective was.

After I had Hannah, I became adamant about taking good care of my body, because it was no longer just *my* body. It was the body that made hers, and it was the body that was feeding hers. It was a body that almost effortlessly healed from birthing her, even after the unexpected nature of her arrival. My body was strong and beautiful, and I committed to loving it. I wanted to love my body so Hannah knew how to love hers. For me, this was one of the biggest shifts in my life. I spent the 29 years prior to having Hannah abusing my body by not feeding it well balanced meals all of the time, not giving it enough sleep, and verbally berating it every single time I looked in the mirror.

The second Hannah came into the world, I released all of this. I no longer saw food as an enemy—but the magic that would help my own body make food. I no longer saw exercise as a chore—but as a way to continue to keep my core strong. This fresh new perspective lifted a weight that I hardly even realized I carried. This part of becoming a mother was—and continues to be—the greatest gift for me. Later you'll read about how I lost sight of taking care of my body and it's part of what lead me into my anxiety. However, the body image issues, need to diet and hating what I saw in the mirror? It's something I've never taken back again. This shift has remained, nearly eight years later.

As I found new gratitude and respect for my body, part of this was really hard for me. My daughter refused to take a bottle. Newborn babies eat about every two hours, but they take essentially 45 minutes to get a full feeding. So almost every hour, I needed to stop whatever I was doing and feed my baby. This is a part of motherhood that I didn't know was coming. I didn't realize how difficult it would be to plan simple things like grocery store runs. I'd get back home just as Hannah would start screaming, and I'd need to leave all of the food in the car to nurse her before putting it away. In the summer, I had to let her cry so I could at least get the cold groceries put away. As soon as I sat down to eat dinner, Dustin cut up my food so I could eat one-handed while Hannah nursed. When we had guests over, I left the table for privacy to nurse and would miss the entire visit.

No one warned me about cluster feeding! When your baby is having a growth spurt (which seems to happen every five minutes in the first few months), all she wants to do is eat! The first few times this happened, it really messed with my body and mind. I questioned everything. Was I feeding her too much? Was I not making enough milk? Should I make her stop? Am I doing something wrong? God forbid if this happened in the middle of the night when my ability to think rationally was on pause until 8 am.

But even with moments of motherhood that required trial, error, and patience, I managed it. I went with the flow and the current of the new parts of my life until I quickly found my groove, and it felt like home to me. I realized there had been a huge part of me that had been missing. I felt fulfilled in it. I felt grounded and connected in who I was.

When it was time to head back to work, I fell apart. It felt like I couldn't breathe. I know that just about every mother experiences this feeling when it's time to go back, and there was something in what I was experiencing in which I needed to respond. When I was back at work, each day became harder. My intuition was telling me loud and clear that I was no longer supposed to be a school counselor.

None of this made sense to my logical brain. I worked nearly eight years to get the degrees required for this position. It was the job I was supposed to be in until retirement. This job was a part of who I was as a person, but that was just it. I was no longer *that* person. I had shifted when I became a mother. It wasn't a shift away from who I was, but rather it was a shift into who I was supposed to be. My job had changed before I left, it continued to change while I was gone, and then I changed, too. I had to walk away from my job and know that it was okay to follow my heart instead of my head and others' judgments.

One day at work, as I sat in the back area of my office where I'd run all of my small groups, I was pumping and sobbing into my baby's burp cloth that held her precious scent. I knew I had to walk away from this job and walk toward my new life. This time in my life was pivotal, and I had to walk toward what was scary and uncomfortable. I had to resign.

While I was home with my daughter, I delved even further into photography. I stand very firm in my belief that it was this practice, the practice of connecting to my creativity, that allowed me to connect even further with my intuition, that "knowing" in which I keep referring. I fully trust that this creative practice, connecting me with my own inner knowing, is what gave me the confidence to trust the decision to leave my position. The decision was full of fear, sleepless nights, and nerves, but I did it. I walked away from a huge part of my identity and walked toward a freedom. I moved toward a new part of my life that I knew would offer endless opportunity to become who I was meant to be.

STAY-AT-HOME MOM

My summer vacation became my new life—the endless summer. Everything felt so aligned and exciting. My photography hobby organically turned into a registered photography business that became a tremendous passion for me outside of motherhood. I had a few lighthearted photo shoots with other mothers, so it was easy to bring my baby along and make it an outing where I got to practice my craft. It felt fun and new. Although I had a couple of photo shoots here and there, I spent most of my time being a mom. I savored every single moment home with my daughter.

Over the summer, my husband continued fulfilling his own passion of flipping houses. This had caused a shift in our life. I didn't understand the gravity of that shift at the time. Looking back, I could feel resentful, abandoned, and angry, but instead I have chosen to forgive Dustin and me for what we didn't know, take the valuable lessons from it, and continue to move forward.

However, it's really important that I share this part of our story. It's the beginning of my fall. It's the part of my life where I didn't have the awareness to know what I needed—let alone the ability to speak up for myself. This is why I'm sharing it—because this is where it can start. No matter what your story is, we all move into parenthood the same way: blind. We have to learn as we go. For me, this was a hard lesson, but one I'm truly grateful to have had because without it, I never would have learned.

At the time, Dustin was a lineman for our local utility. Each morning, he left the house at 6:30 am and came home by 4:30 pm, but he was also on call all the time. At any given moment, he could be called to leave, even in the middle of the night, or, at the end of his shift, he might not be able to come home. During bad storms, he could be shipped away for an unknown amount of time.

Dustin's work schedule was the only one we had ever known, but parenthood brought on a new way of experiencing it. Even with Dustin's ambitious work schedule, we decided to flip another house with his parents. The house we bought to flip was located along Dustin's commute home. Instead of coming home from work, Dustin would stop by the house we were flipping every day to work on it with his mom and dad's help. That left me home alone with Hannah every single day and night. I only saw Dustin for a little bit late at night, and sometimes in the early mornings. At the time, this worked for us. It didn't feel bad or strained. It was our normal routine, so it worked. But eventually, it wouldn't work anymore.

I look back on that summer and remember it being okay. I had a beautiful flow in being a mom. I soaked in my time with my daughter with no other work obligations weighing over me, just the fun in taking pictures. Hannah was a happy baby with a predictable eating and sleeping schedule. I was able to find ease in my house duties, taking care of myself, and being mom. It felt really, really good.

As the fall rolled around, I was nostalgic at the start of the school year, but I also felt free and joyful because I wasn't going back to work. I fell more and more in love with my new life.

Certainly, nothing is perfect. Some days I felt lonely, lacking autonomy as I struggled with giving up my title of "school counselor" and had to find pride in saying "stay-at-home mom." I struggled even more accepting the new title, "professional photographer." My roles were changing. There were changes too in how my husband and I showed up in our relationship, adding the titles "mom" and "dad." While nothing is ever perfect, it was really good—so good, that Dustin and I decided we wanted another baby.

THEN COMES ANOTHER BABY

IT WAS THE FALL OF 2013. Life is kind of crazy, isn't it? Less than two years earlier, we were a childless couple, living in a beautiful new home, working jobs we loved, eating dinner together every night, camping all of the time, and walking our dog on the weekends. Fast forward, and we found a new kind of busy as parents, taking on new projects in our work and hobbies, and jam-packing many more things into the 24 hours in a day—things in which we had a lot of pride and fulfillment. In all of it, we knew we wanted a little boy, and we knew we wanted him sooner rather than later.

It can take time for a nursing mother's body to be ready to have another baby. Because I had a c-section, I was advised not to get pregnant too soon. But Dustin and I decided to let nature take its course and give us our next baby when we were supposed to have him.

We became pregnant with him when Hannah was nine months old, which I find so intuitive of my body, falling in line with the doctor's recommended timeline. They assured me that at this point it was safe to get pregnant, and that's exactly what my body did.

BUT FIRST, PTSD

As a first-time mom, I was a little bit of an anomaly. Many funny memes elude to the fact that first-time moms are very cautious with safety and germs, and second-time moms ease up and aren't as tightly wound with these things. I was a bit of the opposite. I fully believed that a chew toy falling in the dirt would help build the immune system. The first time Hannah had a fever and runny nose, I was oddly excited to squeegee her nose out and soak in the sick-day cuddles. But that December, when Hannah spiked a 103°F fever and appeared to be extremely ill, I knew something was wrong.

It was December 30th, and all of the pediatrician offices were closed except for one. We got the last appointment. As my nine-month-old baby laid helplessly on the table, screaming relentlessly, they checked her for a possible urinary tract infection. It was traumatizing. Dustin and I stood there, never having been parents to a child this sick and having no clue what to do. The doctor looked at us after ruling out a UTI and nonchalantly said, "It might be the flu."

I must have gone starch white, or perhaps green, because the doctor's face mirrored mine, and he put his hands up to express, "No, no, it's okay." But then he said, "Go to the ER."

Dustin and I took Hannah out to our car. I rode in the backseat with Hannah and sobbed. I know that Dustin felt completely helpless in this moment, not knowing how to comfort me or how to fix the problem. I couldn't contain my fear.

After we got to the ER, they took blood and told us to go home. They promised to call with the results. Turned out Hannah did have the flu, and she quickly recovered without Dustin or I getting sick. After seeing Hannah so sick, I was now a tiny bit nervous about germs and people getting my baby sick.

Fast forward to February. One Tuesday, Hannah and I were home alone as usual. We ate salmon, butternut squash, and spinach for dinner. I often cooked for myself and shared it with Hannah. It was a really fun way to introduce her to new foods.

After dinner, we did our bedtime routine of getting her into her footie pajamas and cuddling up in the glider for her bedtime nursing. This was one of those nights where I really needed Hannah to go to bed so I could have some quiet alone time. Desiring my own time without my baby didn't mean I didn't love being a mother or enjoyed our time together. I just needed a few minutes alone, and I remember how badly I wanted them that night.

As I laid Hannah in my arm and brought her to my breast, she was fussy and kept pulling away. Because of my craving to be "off the clock" that night, I began to feel irritated and impatient.

Why isn't she taking any milk? I wondered. Just as I was thinking this, Hannah vomited all over me.

It was a moment in slow motion. It took me a lot of time to process what was actually happening. Being one of four children, babysitting most of my life, and working in a school, I certainly had experience with vomit, but not the stomach virus. It took me a few too many seconds to realize Hannah was vomiting and not just spitting up. I rushed her to the bathroom sink in a panic, and that's when I realized what was going on. As soon as I got us cleaned up enough to get my phone, I called Dustin, who was out renovating as usual, and begged him to come home.

For the next several hours, my body was in a heightened state of fight-or-flight mode. Parents are wired to protect their children, and my brain believed that my daughter's life was in danger. She continued to be sick for the entire night. Dustin and I laid on the floor of her nursery to be by her side. I was terrified she might get dehydrated. Then came hours and hours of panic and fear.

Despite how awful those few hours were, Hannah recovered quickly. She didn't nurse very much over the next 24 to 48 hours, which was a little concerning because of my milk supply, but I trusted my body and hers to do what they needed for one another.

A few days later, on Saturday, Dustin was at the house we were flipping, and I felt churning in my stomach. I called Dustin and asked him to quickly come home as I rapidly declined and developed a very close relationship with my toilet for the next several hours. It was quick moving, and I survived, but the damage to my brain had been done. I suddenly had an intense fear of stomach bugs. I didn't know that even more damage was coming.

Because Hannah didn't nurse for several days, and I got so sick myself, my milk supply diminished to almost nothing. My daughter would suckle her little heart out, only to pull away in frustration, clearly not getting enough milk.

My milk was gone. The moment I realized this, my stomach turned, my throat closed, and I felt rage, panic, and fear completely take over my body. One of my biggest goals in being a mother was to nurse my child to 12 months. It never crossed my mind that I wouldn't be able to meet this goal with Hannah, because it was something that we learned how to do together. I loved every part of nursing and knew that it was our thing. When I realized that I would possibly need to switch to formula for her remaining three months of infancy, my fight-or-flight response kicked in. I'm a fighter. (Note: While nursing was a huge part of my experience with my babies, I am a very firm believer in "fed is best." I share these parts of my story because they are huge parts of my story, not because I believe this is how all mothers should mother.)

I researched every single way to help build milk supply. For the next several days, I was on a mission to find every vitamin, mineral, and ingredient I could ingest to get my milk back. I fought like hell, and I won.

I'll come back to this story later and connect it to my anxiety that will show up about a year from this point. But I want to share with you that this week of my life, paired with the week she had the flu, completely rewired my brain. My brain, for nearly a week, thought my daughter's life was in danger, then thought my own life was in danger, and then the threat of taking my baby's milk away continued to keep my brain in fight-or-flight mode as I fought to get her food again. This is how our primitive brain works. Certainly, I had the logic and rationale to know that we weren't dying, but my primitive brain didn't know that, and so it responded the way it's supposed to. As a result, I would soon begin to experience the symptoms of post-traumatic stress disorder (PTSD).

BY THE WAY, I'M PREGNANT

February 17, 2014, was a weekday morning, but a holiday, so Dustin had the day off. I had a photoshoot about an hour from our home that morning. My photography business was growing, and my photo shoots were becoming more and more frequent. While I was loving its growth and became almost obsessive with expanding my business, I was beginning to lose boundaries in growing the business. I had a hard time deciding when I should work and when I shouldn't.

That morning, my husband was dressing a now 10-month-old Hannah while I got myself dressed. I planned to take Hannah to my mom's house and then head to my photo shoot. But I paused. My period was due in a few days. I had this very calm knowing (there's that intuition again!) that I was pregnant, so I took a pregnancy test. Sure enough there were two pink lines. I walked into Hannah's room as she laid happily on the changing pad with my husband standing above her. I showed him the stick with a soft, genuine smile. I expected excitement, you know, like a big hug and, "Ohmygosh, we're having a baby!" but it was more like, "Oh wow! You're pregnant?" Then we simply went on with our day. It was sadly anticlimactic.

I've learned this is part of the second baby experience, for most people anyway. Especially when your first baby isn't even a year old yet. It's as if there wasn't enough space to do it all over again with the same enthusiasm. Despite our muted response, Dustin and I truly were both very excited to know that another baby was on the way. I learned later that Dustin's response was more caution than lack of excitement. The first time we heard our baby's heartbeat, we felt settled and fully committed to the excitement of having another baby.

As spring rolled around, we celebrated Hannah's first birthday, and we became fully engulfed in our insanely busy life. I learned that I really took pride in saying that I am busy. Looking at a calendar filled with commitments was always a way that I saw success. Not having things to do equated to laziness. Similarly, Dustin thrived off of projects, challenges, and not being still. While this is a strength in both of us, and it can quickly turn into a weakness. We were unknowingly snowballing into a state where our ambition was becoming slightly destructive.

By the summer, my belly was growing, and along with it my business and our flipping opportunities. Around June was the last time I felt calm and aligned. It would be the last time I would feel that for several years.

My fall into anxiety was slow and steady. It's not one step off the cliff. It's many tiny little steps that compound together. It's not until you take the final step that you have an epiphany and realize that you're at the very bottom of a black hole, and you were too busy to realize you were even stepping into one. It was this June that I started to take those tiny steps.

After a big family vacation to the Outer Banks, we came home to our scheduled 20-week ultrasound—the one where we got to find out if we were having that little boy we wanted. Our lives were getting so busy that having a babysitter watch Hannah while we went to the ultrasound was a treat. To sit still in a waiting room, go into a dark ultrasound room, and be asked to lie down? Yes, *please*! When I laid on the table, I realized how tired I was and how much my life had changed. I felt a lightness, surrounded in the much-needed break and quiet with just my husband.

The anticipation of finding out our second baby's gender was a little less heady than it was with Hannah, but for me, it was in part because I absolutely knew I was carrying a little boy. When the tech confirmed with a huge smile and no question that our baby was a little boy, Dustin and I smiled ear to ear.

Although discovering the baby's gender is the most exciting part of the 20-week ultrasound, these ultrasounds are really to check the health and development of the baby. When the tech spent an extra amount of time on one part, I knew something was wrong. My fears were confirmed when she told us the doctor would be in to speak with us. It was an experience, much like Hannah's emergency c-section, that I never considered would happen. I was unprepared to handle what was happening, but I had no choice.

Any time that there is even the slightest possibility that something could be wrong with your child, time goes in slow motion. It's like a rug being ripped out from under you. When the doctor came in, focused solely on our baby, I held my breath. We learned that our son had a condition called singular umbilical artery. A baby is supposed to have two arteries going to the umbilical cord, but our son only had one. This condition can be minor and just need monitoring, or it can be very serious and life threatening. After several weeks of blood tests and an echocardiogram on the baby, the doctor ruled out all of the life-threatening parts of the condition, but our baby was still considered high risk for being born prematurely with a low birthweight. I needed to go to maternal fetal medicine for ultrasound growth scans and checks once a month that were much more in depth than the routine monthly visits at the OB, which I also still had to do.

It's hard to describe how I felt. I think I shut down. Walls went up. I put on blinders, I put my head down, and I didn't allow myself to feel the feelings I had coming up. Instead of slowing down, supporting my mind and body, and taking care of my baby, I pushed myself harder. I was constantly angry. My anger might have actually been fear presenting as anger. This was a far cry from how I felt a few months earlier, living life in extreme joy. I filled my space and time with work. Looking back on my life, this is what I did to avoid anything hard. I piled on the work and kept my mind busy. If I had to be still, I stewed in my own stuff. I kept myself busy at all costs.

Our little guy was due at the very end of October 2014. That summer, as I vacillated between working feverishly and stewing in my own stuff, Dustin wrapped up a flipping project. We discussed possibly moving into town. We loved our home. I was head over heels for our home, but the three bedrooms and lack of neighborhood sidewalks weren't supporting our growing family. We wanted to be closer to people and sidewalks. When we found an opportunity to buy a home in town from a family friend, we jumped on it.

The first time we actually looked at the new house, it was a rainy day in the spring, a few months earlier. The house, previously owned by a friend's grandmother, was completely outdated, run down, and dirty. It was the home of a hoarder—dark and gloomy.

I had a newly pregnant belly and an infant on my hip. The house was so dirty I refused to put Hannah down inside. I felt exhausted walking through the sad, vacant home. Just looking at the house made me tired, but the passion and excitement in my husband's eyes were undeniable.

The house was in a great neighborhood, and it was big with an open layout. I knew my husband could turn it into something amazing. After some negotiating, a lot of legal jargon, and sorting out estates, we finally bought the house at the end of the summer. While moving made sense in my head, my heart was begging me to keep us where we were. Here's where things really began to crumble.

Because I was so numb at this point—so turned off—I wasn't connected to my feelings enough to know that we needed to take a deep breath, stop, and say no. That knowing? It's always there. In hindsight, I can see where it was trying to speak to me, but I didn't hear it because I wasn't connected. Instead of stopping, we just kept going.

Over the next two months, Dustin and his parents worked tirelessly at our new house, attempting to complete a full remodel before we moved in. Meanwhile, I was cleaning our current house, getting it ready to be put on the market, and packing. I was also having steady photo shoots and editing all of my sessions. Hannah was now too old to join me on my sessions, and my business was becoming a true business—rather than a hobby. That summer and fall, I had a constant rotation of sitters coming to watch Hannah as I went to photo sessions—all while having a high risk pregnancy.

In the midst of this uncontrolled chaos, I began to constantly feel resentful. I was resentful that I was left to handle all of the packing, cleaning, working, parenting, and growing a baby all on my own. I was resentful every time I was too tired to clean up the dishes from eating dinner alone—again. I was even more resentful knowing my husband was four miles away, eating dinner with his parents every night instead of with his own family. I was resentful when I couldn't reach something up high or when it felt too hard to bend over. I was resentful when I lost patience with my daughter because I didn't have my spouse to coparent with me. I felt guilty feeling this way, knowing Dustin was breaking his back to get a new home ready for us before our baby came. I was resentful because on some level, I knew I wasn't connecting with my family the way I needed to. I was resentful knowing that we weren't prioritizing correctly. We had fallen out of alignment.

We got comfortable moving through our day-to-day life, hustling to get as much done as we could, but we were completely ignoring the need to slow down, be together, and connect. We ended up in a race against the clock of life. We lost sight of what was really important to us.

One day, I was running around, like any other day. I went downstairs to our finished basement. I lifted my leg to step over the baby gate at the bottom of the stairs, and I miscalculated the height. Before I could correct myself, I took a nasty fall and landed on my back—hard enough that I was actually nervous I could have hurt the baby. In that moment, the resentment and anger fully took over.

Over the past few years, I've learned that I respond to emotional hurt with anger—rather than sadness. I have learned to build up a toughness, independence, and pride to prevent other people from seeing the hurt they have caused by hiding my vulnerability. I learned, instead, to stand by myself and prove that I'm strong enough to do it on my own. In that moment, as I laid on the hard tile floor in pain, I relied heavily on the stubborn, prideful, and wounded woman inside of me. I stood up angrily. I convinced myself that if something was wrong with the baby, they'd find it in the monthly ultrasound I had scheduled the next day. Despite feeling an obvious injury in my lower back, I detached myself from it. I ignored it, soon forgetting that the moment even happened. I would later learn that our bodies don't forget anything.

I struggled every day to do it all, and I was in a state of complete exhaustion and overwhelm. I kept telling myself that once we moved, it'd get better. I deluded myself into believing that this was all temporary. I think that's how we trick ourselves with anything, really. In times of despair, we convince ourselves that the circumstances will soon change, and in turn our feelings will change, too. Little did I know at the time that it's the other way around: I am the one who needs to change how I am on the inside in order for my circumstances to shift. But I didn't have that awareness yet. I continued taking tiny steps down into a black hole.

MAKING THE MOVE

I felt like I was on a conveyer belt—in constant, steady movement. I couldn't go slower, faster, or even get off. I had to continue moving forward steadily, ignoring any desire to stop and take a break. I told myself there wasn't any space to take a break, and because of that my circumstances reflected this. No, I didn't consciously make this decision, but that's the power of our minds. While we have the power to create our best lives, we also have the power to create our worst lives. It happens gradually, through tiny steps and often without our awareness.

While Dustin was gone every day doing renovations, I was building my photography business, taking on wedding clients, packing and moving, caring for a one-year-old baby girl, being nine months pregnant, and serving as my best friend's matron of honor. That was a role I had dreamt about since we became best friends at 12 years old. I was drowning in the responsibilities. I was desperately digging deep to give my dear friend the wedding, celebration, and attention she deserved, and I actually did it—with tremendous help from the other bridesmaids and her mama.

I don't have a damn clue how. Even as I sit here writing this, I truly can't wrap my brain around how on earth I managed to do all of these things at the same time. In about two weeks, I threw a bridal shower for my friend (we all know the planning and DIY projects that go with this), I prepped for the arrival of a new baby, packed our entire house to prepare for our move, took on several photo shoots, and still managed to do all of the day-to-day grocery shopping, cleaning, laundry, meal making, being with my daughter, nighttime routine alone, and so on. It's nearly comical to look back and think that it would have been possible to do this much and stay calm, centered, and happy. I was trying to drive a car cross-country without stopping for gas.

The sad part is that I'm just one out of millions of women who take on this much. This is what we seemingly have been wired to do: to do it all with smiles on our faces—until our smiles disappear.

My resentment wasn't toward any one person—except perhaps myself. My resentment was toward the situation I found myself in, but my awareness wasn't refined enough to fully understand or even acknowledge what I was feeling. I numbed the pain of my emotions by doing more, keeping busy, filling up every moment of the day so I had no time to sit still and reflect on what I was feeling. And I did it successfully.

Of course, not everything I was doing was bad. That's why it's all so tricky. In fact, everything I was doing was good: building a business, moving into a new home that would support our growing family, planning a friend's wedding, and having another baby. It's easy to have clarity in hindsight and completely understand why I fell apart. But in the midst of it all, I didn't know anything bad was happening because I had pushed my feelings down so completely. When you do this, your feelings percolate, and they will find their way out. Sometimes they seep out in a minor emotional explosion. Other times they manifest as physical symptoms such as insomnia or bellyaches. When that happens, if you're as stubborn in your denial as I was, you can push them back down again.

One of my first explosions happened soon after we moved to our new home. I lost it when our dog started barking at a bunny in the yard. Ladies, if you find yourself reacting to something out of proportion of what's actually happening, let this be your first clue that something else is going on in your mind, body, or soul.

Our beautiful Irish setter, Riley, went crazy for bunnies. Fortunately for him, we moved into a property with an overgrown backyard full of bunnies. One day, I was alone in our new home with Hannah, surrounded by what felt like a million boxes needing to be unpacked. I pressured myself to completely unpack before the baby came. I felt disconnected, ignoring the heavy grief I felt leaving our other home. I was also in massive physical pain as I approached the last days of my pregnancy. My back pain was almost unbearable, but I pushed through it. Plus, I was dealing with our 80-pound dog who was anxious over our move. Riley's anxiety manifested in a ton of panting, pacing, and crying out the window, looking for Dustin. It was becoming intolerable for me because I couldn't fix it, and I couldn't take the noise.

Riley went to the bay window in the kitchen. He looked out into the overgrown landscaping, and he couldn't contain himself at the sight of a rabbit sitting still, seemingly taking pleasure in taunting him. Riley lost his mind. I mean, lost it. Have you ever heard an Irish setter cry? It's a high-pitched mix of hound wailing and baby crying. Combine that with pacing of his huge clumsy body and the inability to rationalize, take deep breaths, and calm down. As Riley lost his shit, I unconsciously followed the rule of "if you can't beat them, join them." I lost my shit, too.

My heart felt like it climbed up to the middle of my throat and doubled in size. My stomach did a flip, a heat moved up my body from my feet to my scalp like the wave in a stadium full of fans. Tiny beads of sweat formed over my lip and between the hairs of my over-plucked brows. I grabbed my phone and called Dustin. The second I heard his voice, I yelled. It was like an out-of-body experience. The emotions that flooded my body were so intense, I physically couldn't contain them. It was like I thought I'd vomit every negative emotion out of my body. I cried and screamed into the phone, threatening to open the door and let the dog run away. In that moment, I didn't want our precious first-child-of-a-dog anymore. I wanted him gone and out of the house. That was me crying for help. This was me saying, "I can't handle everything that's going on, and I need help." But once again, I was showing my sadness through anger. My anger would get so big, offensive, and ugly that no one would ever be able to read through my screaming to recognize that I needed help. If I couldn't even recognize it myself, how could they?

During this huge emotional outburst, I felt so out of body that I don't even remember all that I said or how my sweet husband handled it. He was calm on the other end of the line, probably terrified that there was truth to my threats, and he said whatever right thing he needed to for me to get myself together. And I did. As soon as I got some footing, I collected all of those ugly emotions like broken pieces of glass and shoved them right back down where they came from. True to my patterns, I put my anger into action. I began to learn ways to help my dog's anxiety, which was actually the gateway to me finding essential oils, but I'll talk more about this in part two.

This breakdown was the beginning of my emotions finding their way out, but I continued to ignore the signs. My days were still swamped with only nebulous boundaries between my work and personal life. My life was so jam-packed that I couldn't even see straight. When I went into labor 11 days early, one day after we closed on our new house, I stayed true to my pattern of "busy" and "hustle."

LABOR DAY

It was Friday, October 17th. I felt like I was in a space of, "Okay I can catch my breath." We settled on both houses, and Dustin was once again coming home after his workday. I unpacked most of the house. The dust finally settled. I had a few photography sessions scheduled for that week that I guiltily canceled because I didn't want to disappoint my clients. I still shake my head at this. I was heavily pregnant, had just moved, and I felt badly to cancel sessions that I was physically incapable of shooting. I knew I was going to have this baby before his due date at the end of the month, I just *knew* it, and I had to make the call ahead of time. The fact that I allowed myself to book sessions the week we moved while 10 months pregnant is a really beautiful example of having zero boundaries. Take note.

A Friday at home, being able to be still and enjoy a date night with my husband was everything I needed. Speaking of Dustin: One could assume that there was tension and distance between my husband and me. There wasn't. In all of the self-imposed stress and busy schedules, we relied on one another. We always made our relationship a priority. Despite not having the awareness of what I was truly feeling in all of the chaos, I knew how important it was to stay connected with my husband. Probably one of the best ideas I ever had was scheduling a babysitter for a date night every other Friday from August through October.

Naturally, on the day I could finally relax, breath, and mentally prepare for the baby, my contractions started. They were mild contractions, but I knew they would grow into full-blown labor if they didn't stop. So, as I had done when I went into labor with Hannah, I showered and put on my lucky maternity sweater that I wore to the hospital with Hannah, which I still have to this day. Then I took a nap with my little lady. It was a warm, beautiful fall day where summer hadn't quite left, but a crisp fall feeling was in the air, especially after the sun went down. Like labor with Hannah, I chose to not let Dustin know while he was working unless it became an absolute emergency. At 4:30 pm when Dustin came home, my contractions were still mild, but they were now timing perfectly apart, suggesting I was in labor. As Dustin played with Hannah in the yard, I looked at him with my funny smile and said, "I think labor started." Jokingly, he pretended to be annoyed that I'd go into labor the weekend of the Emmaus Halloween Parade, which is practically a holiday for our town. By about 6 pm, I called the doctor to check in. I was planning to have a VBAC (vaginal birth after c-section), which is high risk, on top of my already high-risk pregnancy. Even though a c-section would be the safest choice, the doctors agreed that because my body had labored easily with Hannah, I was a great candidate for a VBAC. While my body healed easily from the c-section with Hannah, it was emotionally very difficult for me and certainly not my preferred way to deliver a baby. Because we lived only a couple miles from the hospital, the nurse encouraged me to labor at home until I could no longer breathe through contractions.

After reluctantly canceling our babysitter for date night, we put our daughter to bed at her 7 pm bedtime, and I sobbed. I can't quite describe the feeling of knowing it's going to be the last time you see your first child as your only child. You know full well that your heart will expand and hold space for both of your babies, but a bittersweet emotion full of grief sits in the pit of your stomach, mixed with guilt and confusion. The emotions you have before giving birth to a second baby are so tremendously different than the nearly ignorant excitement you have before delivering your first. If you haven't been in this moment yet, please know that the second you see your baby, the guilt and grief vanish, and your heart literally doubles in size.

Anyway, after putting Hannah in her crib and closing the door, I sobbed. I cried straight from my heart as I let go of the relationship that I had with my daughter—the one where it was just her and me every single day, just the two of us. Then, I wiped my tears and put my game face on to safely deliver our son.

Dustin's parents came over to sit at the house so we could walk around the neighborhood to help keep labor going. When they arrived, you'd never have known I was in labor. I stood happily in our kitchen, working through contractions effortlessly. They sat on our couch and made themselves comfortable while my husband and I walked out into the dark streets of our new neighborhood. I remember feeling lost, both literally and figuratively. I didn't know where we were, especially in the dark. In the daylight, I knew my way around already, but in the dark, had Dustin left my side, I don't know if I could have made it home. I realized that was a metaphor for my life in that moment, but I couldn't spend time in the complexity of my own thinking as I worked through my labor pain. And back pain.

Today I have the strong suspicion that my back pain stemmed

from that nasty fall I took over the baby gate months ago. But at the time, I convinced myself that it was my sciatica. I theorized that the baby was sitting on a nerve, and the second I delivered him, the pain would go away.

Dustin and I slowly made our way along the sidewalks of our streets. I walked painfully, holding Dustin's hand. My contractions went from mild to the opposite of mild very quickly. I knew I was progressing rapidly. Plus, I had been walking around 3 centimeters dilated for the past three weeks. I looked at my husband, doubled over, clutching my underbelly, and said, "We need to get to the hospital now. He's coming."

By the time we pulled up to the hospital, it took everything in me to breathe through each contraction. There was little to no time in between each one. When Dustin and I walked in the hospital, we realized it was under construction, and we couldn't find the elevator to get to triage. At that point, I could hardly breathe, let alone walk, and we were walking in circles trying to find our way to the right floor. When we found our way back to the front desk, I felt a rage that only a woman in labor can feel. The woman at the front desk explained to us how to find the elevator, but apparently she decided to give directions in slow motion that day. They're lucky I was too doubled over in pain to swing a right hook, but I digress.

Once in triage, the resident asked me if I wanted an epidural.

"It's too late," I said.

When he checked me and found that I was at 8 centimeters dilated, there was a mad dash to get me into a room to deliver the baby. I had become so focused on breathing through the pain that my fear of anything going wrong during this delivery was swept away.

I'm astounded at the body's physical, mental, and emotional ability to prepare for labor. Through my breathing, pushing, and focus, it felt like it was only moments later that I held our new son in my arms—before midnight. It was a high I wasn't prepared for. I was "the one" who delivered a baby like the speed of light after coming into the hospital—without pain meds. I'd be the talk of the floor for the rest of my stay.

For a fleeting moment in the delivery room, I felt like I was through the messy middle of all of the stress and chaos. John Paul, our baby boy was finally here, the move was over, and we could focus on being a family.

But within 24 hours, I was painfully brought back to my new reality—a low that I couldn't seem to get out of.

THE HOSPITAL STAY OF HELL

My labor and delivery were seamless. I actually couldn't have asked for a better experience. It was superfast. After delivering John Paul, I laid in my bed, no shaking, no vomiting, no catheter. His birth was the opposite of my labor with Hannah. I naively expected that our hospital stay would be just as beautiful. But my hopes were shattered when I found myself alone the next day.

The next day, after Dustin and I woke, we decided that he would go home to be with our daughter, and I would stay in the hospital alone that day and night. We expected that I would be discharged the following day. After Dustin left, my loneliness was louder and bigger than I could have ever anticipated. I was so diligent about filling my time and space to avoid my emotions, but now I was forced to lie in a hospital bed with nothing else to do but reflect on my feelings. They were big and ugly.

I began to pity myself. I felt sorry for myself that I was sitting in a hospital with no visitors. No one. I am from a family of six, and no one visited me or came to meet my precious baby boy. Later in the day, my mom came alone for perhaps an hour or two. She was there long enough that I was able to finally take a shower. In the shower, I realized my back still hurt badly. After my mom left, I continued to pity myself, but I pushed it down again, coercing my heart to feel strong and independent. But my pity and pain kept popping up like a broken jack-in-the-box.

That afternoon, I was mandated to attend a baby class in the hospital to be taught how to put the baby in a car seat and give him a bath. I was insanely annoyed in having to attend this class, considering I just went through this a few months prior with our daughter. But like a good student, I went. The class was at the opposite end of the hallway. I had a corner room, and it was fabulous with windows across two walls that looked out to the back of the hospital. I had the perfect view of the mid-autumn foliage. I was away from the noise of the nursery and nurses' station. My room was big to boot. But I had no one to share it with. And it was far from the classroom.

As I made my way down the hallway for class, I was hurting. Every single step felt like a knife was being driven further into my left lower back. I had delivered a baby med-free less than 24 hours earlier, and this pain was more than I could handle. It was bad, yet I continued to hide it and somehow convince myself that it was going to go away.

As I sat in class, I shifted in my seat relentlessly, trying to find relief from the pain in my back. A part of me desperately wanted someone to ask me if I was okay, but I was in a room full of women who just pushed a watermelon out of a hole the size of a lemon. None of us were sitting comfortably. So, while part of me was agonizingly uncomfortable, another part of me was grateful that I wasn't seeking the attention from someone asking me if I needed help. God forbid I admitted I needed help—let alone accept it.

When the class was over, I stood up, hoping to get some type of repose from my back pain only to find that taking a step forward felt nearly impossible. Holding my breath, I made my way down the hallway. My throat began to close to prevent tears from coming out of my eyes. When I rounded the corner, I brought my entire body to the wall, leaning on it for any support it could give me. Realizing that the only way to escape this pain was to lie flat on my back again, I courageously put out my right hand, gripping the flat surface of the wall. My knuckles turned white as I desperately tried to find something to hold onto. I moved my feet one in front of the other with the most intention I've ever needed to walk. Something was very wrong.

I got back to my room. The grief was filling me up like water dripping into a bucket from a leaky faucet. I was slowly, steadily filling to overflowing. I grieved because I felt that no friends or family wanted to meet my new son, that Dustin had to be home with our daughter because we didn't know how else to give her normalcy in all of the changes, and that my perfect delivery experience was being marred by my inexplicable back pain. To add more drops to my grief bucket, I was having trouble nursing my son.

Breastfeeding, which came so effortlessly for my daughter and me, was not coming easily this time. I laid there with my tiny baby boy, who was not latching on in a way that felt right. He kept falling asleep at my breast. My pride wasn't as strong as my need to feed my baby, so I called in the lactation nurse. She confirmed I was doing everything right, and she urged me to keep trying.

I had never felt so alone in my life.

As the sun set, my room became dark. The halls quieted. I laid in my bed with my baby boy lying next to me in his hospital bassinet on wheels, and I cried. I wanted my husband. I wanted somebody, anybody, to help me. Not many people warn you of this when you have a baby, but the second night is often a bad night. The first night after having the baby, the baby sleeps well, and the mom often does, too. Giving birth and being born? That's hard work! We need a good long nap after that happens. And then night two comes. The baby realizes how flipping hungry he is, and all he wants to do is eat. Welcome to cluster feeding.

By around 10 pm, I knew I was going to be up all night. I had experienced night two with Hannah! With my back pain, and having just given birth, I didn't have enough core strength to pick up my son out of the bassinet to nurse him. My grief bucket overflowed. I couldn't stop the leak, and I had no more room to collect the drops.

I found myself in a state of complete despair, isolation, and helplessness. I was in so much pain I couldn't even roll over to pick up my son and feed him. I called Dustin, sobbing. He made a very rational suggestion, "Why don't you call the nurses when he needs to feed so they can come in to give him to you?"

This added salt to my prideful and stubborn wounds. Me? Ask for help? Ask someone to hand my son to me when I need to nurse him when that's something I should be able to do myself? Not a chance in hell. So, when I answered Dustin by sobbing some more through incomprehensible words, begging him to come to me, he did. It wasn't easy, and we had to rely on his parents tremendously (they are saints), but he came.

While I was incredibly grateful he came, I sat in guilt and shame that I needed him at all, that I was inconveniencing our family so that I wouldn't be sitting alone in a hospital bed incapable of picking up my son to nurse him. My outside experience was a direct reflection of how I felt on the inside. I was insecure in who I was. I was constantly worried of what others would think, and I perceived vulnerability as weakness. Today, I feel heartbroken about how I allowed myself to experience my son's birth. I feel angry that so much of what happened was in my control, and I refused to pay attention to it. I was broken in that moment, sitting in that hospital bed, in the corner room with the views.

The pieces of glass that I was picking up over and over again and shoving back down were shattered into complete shards by this point. I couldn't even collect them anymore to be able to hide them. But I didn't know what else to do with them. I let them be shattered in front of me and ignored them the best I could.

5

AND THEN COME OVERWHELM AND ANXIETY

TRANSITIONING HOME WITH A SECOND BABY only 18 months after the first was less than happy, easy, and exciting. To make matters worse, I chose to experience this new transition by throwing myself into busyness. I know that I am no exception to the rule. Mothers work hard to earn their busy badges of honor by shouting from the rooftop how many loads of laundry they've washed, cookies they've baked, and songs they sang with their kids before 9 am.

Society applauds the mother who is "out and about" with her one-week-old baby in her pre-maternity jeans. Quite frankly, this is the problem. Society isn't compassionately looking at these moms saying, "Hey, Mama, you're doing too much." Society isn't applauding the mom who didn't leave her house for four weeks after having her baby, or the mom who slept until 9 am with her baby because she was up so many times nursing. We applaud and encourage the wrong things. We are annihilating mothers' health and wellness as they attempt to live up to these standards and achieve the desired praises.

Think about every other animal who gives birth, a dog for example. When a dog is close to going into labor, that mama lays in the whelping box and does nothing else. She rests her body. She's not shopping, cleaning, doing laundry, and making a month's worth of dinner to put in the freezer. She's letting everyone else do that stuff for her, cause she's getting ready to give *clap* birth *clap*. And then after she has her babies, she continues to lie there and nurse them for weeks. She only gets up to "use the bathroom" and eat. That's all. Nothing else. She lies, feeds, and heals. She's not getting up and running five miles with her owner or galivanting around the backyard. She's recovering. We, as a society, have strayed so far away from what our bodies are supposed to be doing that it's no wonder our bodies respond with anxiety, depression, and diseases. How else is your body going to get your attention?

WHAT MATERNITY LEAVE?

After arriving home with my son, I could no longer ignore my back pain. Your body will continue to decline to get your attention until you finally *have* to listen! I reluctantly called my OB office. The shame, hesitation, and nervousness I experienced on that call were pathetic. I was so ashamed to have to admit I hurt, to admit I needed help and admit that my body "failed," that I almost couldn't call. When I finally reached a point of being brave enough, I convinced myself that they would help me.

When the nurse took my call, she asked me to describe what was going on. I knew immediately that they'd say it was my sciatic nerve, so I was sure to explain at a level of desperation that I knew (oh, hey there intuition!) that it was not a nerve but something wrong with my bones, like something moved. So, when they called back with a script for a muscle relaxer, I wanted to fall apart in tears. It took so much courage to even make that call, for them to provide a muscle relaxer, while I'm breastfeeding no less, made me want to scream and give up on life. In my true form though, I stood right back up and kept fighting.

Like many a mother in a quarrel with herself and her medical providers, I turned to the mom groups on Facebook. It's necessary to weed out the good advice from the bad, but I'm always amazed at the willingness of mothers to share their knowledge and support with a fellow mother in need. On that forum I discovered a local chiropractor who specialized in mothers and babies. Bingo!

I believed in my heart that I would walk into my appointment, she'd do a quick adjustment, and I'd be good as new. Wrong. About five days postpartum, with my son in hand in his car seat carrier, I slowly hobbled my way into her office, which was in the bottom of another building that required walking down a short flight of stairs. Standing at the top of them, I stopped to collect my strength so I could make my way down into the office. With the window on the front door offering the doctor complete transparency of my pain, I made my way down the stairs, doing my best to not fall and also to hide how hard it was to actually make my way down.

My appointment was for a consultation. To my tremendous disappointment, I learned that the damage to my back was going to take intense work to repair. It was another shard of glass that I couldn't clean up. I felt like with every step I took, figuratively and literally, I was falling apart more and more. I couldn't bear the thought of being in this physical pain for another day—not because I couldn't handle the pain, but because I couldn't handle the humility. I couldn't handle needing help from other people throughout the day because I couldn't walk. I couldn't handle that the pain slowed me down when all I wanted to do was stay busy. Staying busy meant I didn't need to deal with the pain—the emotional pain that I was shoving down daily. I was being forced to stay still.

After that day, I found myself in an intense rotation of chiropractic and physical therapy care, going to them about three times a week each for at least four weeks before being able to taper off from my appointments. It turns out that my left sacroiliac joint was severely dislocated. Or something like that. I was in such a fog I don't actually know what the injury was. It hurt like hell. I had no idea that this part of my back would end up being my weakest link, and the biggest gauge of my health for the next five years.

The pain was unbearable. The only way I was able to walk was to use my son's stroller as my walker. I USED MY SON'S STROLLER AS A WALKER. I never wanted to admit my pain to the world or myself, so I put all of my weight into those handle bars and fought like hell to distribute my weight evenly between each step, faking an even gate and holding my breath through every painful step. Because of shame. Because we have a society that doesn't condone weakness.

Despite showing up for every single appointment and doing my exercises at home, I likely prolonged my injury because I never stopped working. In fact, I looked back at my work to see how long of a break I took only to find that I didn't take one. I had an 18-month-old daughter, had just delivered a baby, had just moved, my back was nearly broken, and it still wasn't enough to get me to take a damn break. Recounting this is infuriating. Even though I'm fully responsible for my own actions, I was fueled by society's expectations and kudos for women who overwork themselves. I was steadily working toward a gold medal.

Those photo sessions that I had to cancel because I was practically in labor? I rescheduled them for three weeks postpartum. Three weeks! I arranged to have my best friend with me to take care of John Paul for one session while Dustin stayed home with Hannah because he was too young to be away for too long without nursing. For the other session, Dustin came along to be with John Paul while we arranged to have his parents stay with Hannah. Those engagement sessions ended up being two of my favorite sessions, and they were with two of my very best clients and friends. The sessions gave me plenty of joy and gratitude, so this creates a lot of dissonance, but I can't help but feel sad remembering me as the mom who was in excruciating pain, lugging her three-week-old baby around in cold and flu season so she could do a couple engagement sessions. Not to mention, that November I was away for my best friend's bachelorette party, and then for her wedding on New Year's Eve. Thinking back, my head spins at the thought of all that I allowed myself to do without any boundaries, no's, or permission to rest and heal. It breaks my heart, but I am not an unusual case. This is how so many women function in our society. It's not okay. This is what's breaking us.

From this point, despite having the holidays in between, I steadily continued to work and build my business. I was fueled by pride and stubbornness. I didn't have the ability to recognize how much my children, home, and marriage needed the energy and focus that I was putting into my business. In hindsight, I understand that this work and drive were part of my defense mechanism to avoid dealing with the parts of me that needing healing: like the part of me that pulled my daughter out of preschool because I was scared she was going to get sick. And the part of me that began to feel betrayed by my family, because I felt like they were never there for me. The part of me that would scrub every surface of every part of the house even though no one was there to bring in germs. And the part of me that would drink too much red wine at night after the kids were asleep. The part of me that would literally crumble at the notion of a possible stomach bug, not even acknowledging that my fear was a full-fledged phobia that was interfering with my daily life. The part of me that was completely broken.

I didn't have the strength to see her and hear those broken parts of me. I hid in my perceived strength, working and wearing a Super Mom cape every single day as I continued to ignore the shards of glass that were piling up around me.

I NEED HELP

As winter settled in, I found myself racing to keep up the relentless pace of life raising two kids and running my own business. No matter if you work from home, work out of the home, or work full-time as a mother, you are going to find yourself in this space. Bringing home a new baby for the first time is something of a honeymoon. It's not all rainbows and unicorns, but it is new and exciting. You are delving into a new part of your life and learning as you go.

Certainly, everyone's experience is different, especially those with severe postpartum depression, but for the most part, moms with a first baby are excited for each milestone, every new set of clothes, and each new batch of toys the baby is old enough to play with. We're excited for the chest naps, the new smiles, and giggles. It's not to say that we don't adore all of these moments with our second child, or they're not as special (I can talk about this, I'm a second child), but the second go round is different, and the newness has worn off. And quite frankly, I don't even think it's about two kids. It's about moving into that second stage of parenthood when your baby is no longer a newborn, the dust settles, and you find yourself in a mundane routine that wears you down to exhaustion.

By January 2015, I felt like I was drowning—in dirt, toys, laundry, and sleepless nights, breastfeeding a very healthy baby—yes we got our breastfeeding all figured out!—grocery shopping, and keeping up with my to-do list. I couldn't figure out when to clean the bathrooms or mop the floors. Our dog never got walks anymore. We didn't have a fence, so I had to constantly find time to safely take him outside to do his business. I also had to find time to edit all of my photo sessions, answer e-mails, send out contracts, and write blog posts. The list goes on. I literally felt like I couldn't breathe. I found the perfect solution: hire a nanny.

Dustin agreed. With his work schedule, which resulted in him being called out often, he could see that I needed another hand. I couldn't do it all myself. He had no choice but to agree. Between my constant emotional breakdowns and tears, I was a fraction of the woman I used to be. I needed help.

After interviewing several young women, a 20-year-old college student sat in my living room, three months pregnant herself; we'll call her Katie. I felt a connection. Perhaps it was my intuition again. I knew Katie could help me.

Almost immediately, Katie began coming to our home every

Monday from around 7 am to 3 pm, before heading to her college classes as she worked to complete her bachelor's degree before her own baby arrived. For nearly six months, Katie came into my home weekly, never complaining and doing more than what I asked of her—laundry, cleaning, and caring for my babies—so I could work and take time for myself.

After taking a little time off to have her own baby, Katie continued to help me on a weekly basis for more than a year. She became a part of our family, and she will hold an incredibly important place in my heart forever. Hiring her, asking for her help, and accepting it were some of the best things I could have done for myself in those years. Along with her help, I also invested in hiring cleaning people.

Though I found myself in a space to ask for and accept help, it came from a place of desperation, trying to figure out how to make it all work. I would, and still do, painfully think of the time before children—when it seemed so easy to clean my house weekly. I had so much pride in the organization, tidiness, and cleanliness in my home. Because I learned to put my worth in this, having an untidy, dirty home and asking for people to help clean it left me feeling worth*less*. So, even though I accepted the help at that time, it came from a very wounded part of me.

AND THE BUSY BADGE AWARD GOES TO. . .

You guessed it! Me! Gosh, I was doing a phenomenal job at *everything*! I was building my business, steadily gaining more and more clients and photo-shooting opportunities, including taking on more weddings. It was unbelievable how much opportunity and incredible work continued to come my way. I was determined to find time to do it all. Looking back on this time, I am proud of my drive and ambition. But I'm not proud of how it blinded me and stole me away from so many other things, mainly from being a stay-at-home mom.

I had left my position as a school counselor because I wanted to be home with my daughter. My only dream was to be a mom—to be home with my child watching *Sesame Street*, going to playgrounds, and doing crafts together. I made this a reality.

I had not set out to start a business, but as my photography hobby grew into a business organically, I was fed by my obsession with the craft of photography and my entrepreneurial spirit. Later, I realized that an unhealed part of me defined success and self-worth through my work. In order for me to feel successful in life, I had to work enough to earn the salary I walked away from. I didn't need to do this because of our finances or because that was a deal Dustin and I made. I needed to do this because the little girl inside of me was convinced that if I didn't hit that number, I'd fail. But even when I hit that number, I felt compelled to keep going.

This drive, this thirst, this unhealed wound that I had, took me away from my biggest dream of all: being home with my kids. I realized it in June of 2015. I sat at my desk in front of my beautiful iMac that faced out into the gated play area. I watched my two-year-old daughter and eight-month-old son occupy themselves with the TV and toys. I looked at my editing queue and sessions coming up, and I broke down. The pain that I pushed down over and over began weeping out of my heart and soul in convulsive sobs as I grieved over the position I put myself in. All I wanted to do was experience the love and joy of being a present and grounded mother who could play with her children without the stress of work and house chores, but I had so much to prove (to no one but myself) in building my business. Once again, I swallowed my pride to ask for help. I knew on some level that once I relinquished my pride and asked for help, I would receive the help and answers I needed.

I knew that I could find validation and support in photography forums, where many of the photographers are mothers. With swollen, red eyes and a face full of drying tears, with my two bored and tantruming children a few feet away, I posted in the photography group with my tail between my legs. I found the original post:

"I'm a mama to a 2 year old (turned two in March) and an 8 month old. They're precious, well-behaved kiddos, but they're babies, obviously! I have a budding business, too. Both my babies and my business are my life in the most amazing way and I wouldn't change a minute of it. However, I'm really struggling with the whole "only 24 hours in a day" thing. Right now, my priorities are being sure to spend time with them (usually morning to nap) then edit my tail off during nap and then after their down. The baby isn't sleeping great at night so I'm running on fumes right now. With those as my priorities, I'm left with absolutely no time for anything else. Laundry, cleaning, me time (aaaah!), sleep, quality time with my amazingly supportive husband. Some weeks are totally better than others, but more than not lately, I'm feeling super exhausted like the little engine that just can't anymore. (But I will, I just feel like I can't!) Has anyone else ever been through this or going through this... anything you've done to help your workflow, time management? I should also mention I have regular sitters/family who come a couple mornings a week so I can work, but I have a desk top and let's face it. When Mommy's home, I can't just sit here and work without any distractions or kids climbing on my lap no matter how great my sitters are. Thank you for listening! —Signed, One happily exhausted mama photographer!'

I waited for someone to give me the answer to life. But instead, the comments were filled with what felt like passive-aggressive, unsupportive responses. One woman was doing all the same AND working full time. Another woman was doing all the same but had FOUR kids. Still another woman reminded me that everyone feels that way, which I read as "buck up." Others told me that I was taking on too much and had to slow down. This response was truth, but it was one I didn't know how to do because I didn't know what my boundaries were or what it meant to take on less. Remember, I put my worth inside of how much work I was doing. It wasn't as easy as saying "Eh, I'll just do less." Because what this statement actually meant to me was, "I'll BE less."

I had put aside my pride to ask for help, only to hear that apparently it's just always this hard with kids the age mine were. I decided the best thing for me to do would be to push down my feelings again, grab the damn duct tape, and close the broken jack-in-a-box so I could get a break from all of the feelings I didn't want to deal with.

Fall of 2015 rolled around. I continued to run myself ragged. I took on session after session and one opportunity after the next. I was pumping my breastmilk as I was driving, carrying my son on my hip for some sessions, leaving Hannah at home with a grandparent, and gloating every single time my clients and friends would say, "You're SO busy! I don't know how you do it all!"

That's like saying to a person with an eating disorder, "You're SO skinny! You must not be eating anything!" The wiring in the brain that causes a person to engage in addictive and self-destructive behaviors is reinforced when we hear someone notice what we're doing and recognize it in a positive way. That validation reinforces those little short-circuited wires. Sadly, many of us have it. It's why everything is labeled "hustle," because it's applauded and promoted as a way to live. When I heard these amazing compliments, I thought to myself, *I'm doing such a kick-ass job. I'm doing so much work, momming hard, and it looks like I have my shit together!*

By this point, I was so busy, I didn't eat much. I remember a friend saying to me, "You look thin." I smiled and replied, "I don't have time to eat!" The sad part was, I wasn't saying this in a way of explaining that I had a problem but a way of saying, "I'm so awesomely busy that food isn't even a priority anymore. By the way, have you seen the busy badge I've earned?" I didn't hear this comment and think to myself that I had a problem I needed to fix. I heard the opposite.

When my sweet John Paul turned one year old in October 2015, I found myself in the tug of war of having an October baby and being in the midst of the busiest photographer season. I definitely didn't plan the timing of his birthday very well, now did I?! Instead of prioritizing my time with my family, I continued to add in a tremendous amount of work and sessions to accommodate all of the inquiries I was getting. I began eating less and not prioritizing my body. From early 2015, through the time of my initial anxiety attack in 2016, I became very thin. People regularly commented on how thin I looked, but in a positive way like, "You lost all that baby weight!" which, again, is society's way of supporting a woman who is unhealthy and actually quite sick from not taking care of her mind or body.

For John Paul's entire first year, I juggled all of my to-dos on little sleep, not eating nourishing food, taking on more work than I should have, and putting a smile on my face. I found a new normal and routine in how I was approaching life. Even though my body was giving me signals that I wasn't taking care of myself, they were subtle enough that I could ignore them and hide them away. Two big clues were twice or thrice yearly emotional breakdowns and unintentional weight loss.

But the biggest clue was my constant phobia of stomach bugs. I read article after article, trying to understand the virus, how it was spread, how it was contained, what chemicals killed it, the incubation period, and how to avoid getting it. I refused to get salads from salad bars or take my kids to the grocery store from about October through May. I washed all of our hands raw every single time we went out. I carried my own Clorox spray to clean surfaces and handles everywhere I went, especially with the kids. I didn't allow them to go to birthday parties or have play dates. If anyone in our family showed signs of the norovirus, my body went into fight-or-flight mode. Hearing the words "tummy" and "belly" made my heart rate skyrocket. If I read "stomach bug" in a mom group, I had to close down social media and catch my breath. Often, it would ruin my night because I was feeling so much anxiety—even though I didn't realize that's what was happening.

By the winter of 2015, I was constantly afraid of becoming sick. This is part of why I lost so much weight. I felt too sick with worry to be able to eat. My worry made me so sick I thought I *was* sick, and thinking I was sick made me worry more. This vicious roller coaster turned into unbearable anxiety without me even realizing that's what I was dealing with. I found myself regularly asking other mothers, "Do you get this worried?" hoping my feelings would be validated only to find out that, nope, I was not normal in my stomach bug fears. Instead of doing anything about it, I continued to move through life in a constant panic. I tried to numb it with so much work I couldn't see straight.

When I think back on John Paul's first year, I'm thankful I took so many pictures because I don't remember it. I joke that I blacked out to get through it, but I don't remember it because I was in survival mode.

DO YOU HEAR ME NOW?

Time continued to progress. By early 2016, I was a walking shell of myself. From the outside, everything looked amazing. Despite my struggles, Dustin and I continued to have a strong relationship. My business was growing and thriving. We had two happy and healthy kids. We took amazing vacations, had a beautiful home and great jobs, and we looked happy. We painted the picture of the perfect family. I painted the picture of a perfect mom. And this is where it becomes even more complicated for me to be able to articulate. None of this experience is black and white. My days were filled with anxiety and stress with everything feeling so hard. But even in all of this, I was still in love with being a mother, I adored my children, and I was madly in love with my husband. I think a lot of women feel these contrasts, and I also believe it's why it was so hard for me to admit that I was having anxiety. I never wanted my anxiety to be all of me or to take away from the good in my life and I was afraid that admitting this part of me, it would be that. I was afraid I'd be admitting failure, and it would seep into everything I had done right in my life and the things that truly brought me joy, namely Dustin, Hannah, and John Paul.

Inside though, I was completely crumbling. My pride and stubbornness were beginning to lose the battle against the parts of me that had to be seen, released, and healed. When we ignore our intuition and signs from our body telling us what we need, our symptoms become greater until we listen. I suppose we all have different thresholds for when we choose to wave the white flag. For some, it's getting a few too many colds. For others, it's having anxiety daily until they can't take it anymore. For still others, it's a diagnosis of cancer. My goal is to help you gain the awareness to remove this threshold and hear what your body, mind, or soul needs when it's only a whisper.

After my anxiety attack in March, my body finally got my attention. I was listening. I think the hardest part in all of it was that I had ignored my body and feelings for so long that I was deep down a black hole. It was going to be impossible to climb out of the dark hole with willpower alone. It wasn't as simple as, "I just realized I'm down here, and I'm ready to get out now." To get out of the black hole would require a steady, slow, and consistent climb with the help of a lot of people holding the rope.

On that life-changing day in March 2016, after my trip to urgent care, I found myself in a state of complete physical, mental, and emotional exhaustion. In reflection, it was absolutely devastating to see where I was and to think of what my life looked like only four years before. I was literally gliding through life on cloud nine, my ducks were always swimming in a row, I had no sock without a mate, and not a spec of dirt or a bill was unpaid. I was desperate to create a family, to be a mom, and to live the life of my supposed dreams. But as I sat there, I thought, *This is so far from what I ever dreamed. This can't be happily ever after, because it feels like hell.* This thought brought me to my knees. It was the most confusing emotion I had ever felt in being a mother. My soul aches for my children. There has never been a moment that I wouldn't die for them. My heart literally bleeds for my kids, yet there I sat with my body failing me, my mind attacking me, and my soul crying. Something didn't make sense. This wasn't adding up, and I had to get to the bottom of it.

I made an appointment with my primary doctor to talk to him about what happened and what to do. While I'm a huge fan of Eastern medicines and holistic approaches, I also believe there is place for Western medicine. Finding a doctor who hears you and sees you is necessary to get the best care. I don't know if my family doctor understands the kind of extraordinary human he is.

As I sat in the patient room, with my long legs dangling from the old patient bed, white paper crinkling with each nervous movement I made, my doctor sat and listened to me. He explained the brain to me, and he brainstormed with me. He didn't say, "Here's your script." He showed compassion. He begged me to call the office if I ever had another anxiety attack, rather than going to urgent care. He sat in that room with me for 45 minutes as we discussed my health and different ways to rule things out so we could get to the bottom of why I was having so much anxiety.

I know that my family doctor is special: He's a unicorn. I beg you to find a doctor who treats you like the person you are. It will change your life as you find your physical, mental, and emotional wellness.

As I talked with my doctor, we pieced together that I had stopped nursing my son that January. My body had been either pregnant and/or nursing from July 2012 through the beginning of January 2016 and was now sitting in a space of not needing to grow or feed a baby. There was something hormonal happening. My doctor used the term "post-nursing anxiety."

There is little information out there about this phenomenon and, again, it's a disservice to mothers that we aren't educated on how powerful our hormones are and how much they may affect how we feel. I learned that the oxytocin that is vital for milk production begins to decrease and level out after weaning. Oxytocin is the "love" hormone, so naturally, as this is decreasing, we are going to feel sad, depressed, or anxious. Additionally, our prolactin, which is the hormone that also produces milk along with a calm and happy feeling, begins to decrease. So, yes, when you wean and lose two major happy hormones, you're going to feel the effects of it.

Although my doctor and I concluded that there was likely something hormonal happening, he also did many tests, including an EKG and full blood panel, to ensure that the rest of me was healthy. The tests showed my levels were in normal range, and my heart was beating the way it was supposed to. I checked out. However, there was no conclusive hormonal testing done to confirm our suspicions. In fact, I've since learned that most hormonal testing isn't offered and insurance doesn't cover testing such as the DUTCH test (Dried Urine Test for Comprehensive Hormones), it leaves the patient to their own devices to learn about this as an option and seek out a certified practitioner to offer the test and read the results.

My doctor and I also discussed medication and agreed that it was an option for me. He encouraged me to read more about it and really *feel* out if this was something I needed to support me through this time. Ultimately, my answer was no. I trust and believe in medication, but my body has such adverse side effects to so many medications, I wasn't willing to exchange some symptoms for others. I decided that I wanted to keep my feelings as they were to help me find the root cause of where they were coming from. Muting my feelings with medication could prevent me from figuring that out.

After several intense weeks of testing and doctor's visits, the diagnosis of a hormonal imbalance ate away at me. I believe my intuition was guiding me, asking me to take this route. I researched hormones while this sat heavily in my gut. A good friend of mine mentioned that she was working with a hormonal nutritionist to help with some digestion issues. It took me less than five seconds to find her contact information and get in touch with her. When I connected with her, there was never a question in my mind of, "Can this woman help me?" It was that knowing again, the realization that God-Universe led me to her. My work with her couldn't start soon enough.

I had no idea at the time, but working with her was the tip of the iceberg in my healing journey. She held the rope as I began to climb out of the dark hole. To this day, she is a tremendously important person in my life. Without question, she's a soul with whom I was meant to be connected.

THE NEXT FOUR YEARS

I think the hardest part in finding physical, mental, and emotional healing is that it takes a really long time—maybe even a lifetime. I refuse to sugarcoat it, because that would be cruel. Removing anxiety, finding our joy, living with less overwhelm, and being aligned with who we are meant to be and what we are supposed to be doing are things that take work. The journey isn't linear. It's not a gradual climb up—rather it's a zigzagged line of highs and lows. Some highs will be very high, and some lows will be very low. It's crucial to remember that a low is not failure. A low is not a setback. A low is *feedback*. A low is *still* moving forward.

Over the rest of 2016, I worked intensely with my hormonal

nutritionist, learning a lot about my body and how to heal it with food. What I learned and the shifts that I slowly began to feel were remarkable and very eye opening. I learned that my estrogen and progesterone levels were completely plummeted, and my adrenal glands were on overdrive. Because I had no fuel from any of my hormones, it took practically nothing to push my body into a state of panic. It was a relief knowing that something physiological was causing these horrendous emotional responses and feelings that I had every single day. It was a relief knowing, "I'm not crazy."

In addition to changing my hormones simply through adjusting my diet, I also started therapy once a week. I would continue therapy for a year and a half. In therapy, I completely broke down, investigating all of the sad parts of me, my relationships, and my roles.

This was also when I learned that I was suffering from post-traumatic stress disorder (PTSD), which was triggered when Hannah had the flu and then a stomach bug. My primitive brain perceived these events to be life-threatening, and so it turned the switch onto, "you must survive," which is also the anxiety switch. Yup, same switch. Sometimes our brains get a little over-zealous in their quest to keep us safe. In PTSD, your brain is looking for the same signals that happened in the original traumatic event, believing if those happen, the traumatic event will happen again. If your brain detects those small clues of the trauma repeating, it will turn on the flight-or-flight response to protect you from it happening again. Pretty amazing, right?

After my daughter and I were sick, my brain watched tirelessly for anything, *anything*, that looked remotely like a stomach bug 'cause by God, my brain was going to keep us healthy! This, my friends, was my anxiety. My body's essential hormones that kept my brain calm and happy were gone, my estrogen and progesterone were gone, my stress was through the roof, and my adrenal glands were completely out of whack. What does this all mean? I was a dang mess.

Through a lot of therapy, I was able to slowly rewire the neurotransmitters that were wired in a way to flip out thinking it was keeping me safe. The healing, discoveries, and tools I gained in therapy were crucial in my repair. The "magical" formula I found combined the physical healing I was getting with healthy eating with mental and emotional healing in therapy.

As a bonus, both my nutritionist and therapist, synchronistically, introduced me to the world of Gabrielle Bernstein and Marianne Williamson. The wisdom and teaching of these women began to completely change my perspective in life and allow me to look through a lens of love instead of fear. They were my gateway into the world of personal development and personal growth.

Personal growth became my new obsession. I began to learn more about holistic healing through understanding our chakras. I became committed to removing toxins out of our home. I started reading again, and I began creating more boundaries around my home, professional, and personal life. I found joy and connectedness in motherhood—which I had craved my entire life. My journey then led me to hire a life coach. This moved me completely out of survival mode. Coaching pushed me to begin to thrive and ultimately to live my best life. I slowly but surely began to feel less anxiety.

The anxiety didn't go away in a steady decline. It has returned at times in the past four years. And it likely will again. But with all of the tools I've learned in the past four years, I'm able to tackle anything that comes up and do it with more ease each time. And now I'm grateful to share all of these tools with you.

PART TWO

foresight

fore·sight

/ˈfôr-sīt/

noun

1. the ability to predict or the action
   of predicting what will happen or be
   needed in the future.

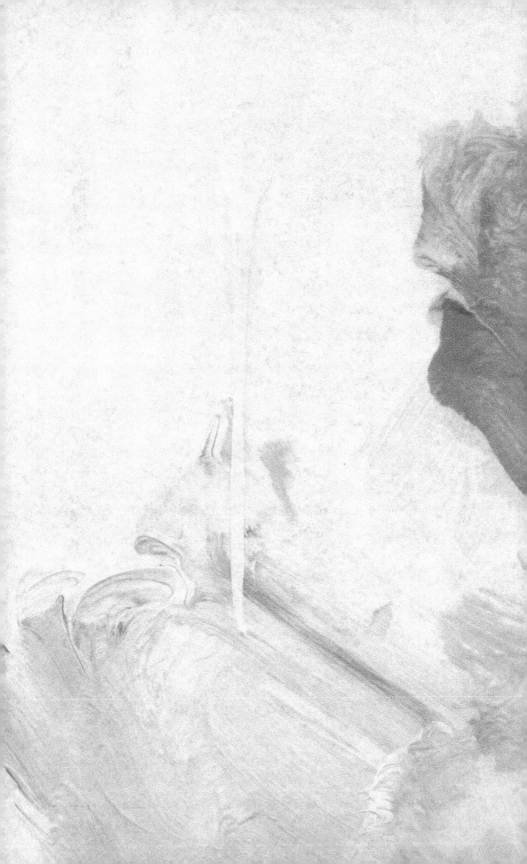

THE LAYERED
GROWTH METHOD

AN IMPORTANT NOTE I want to share with you, my beautiful reader, as we begin part two is this: You are enough. You are an amazing mother. I want you to stop, go back, and read that line again. Commit to saying this out loud every single day. Whether you gave birth to your children or not, whether you have postpartum hormonal fluctuations or not, you are still a mom. And being a mom is hard. You are pulled in a million different directions, the stress, lack of sleep, and big life questions that create our overwhelm or anxiety come with motherhood no matter how you've become a mom. And just because this happens doesn't mean we are weak or bad mothers, it means we are human. It means that we get to *choose* how we want to move through the healing journey and how we want to experience motherhood. And there is no wrong choice. Please know this.

The most important part to my journey, and likely yours, was truly recognizing that I needed help and healing. I just wrote half a book talking about my lows, from an emergency c-section, working too much, moving, hurting my back, feeling isolated, not eating, and the list goes on. But in the midst of all of this were also really good days. We took amazing vacations. I always had my in-laws help when I needed them. My husband and I had a relationship with open communication and a close connection. I was taking beautiful pictures of my children and finding something to enjoy and appreciate every single day. My highlight reel in life wasn't a lie. These were my truths mixed in with my struggles. Our good times, moments, and feelings allow us to convince ourselves that we're okay.

It's okay to not be okay. There is nothing black and white in this world. Even in a state of anxiety, overwhelm, and exhaustion, you can still feel an indescribable amount of joy and love for your life and your kids—like I did. The fall to anxiety and overwhelm is slow and steady. It's imperative that we stop to take notice of the state we're in—and to recognize if we need to make a change. I found my anxiety and overwhelm interrupted my daily life. That's when I knew it was time to make a change.

My healing journey is very specific to me. No one else will experience the same type of healing that I did, and no one will use the same exact tools or the same order of tools that I did. Your journey is like a snowflake; it's going to be specific to who you are and how your life is supposed to be lived. Know and remember that life is happening *for* you, not *to* you. You are in the driver's seat. As you find healing for your anxiety and overwhelm, as you find purpose in your motherhood journey, remember that it's yours and yours alone. Live it for *you*. Now that I've shared my story of my struggles with anxiety, I am going to share the tools I've used to heal it. I wish I had the foresight before my children were born to know these things. But I didn't. But you can learn from my hindsight.

We will never be able to live our life with hindsight vision.

Foresight is simply having intention. It's having an awareness and a grounding to enter a situation or make a decision with purpose. I believe that most women become mothers without enough preparation. Our society focuses on all of the good stuff, rightfully so because it really *is* good stuff. And we struggle with too much shame and embarrassment to talk about the real stuff. Plus, we fear talking about scary stuff saying, "We don't want to scare or overwhelm new moms."

Maybe it's not any of those things. If I had read this book before having my children, I might have responded with my know-it-all attitude of "that won't happen to me." That's okay. My hope is that from reading this book, from hearing the authentic, the raw, and the honest, it will plant a seed—the seed of a tool that you don't need yet, but will be ready to harvest when you *do* need it. I hope this book gives you the awareness so that when you reach a point of having anxiety or feel overwhelmed by motherhood, then you can pick up this book again and thank me for being real with you. I love motherhood, and I hope that as a collective of powerful women, we can change the story of motherhood and anxiety. I hope that we can stand empowered in our roles, not defined by them or disempowered by them. We can do this together. We can do it with foresight.

And for you, Mama, who's reading this in a state of overwhelm, exhaustion, and anxiety, you are going to be okay. You are not alone in this. I promise. Please take your next step, let it be small but mighty, and ask for people to hold your rope so you can be secure in your climb. The climb isn't easy, and it's not quick. But when done with steadiness, consistency, and faith, you make progress and slowly find your way out of the black hole.

Now, I am going to break things down for you in a simple way. I'm going to share a LOT of information, including ways to schedule, communicate, set boundaries, care for your body, support your energy, and heal your energy. I'll give you enough information on everything to get you started and make progress. Know that there is so much more to learn about every one of these topics, so don't be scared to start your own learning journey on the pieces that light you up. I have a lot of therapeutic approaches, certifications, and education to back up a large percentage of what I'm going share, but much of it comes from my own experience. It's my goal to bring these things to your awareness. You do NOT need to become an expert in every single thing. Focus on strengthening your foundation, hiring professionals when needed, and learning more about the practices that resonate with you. Follow your intuition to know how and what to navigate, beautiful soul!

ANXIETY AND OVERWHELM

First, I think it's really important that we have a very clear understanding of what anxiety actually is.

When I got home after my anxiety attack, Dustin and my mother-in-law seemed uncomfortable, not knowing how to respond to what just happened to me, even though they were full of love and compassion for me in that moment and ones that followed. I think a large part of it is because we, as a society, don't fully understand what anxiety is. Many people perceive it as an emotion that can be turned on and off, or a weakness, when, in fact, it's a physiological and neurological response. It's very far outside of our "control." Let's break this down so we're clear. If you are suffering from anxiety, it's imperative that you know what's actually happening to you.

Talking about the brain can become complicated, although I could easily sit and listen to hours of brain talk. It's the geek in me, but I can't assume you're a brain geek, so let's chat about it quickly and then move on to the stuff that is going to help you.

The various parts of your brain hold their own jobs, with many of the parts working together to make things happen. The brain is easily the most complicated organ of your body and, despite it being 2020 (as I write this book), neurologists only know 10 percent of the brain's function, according to scientificamerican.com. This leaves 90 percent of the brain as an unknown, which blows my mind. (Did you see what I did there? heh) Anyway, the two parts of your brain that are involved during anxiety are the amygdala and the hypothalamus. You hold memories in your amygdala, which then connect to your hypothalamus. These parts of your brain tell your body how to respond to an event.

Let's use my fear of the stomach bug as an example. I had a perceived trauma with my daughter getting the stomach bug. This perceived trauma and memory was now stored in my amygdala. Any time my brain perceived something remotely similar to this memory, it told my hypothalamus, which then decided, "Woah there! This is dangerous! Let's protect you!" and then turned on that little switch, it's called fight or flight. It floods my body with cortisol, which is the stress hormone, and norepinephrine so that my reflexes are faster. My heart is racing so that it can give more oxygen in case I have to run. My body is now in survival mode. Typically, I'm not actually needing to survive anything and utilize the hormones my brain is pumping out for me, so they result in other symptoms like shaking, clammy hands, light-headedness, and nausea. We call this feeling "anxiety."

Consider the fact that your body is giving you the response for survival—even if all that created this was a thought, a worry. There isn't actually anything to survive. There's no tiger chasing you! You can't use up any of the survival hormones to save yourself, so where do they go? They create all of those symptoms, and, ultimately, it's creating your anxiety. Your body isn't able to fulfill the job that the brain is telling it to do.

As I struggled with anxiety, I found it very helpful to understand what was happening to my body. Remember that in addition to this short explanation, there could be other hormonal fluctuations contributing, too, and also environment factors, which we will unpack very soon.

It's important to address the fact that some mothers don't experience anxiety, but they do experience overwhelm. A study by Forbes-Women and TheBump.com found that 92 percent of working mothers and 89 percent of stay-at-home mothers felt overwhelmed with work, home, and parenting responsibilities.

According to the Oxford dictionary, overwhelm means to bury or drown beneath a huge mass. Yup. That's actually pretty much what it feels like. It's having one kid asking for homework help while another is screaming and crying that he has a stain on his pants, the burner is on, the phone is ringing, you just remembered you forgot to reply to an important e-mail, you still need to sign your kid up for something before the deadline, and you just realized you forgot to move the clothes to the dryer—again. Or you have a cranky baby nursing nonstop, a toddler climbing furniture and writing on the walls, the UPS guy ringing the doorbell at naptime, you haven't showered for three days, and you can't remember the last time you cleaned the toilets. It's *overwhelming* to say the least.

It doesn't have to feel this hard. I repeat: It doesn't have to feel this hard.

Am I going to write out a magical methodology that when applied you'll live your life as a mom with ease and joy 100 percent of the time? No, absolutely not. Anyone who tells you that motherhood can feel good all the time is lying. That's not a human experience. Being human means feeling emotions, having good days and hard days, and experiencing imperfection. If your goal is to live a life of perfection, you will inevitably burn out. Perfection is not attainable, and your climb to try and reach it is not sustainable. Enter burnout.

Whether you suffer from overwhelm, anxiety, or both, know that while it'll never be gone 100 percent of the time, you can embrace the zigzagged growth chart knowing that another high will come. Eventually, you'll have more highs than lows. Consistent effort, faith, and support can almost guarantee steady growth forward.

To find our steady growth forward, I'll share information about physical, mental, emotional, and spiritual wellness. While I'd love to compartmentalize them, they are completely interwoven. I've found you need to work in a foundational way, as if you are stacking layers, to build up from the bottom. You can't build a strong house on a weak foundation. I see personal growth as a ripple effect with you being the rock that is thrown in the water. The bigger and stronger you are, the more profound your effect will be on the water around you. Each ring in the water affects the next, and these are what I see as our layers. We are the foundation, the rock, or what I refer to as Layer One. The rings that follow after us are Layer Two - our relationships and boundaries, Layer Three - our personal development, and Layer Four—our expansion. I've coined this method as The Layered Growth Method. I believe these should be worked on in order, and so we'll discuss them in order. You don't need to master one layer to move to the next, but you should at least feel a sense of clarity and ability to move forward. Each layer is going to need your regular attention and consistent work. You might never master one, but you should have a handle on it, an understanding and awareness before moving to the next step.

All of these pieces work together like a beautiful dance. If you're meditating every day but skipping meals and not sleeping, you'll never meditate away your anxiety or your overwhelm. At some points in your life, some layers will clamor for your attention, and then later another layer will take the lead. That's okay. What's important is having the awareness to know when it's time to move between the different layers. Trust yourself; trust your body and what it's telling you. It's always talking to you and guiding you. Good? Good. Let's get started.

LAYER 1

YOUR FOUNDATION

WE ALL HAVE A FOUNDATION, and a good one at that, but none of us have a perfect one that's unaffected by life events. No matter who you are, you have a foundation that is functioning and doing its job. Like any foundation, though, the earth around it can get saturated, move, settle, and change, causing the foundation to crack, shift, and become a little less sturdy in some areas. This is a normal process of a building. If these cracks and weak parts of the foundation are ignored, over time they will become worse and nearly irreparable. To keep a structure strong, it's necessary to remove the stressors of a foundation, fix the cracks, and strengthen the weak areas.

What are the components of Layer One?:

- Meet your basic needs
  - Air
  - Food
  - Shelter
  - Sleep
  - Water

- Remove toxins
- Increase your self-care
- Improve your self-worth
- Be present
- Be grateful

MEET YOUR BASIC NEEDS

Psychologist Abraham Maslow theorized that humans have a hierarchy of needs, with basic needs needing to be met first before any others. Meeting our needs drives our behavior, but people are so complex that things aren't always black and white. Consider a wild animal that's not getting enough food. The animal will work tirelessly to find food and spend its energy on nothing else. In fact, it'll instinctively conserve energy if it's not getting enough food. People are phenomenal at ignoring their own needs and their bodies' innate instinct to meet them.

Let's go back to how the brain works. Despite how socialized and evolved we've become, we still have a primitive part of our brains, and, if our basic needs aren't being met, it's going to prompt us to believe we are in danger. What does the brain do when we are in danger? It turns on our survival switch. And here, my friends, is where our anxiety shows up. So, if we aren't getting enough food, instead of listening to our body and focusing on meeting this priority, we have learned to be able to ignore our primitive instincts and convince ourselves that we are capable of surviving without fully meeting this need.

I found myself eventually in a place of being sorely mistaken. It didn't happen overnight, but my hormonal imbalances and daily anxiety didn't happen by accident. My lack of nutritional care played a very important role in how my body responded. Not eating well is like not putting gas in a car. It's asking your body to run on fumes until it completely runs out of gas, then throwing it in neutral and pushing it from behind. It's not sustainable. Eventually, if you want to keep going, you are going to crash and burn with no other choice but to find a damn gas station. And believe me, you're gonna want to fill the whole tank because if you only put in three bucks, it won't be enough to gain your strength back before you have to start pushing again.

All of this isn't to say that if you meet your basic needs, your anxiety and overwhelm will dissipate completely. If this were the case, this book would be a lot shorter. Just like a car has other fluids to check and functions to monitor, you need more than food to run the right way. We'll discuss these other layers in later chapters. But first and foremost, your body needs gas. If your basic needs aren't met, any of the other work you do to support yourself will either not work or take no effect because your brain is doing everything in its power to keep you safe and help you survive. In order to survive, you need to meet your basic needs.

Mothers become accustomed to not giving ourselves our oxygen first. It's the first rule in survival: Put on your oxygen mask first because you can't save others if you're dead, right? How have we become so used to skipping meals, forgetting to drink water, not allowing ourselves to sleep in or take naps, and not moving our bodies? It's absolutely no wonder to me that we are falling apart. We must mother ourselves by meeting these basic needs. We'd never allow our babies to go unfed or deprive them of crucial sleep and exercise. Why do we do it to ourselves?

We do it because life feels too hard. No human, in their right mind, would do this to themselves on purpose. It's come to a point of it simply feeling too hard. I get it, Mama. We fall into a routine of bad habits and putting ourselves last. And, honestly? I believe that we think we'll "get to us" at some point, but day after day we move to the bottom of the list. We never get to ourselves. This decision compounds, and slowly but surely it will catch up to us. Our bodies will let us know by responding in all different ways from thyroid issues, adrenal issues, acne, insomnia, extreme fatigue, fibromyalgia, anxiety, and depression. If it were as simple as saying, "go eat," you would.

The reason it feels so hard is because we're not making it a priority. What do I mean by this? A priority means that nothing else is more important than that one thing. In a day, we need to do a million and one things, or so we've convinced ourselves. I put laundry, cleaning, my kids' needs, editing, and answering e-mails before eating—always. I'd wake up to my children's "Mom!" I'd nurse and make breakfast. I'd maybe pick at something they left behind or take a handful of cereal as I was putting the box away and drink cold coffee all the way until noon. I'd spend the morning playing with them whilst working on house chores and tidying, bringing us to lunchtime like the speed of light. It always felt like a fire was lit underneath me. I'd race against the clock to get my kids something to eat for lunch, empty the dishwasher, and clear the dishes from the sink as they ate, taking us right up to nap time. I'd eat their last bite of mac and cheese or chicken nuggets, kind of wishing they had left more for me to eat, and then rush to get them down for nap so that I could use every single minute I could to work. There was no time to eat! If I even took 30 minutes to eat, I feared I wouldn't get all of my work done, and God forbid I made it to the end of the day without being able to cross everything off my list. By the time my kids woke up from a nap, my energy was depleted, and I was no longer hungry because my body was shutting down and conserving. Our bodies are smart, aren't they?

I know the story, my beautiful fellow mama. I know how hard it can be to get nutritious food into our bodies. I can't stress enough how important it is to make time for it. The time is there! We choose to use our time on different things. So, it's a matter of choosing to use our time to eat. We are skipping it, thinking we are making more time and getting more done, but I *promise* you, if you make eating a priority, you *will* find more *sustainable* energy, which helps you get more stuff done.

But *how*? How do you make it easy to eat?

I should preface every section in this part with this: Find a professional to work with to give you even more information—specifically on *you*. No minds, bodies, or souls are the same. It's important to work with professionals—such as a nutritionist, naturopath, medical doctor, coach, mentor, therapist, or trainer—to help support you through the process. Even better, find someone certified in running different tests to learn exactly what your body needs, which will undoubtedly lead to full body health and take the guess work out. Test, don't guess. Three tests that I have found to be the most informative are the GI Map, Hair Tissue Mineral Analysis (HTMA) and the previously mentioned DUTCH Test.

I want to remind you of this: If our minds are powerful enough to convince ourselves that we can live without meeting our basic needs, then our minds are also powerful enough to find a way to actually meet them. It's a matter of making the choice to do so.

Let's talk about the five:

- Air
- Food
- Shelter
- Sleep
- Water

AIR

Air seems obvious doesn't it? We breath automatically. We don't have to make a conscious decision to breath, and because of that, we lose our intention with our breath. This is where your air can be so important in managing your anxiety.

When we are short of breath, pulling in shallow air just into our chest, short of our belly, it's an immediate signal to our brain that we are in danger and another cue to turn on the fight-or-flight switch.

I remember when I first learned this, I think my mouth fell a little. It seems so obvious and such a tangible and easy way to support my nervous system, yet for my entire life, I had never taken control of my breath. This actually felt funny to me, considering how many students sat in my counseling office and learned to "belly breathe" with my teaching. Yet here I am, totally ignoring my body's cues to belly breathe.

For me, and in teaching my clients, one of the first things I remind them to do, always, is to breathe. This needs to be practiced and used daily. Do guided meditations offering breath work, breathe before getting out of bed, breathe in the middle of the day when you feel frazzled or edgy. Just breathe! There are three go-to breath techniques to really help create intention in your breath. It's easy to stop and take deep breaths, but I find something more guided helps really ensure I'm slowing my breath down the way it needs for my brain to calm my nervous system down.

BOX BREATHING

This is my favorite breath work because it can be done anywhere and not make you stand out. Whether you're in your car, grocery store, making dinner, or laying in bed, it's one of my favorites. Think of drawing a box and each side being four counts. Imagine drawing a box. Take four counts of deep breath in, hold for four counts, slow four counts out, hold it out for four counts, and then keep going until you begin to feel your heart rate lower.

NOSTRIL BREATHING

In this breathing technique, you are going to take one hand and hold your thumb over one nostril and your pointer finger over another in such a way that if you squeezed them, you'd be holding your nose closed. What you're going to do is use your thumb to only hold down one nostril. Take a deep breath in through the open nostril and then you are going to release your thumb and then press down your other nostril with your pointer finger as you release the air out of the opposite nostril. Keeping your fingers where they are, now breathe in through the open nostril, then close it and release out of the other. Continue doing this for a few rounds, and then find which nostril is hardest to breathe through and take in a few full breath cycles out of the one nostril before completing.

STRAW BREATHING

It's literally as it sounds. Take a straw and breathe in and out through the straw. The smaller pathway forces you to breathe slower both in and out.

No matter your technique, remember you always have your breath, and you always have control over it. Create the intention to come back to your own breath when everything else around you feels unsteady.

FOOD

Every single thing we eat is either going to support your body's functioning or hinder it. Your body is a very complicated machine designed to need certain vitamins and minerals to flush out necessary toxins, maintain blood sugar levels, sustain proper energy, and design the correct ratio of hormones. With today's choices and availability of processed foods full of sugar and toxins, your body's response is going to be defensive. It will defend itself because it's incredibly intelligent, but to defend itself, your levels and functioning become compromised. There can be many results from this compromise, one popular one being anxiety.

Understanding exactly what our body needs can get a little complicated because there isn't a single diet or vitamin protocol that fits all. I highly recommend working with a certified, trained practitioner, who can assist you in finding the food your body loves and with which it can thrive. Is it absolutely necessary in order to change how you're eating? No, but having someone run tests and create an individualized protocol is going to help your body thrive.

I found that eating gluten and dairy isn't ideal for me. Too much caffeine, alcohol, and sugar aren't ever good for you and should be consumed in moderation. For people suffering from anxiety, the results from cutting back on caffeine and alcohol or eliminating it completely will shock you—in a good way. Truly. It's alarming how much caffeine and alcohol contribute to the body's anxiety response. The thought of this is terrifying for us coffee and wine lovers, but the benefits far outweigh that second cup of coffee each day or glass of wine each night. Try it.

Next I'll structure how to build meals for you, share easy ways to make it happen during the day, and even look at some meal ideas.

Build each meal with these components, adjusting for any food allergies.

1. Protein
2. Vegetables/Fiber
3. Starch
4. Healthy fat

Have go-to foods in each of these areas for every meal. Here are mine. I buy the foods marked with an asterisk in bulk.

Protein: Eggs, frozen chicken,* frozen fish,* organic ground turkey,* organic ground beef,* organic lunch meat (turkey), tuna

Vegetables: Power greens,* frozen veggies (green beans, broccoli, peas), baby carrots.* (My dog loves these, too.)

Starches: GF bread, rice packets, sweet potatoes, purple potatoes, red potatoes, spaghetti squash, quinoa

Healthy fat: Avocado, chia seeds, seeds for seed cycling (more on this next!), coconut, extra virgin olive oil (EVOO)

Below are some ideas for each meal of the day.

BREAKFAST

BREAKFAST SMOOTHIE + A PIECE OF GF TOAST

- Plant Based Protein Powder with added greens
- A green powder supplement
- Chia seeds
- Half avocado
- 2 seeds for seed cycling*
- $\frac{1}{2}$ cup strawberries
- $\frac{1}{2}$ cup blueberries**

* Seed cycling has been a game changer for my body. It's one of the best ways to naturally begin to balance and regulate your progesterone and estrogen. Finding this balance can help regulate weight, acne, hair health, hot flashes, and more, according to healthline.com. While more evidence based research is happening to support this naturopathic method, at the very least, having seeds in your smoothie is a great way to get healthy fat in there.

To do seed cycling, eat 1 tablespoon each of flaxseed and pumpkin seed from days 1 through 14 of your cycle. Day 1 is the first day of menstruation. If you're a woman without a regular cycle for any reason, your day 1 is going to be the new moon. On day 15 through the end of your cycle or up to the next new moon, you are going to have 1 tablespoon each of sesame and sunflower seeds. It's that simple! There are a lot of articles and research out there, so if this is something that interests you, I definitely recommend researching more and talking to your nutritionist about its benefits.

**You might have noticed this smoothie has no banana! I do not eat bananas because of my blood sugar levels, but this may be a great carb option for you. Know your body!

EGGS AND VEGGIES

- Sauté sweet potatoes and peppers in EVOO.
- Add spinach and sauté.
- Add in whisked eggs.

BREAKFAST MUFFINS

Pinterest has a ton of recipes on egg muffins or oat muffins that are fueled with nutrients for sustainable energy. I love to make things like this when I have a busy week ahead or we are going on vacation. It makes an easy grab-and-go breakfast, ensuring that I'm nourishing my body even when things are busy or junk food is tempting. Be sure, as you're looking at recipes, that you have all of the four components mentioned of protein, vegetables, starch, and a healthy fat. Sometimes it's hard to get a starch in there, so I'll have that separately, like a piece of toast.

LUNCH

I always piece together each component of a meal, often sauté and mix it all together in a bowl.

Examples:

- Sautéed ground turkey, greens, carrots, avocado, rice, EVOO, and Himalayan or sea salt (Use natural salts for the minerals!)
- Sautéed ground turkey, greens, quinoa, and EVOO
- Runny eggs, GF toast, avocado, and greens
- Grilled chicken, greens, carrots, sweet potatoes, and EVOO

For super easy lunches all week, I often cook a pound of ground turkey on Monday, mix it with a starch (rice for example), use a quarter of it, and put the rest in a container to enjoy for the next three days or so.

DINNER

This is where I plan. I have all of these ingredients on hand so we can make a dinner quickly with no planning if needed.

Examples:

- Fish with broccoli and rice, using an oil during cooking.
- Chicken with baked potato and green beans, using oil during cooking.
- GF spaghetti with organic ground beef and sauce (I always keep several types of GF pasta in the house and vodka and marinara sauce.) I usually add oil to the ground beef.

To plan meals that are more exciting...

- I go through my planner to see what days I'll be home and know that I'll have the energy to cook a new recipe. This is something I really enjoy doing, so I like to make time for this. (I did not do this when my kids were under the age of four.)
- Find your recipe! My go-to sources are cookbooks, Pinterest, and allrecipes.com.
- Make your grocery list.
- Write out your menu so it's an easy reference throughout the week, and your significant other can start dinner if needed.

I do NOT do crazy meal prep on Sundays. It doesn't work for my energy, but for you, it may be perfect. Play around with your prep style, and stick with what works for you. Don't worry about what other people do; do you.

I often plan dinners that make enough so that we have leftovers at least twice a week. By doing this, I have to cook only four weeknights a week, which has been a very efficient use of time whether it's extra time with the kids, less rush after an extra-curricular activity, more time to get other house chores done, or more leisure time.

If you don't prioritize food at all, this is going to feel overwhelming. Of course it is! Remember, ask yourself, "How can I?" Start with one meal. Fix *one meal.* Choose the one that feels the most attainable and sustainable. Get that down, find your footing, and then move onto the next meal. It took me about a year to revamp my meals and find a rhythm in crafting meals without gluten or dairy, but my consistency and small action steps helped me ease in all of it. You can, too—one baby step at a time.

SHELTER

Without question, if you don't have a place to live, your brain is going to work overtime to help you find one and to keep you safe. In terms of shelter, I see it more as our environment, or the state of your space, supporting the management of anxiety and overwhelm.

If you're like me and clutter and disorganization in your home creates stress, know this about yourself, accept this about yourself, and find ways to create more organization or at least have a sacred spot just for you.

As a mother of small children, I've come to the realization and acceptance that my home likely won't be clean and tidy to my liking until my kids are much older. I didn't come to this realization on my own; it took hours of sitting on my therapist's couch to find this acceptance.

So, instead of focusing on what is out of your control, focus on what is. Since finding that acceptance on that sunken couch, I've made it a priority to always have my own space—whether it's a corner in your bedroom or an entire room in the house that is yours. Find your space, and make it sacred.

In my old house, I really needed this. We chose to make the fourth bedroom my office. As I picked out the furniture, decor, and inspiration, my mom shared a story with me. She told me how a friend of hers always wanted to go to Arizona; it was a place that had her heart and made her feel joy. So, this friend of hers made a space in her home decorated to feel like Arizona, and she called it her "Arizona." As my mom shared this with me, she encouraged me to have my own "Arizona" in my home. And now I encourage you to do the same. Make your "Arizona," the space in which you can be to feel your joy. This type of shelter is a basic need.

SLEEP

It's hard for me not to laugh at this because I was nursing my daughter from 2013 through 2014, then nursing my son from 2014 through the beginning of 2016. I basically didn't sleep through the night for three years, especially with my son, who was so darn hungry at night! And then my babies were up at the butt crack of dawn, and I felt like I had been completely railroaded.

I'm not going to lie to you: Those first few years as a mom, you are going to feel tired, especially if your kids don't sleep through the night. I'm not going to write about how to sleep train your kids, or if you should. But I *am* going to talk to you about how you can take care of yourself the most in those first few years of parenthood.

My very first suggestion, and by suggestion I mean DO IT, is having an evening routine. I think every single mother can agree that the nighttime, from about 10 pm until 12 am, are sacred hours of complete quiet. It's usually the time that our kids are actually asleep, our spouses are often asleep, and even the dog is asleep. It's like hearing singing angels to sit in a house by yourself and not be bothered by a single soul.

I value this time *more* than sleep. I relish in hearing the house creak as it settles in the darkness. I sit quietly, watching the lights from passing cars dance across the walls. I'm hypnotized by the TV's bouncing light as it casts a mind-numbing reality show. I slowly taste each sip of sleepy-time tea that I bring to my lips, helping me to quiet the monkey mind from the day that passed. (Not familiar with the term "monkey mind"? It's that feeling where your mind is racing, jumping from one thought to another like a monkey through the trees. Monkey mind is often associated with anxiety.) It's like a vacation every night. But, inevitably, you wake up before the sun to regret that last show that you watched and wish so badly that you could have another hour of sleep.

These quiet evenings are gold, but I recommend having them in moderation because nothing in excess is good. Schedule them weekly as something to look forward to, and, in turn, you can enjoy them with less guilt. If you wake up tired, you'll know that getting to bed later than usual was something you did with intention because you love it. It filled your cup instead of doing it mindlessly in habit and having it drain you of all of your energy. How we choose to show up in our day must come from a place of intention, not mindless habit, to obtain and sustain our energy.

What should you do the other nights of the week? Personal development experts often tout the importance of having a morning routine. I'm sure that the man who wrote about the *Miracle Morning* wasn't breastfeeding a sumo wrestler infant five times a night and getting zero hours of restful sleep. Once your kids are older, you will likely find true value in the morning routine. But I don't think it's really that valuable to a mom who is waking through the night. Instead, for her the evening routine is even more valuable, in my opinion.

Creating an evening routine is about finding intentional habits to replenish your energy and prepare you for a restful night's sleep. Here are some ideas:

- Taking a bath or a long shower
- Applying lotion to your body
- Doing a skincare routine
- Using essential oils to stimulate sleep
- Having a cup of your favorite tea
- Journaling
- Meditating
- Lights out by 9:30 pm

If you crave those quiet nights in the living room watching TV, you might need to rewire your brain to crave a routine like this instead, which will help you sleep better and reenergize you. Consistency is what will rewire. Finding a fulfilling routine will help you wake up with more ease, less exhaustion, and renewed patience. Find an evening routine that feels good to you. Remember this is for *you*. It can look however you want it to look, and you can also change it however and whenever you want to or need to.

Another way to get more sleep is to nap. I know, so many people told us "nap when the baby is napping," and we laughed because they clearly didn't know how much we need to get done. Remember, our basic needs are the priority. I promise you, I seriously promise you, that the stage with young children of the messy house, piles of laundry, and toys all over the place will not last forever. It feels like it will, but it won't. And when you tell me, "But I can't sleep knowing the house is a mess." I call bullshit. I've been type A, too. I've been the overachiever, too. It's not "I can't" it's "How can I?" We'll get into delegating and boundaries later, but for now, trust me, and find a way to nap. You certainly don't need a three-hour nap, but let yourself snooze for 20 minutes, and then go fold the laundry if you still want to.

WATER

Let's keep this simple. Drink it. I know the limiting beliefs you likely have:

- I forget during the day.
- I don't like it.
- I have to pee too much.

Okay, I hear you. I do! But it comes down to this. Are you willing to trade these excuses to get rid of anxiety, dull skin, and bad digestion? You choose.

The number one thing that I tell my clients and children is: Don't say *I can't*. Ask yourself *how can I?* How *can* you drink enough water? Here are some ideas.

- Drink a large glass as soon as you wake up.
- Get a water bottle that makes you excited to drink.
- Make it a daily competition with your friend or spouse.
- Add lemon or fruit to your water.
- Set a timer throughout the day reminding you to drink.

According to *Medical News Today*, drinking water:

- Lubricates the joints.
- Delivers oxygen throughout the body.
- Boosts skin health and beauty.
- Cushions the brain, spinal cord, and other sensitive tissues.
- Regulates body temperature.
- Improves digestion.
- Flushes body waste.
- Helps regulate blood pressure.
- Makes minerals and nutrients accessible to your cells.
- Is essential for breathing.

These all sound like really important functions, don't they? If I have to pee a little more frequently to get all of these benefits, you bet your butt I'm drinking a lot of water each day. This isn't a suggestion; it's a *basic need* for your body to function. This is a *priority*. It's so easy to let this fall down on our priority list because it truly does take intention and effort to get in enough water every single day. Understanding how it can support your anxiety, though, may help give you a little more motivation to get it higher on your priority list. Earlier on, I shared the metaphor of how our body will shut off all other systems in order to survive, comparing it to an animal in the wild making sure all of its needs are met. If we aren't meeting our basic needs that make our body function properly, our body's energy is going to immediately go after what's missing. So, with this in mind, if we are lacking on our water intake and are dehydrated, our body is going to be alerted that something's wrong; a basic need for survival isn't being met. And when we pile on signals of distress, such as not eating, not sleeping enough, not breathing deeply, and then not getting enough water? This will, without question, give our body more reason to turn on our anxiety. Also, water has calming properties, and our brain and body are made up of mostly water. For this reason alone is why we should be filling ourselves with water.

To really enhance the benefits of water, it is strongly recommended to drink clean water. So much of our water is contaminated with chemicals that are dangerous for our body, and, if we are drinking a ton of toxins with our water, it becomes counter-productive. I recommend drinking spring water or using a filtering system such as a Berkey.

REMOVING TOXINS

Removing toxins from my environment has been a very slow and steady process for me, and, the more I learn in this area, the more passionate I am about sharing how important this is in your anxiety journey. When my son was a couple months old, I bought a starter kit for Young Living essential oils. It was a slow start for me, feeling overwhelming and only assuming that the new oils were trendy and a new way to make my house smell good. However, the more I learned about how we can use essential oils in place of toxic products and saw the astounding results from something as simple as an oil, like eliminating headaches, seasonal allergy symptoms, or a weird rash only a kid could get, I continue to become more and more convinced.

I have always been in love with lotions, candles, beauty products, and makeup. I remember being a young teenager walking to the local shopping center to spend my hard-earned baby-sitting money on a favorite perfume or new mascara. Does anyone remember the perfume Sunflowers by Elizabeth Arden or when clear mascara was all the rage for a hot minute in the 90s? Little did I know, this beloved hobby of mine was constantly dumping toxins into my body and disrupting its ability to function properly.

According to multiple sources, of 84,000 known chemicals that can cause cancer, birth defects, and more, only 11 of them are banned in the United States. That means nearly 84,000 chemicals that can make your body very sick are essentially allowed to be used in our daily products like suntan lotion, shampoo, baby wash, and makeup. The number of how many known chemicals is often up for debate in an effort to debunk this controversial statistic. To put this statistic into even more perspective, of the same chemicals, about 1,400 of them are banned in Europe. This means, 1,389 chemicals that are banned in Europe being deemed unsafe are not banned in the United States. This statistic alone made me realize how important it is to be my own advocate in understanding what I'm putting into my body and into my family's bodies.

The unsafe chemicals, aside from possibly causing cancer and birth defects, are called endocrine disruptors. According to the National Institute of Environmental Health Sciences endocrine disruptors are natural or human-made chemicals that may mimic or interfere with the body's hormones, which is our endocrine system.

Our endocrine system is comprised of glands that secrete different hormones, such as our pituitary gland, adrenal, and our ovaries. A hormone that is secreted from our endocrine system is the stress hormone cortisol. What this all means is that the system responsible for our hormonal functioning, including anxiety, is being tampered with by the chemicals we are ingesting through our diet and lifestyle. However, all of the products we are buying aren't properly regulated to ensure our health, so we need to do this ourselves.

I hope that this information is eye opening for you if it's something you've never known. It's not to be scary, it's a section to be interpreted as, "The more you know." This isn't about making a complete overhaul of your products in one night; it's about having the awareness and taking control of things that you buy and use to support your body and its functioning.

I am a huge believer in what I call "Ditch and Switch." This is taking the time to learn about one product and switching it out with a healthier option; just do a little at a time. The companies in which I have invested have been Young Living and BeautyCounter. By using the oils, supplements, and cleaning products of Young Living and all of the makeup, hair, and skin care of BeautyCounter, my family and I are living in much less toxins. In fact, since eliminating my use of candles and perfumes, I have been able to stop using a daily inhaler for asthma, which I've had to use for the past 10 years. If you aren't sure where to start and want to simply begin understanding what products are good and which aren't so great, an app that I love to use is called Think Dirty. This app allows you to search different products and rates how toxic the products are on a 0-10 scale.

All in all, its about educating yourself and taking control over the things that you can, and this is an area you absolutely can. Just a little at a time.

INCREASE YOUR SELF-CARE

Another imperative piece to your foundation is self-care. This term has become very trendy and synonymous with pedicures, massages, facials, and girls' nights out. We all deserve those luxuries and should absolutely plan and schedule if it fills your cup, but I personally don't believe they fall into the realm of self-care.

I believe that self-care is a demanding and difficult practice of self-discipline. While it takes a lot of effort to implement and maintain a self-care practice, it's worth every bit of it. In today's society, I add it into the basic need of motherhood. It's a part of motherhood that we quickly talk ourselves out of through our guilt of feeling indulgent and possibly abandoning our children, but what if I told you that a faithful and consistent self-care practice was more for your children than it was for you? Here's how I see it. Stay with me.

Our lives are a series of experiences, which are like blocks placed one by one on top of each other. As we grow, our lives begin to take shape, each experience building on a previous one. We eventually realize how life is a compound effect of everything that's happened before. One example is realizing you have guilt over sleeping in only to remember that as you grew up, your mother never slept in and was always up early working hard in her role as a mother. Or that your family values come from those family dinners as a child.

I realized something that is incredibly empowering. Mothers are the first blocks for their children. Their first life experiences are from us. Now, I realize that this is also a little terrifying because no matter who you are, you're not perfect. Some experiences will feel ugly and detrimental to their growth, but we have the power, in these early and formative years, to place the next block on top of that one, creating something stronger.

For example, let's say hypothetically that one day I'm feeling really exhausted, run down, and getting sick. My patience is non-existent. Then let's say my son spilled his yogurt all over the kitchen island and the floor, and I lost my shit. Like, full on mom-page. Queue in a block that will eventually require therapy to fix, right? Wrong. Before that block was fully set, I used this experience to talk to my child (or I would have if this actually happened, ha) to explain why I lost my marbles, tell him that he wasn't bad, and that it's no big deal that the yogurt spilled. I helped him realize that my response was a direct correlation to how I was feeling, and the lack of self-care I had implemented. It had nothing to do with him.

The block that was just laid down in his foundation is now a powerful one. It's one that has taught him that peoples' reactions and responses, even if directed toward him, likely have nothing to actually do with him.

The reason I was able to make this life experience a teaching one, powerful, and part of a strong foundation, was not by accident. It's not because I went to school or because I have a master's degree. It's because I work EVERY DAMN DAY in a grounding practice, in my faith, in my awareness, in meeting my basic needs and practicing self-care. I am constantly striving to understand myself more and in turn understand my children more.

Our children, who grow incredibly fast, will soon enough start to gather experiences that we are no longer a part of. Our kids will be off to school, building blocks from the relationships with their teachers and peers. Eventually, they'll be building blocks that we will know nothing about.

Our children will have life experiences that challenge them, such as experiences with drugs, sex, career choices, relationships, and finding their autonomy. In these parts of their lives, each experience is built on top of the other. With a strong foundation, a bad experience later in life doesn't have to break them. The blocks don't have to come tumbling down. They will have the tools to navigate these challenges and stand back up because you can teach them through example. And this, Mama, is why we need to take care of ourselves. Self-care isn't about treating ourselves. It's not because we deserve it, even though we do. It's not something that we can do when we have enough time. Self-care is investing in our children's foundation. A mother's self-care is vital for her own health so that her children are healthy in their bodies, minds, and spirits.

Self-care isn't pedicures and massages. Here's what self-care is: (We'll go into greater detail on some of these in later layers.)

- Eating three meals a day
- Understanding female hormones and how to eat to balance them
- Finding 20 minutes of alone time in your day to meditate and journal
- Moving your body when all you want to do is sleep
- DELEGATING, advocating for yourself, and recognizing mothers don't HAVE to do EVERYTHING

- Setting boundaries that feel really uncomfortable
- Having a physical, mental, and emotional awareness that can only truly be obtained and maintained through a self-care routine, like morning and evening routines
- Choosing tea instead of wine
- Going to therapy
- Deleting social media because it sucks up your attention and makes you spiral in comparison
- Taking vitamins
- Leaving dishes in the sink so you can take a nap
- Choosing a personal development podcast over a reality TV show

Self-care is hard. It requires discipline and hard work. While I know that mothers are the primary beneficiaries in our self-care practice, the reason we need to do it is for our children. A mother's self-care allows more patience. It allows more understanding. Self-care fills your cup so you can pour more. Most importantly, your self-care practice is a model to your children so they know *exactly* how to take care of themselves starting *now*. Your self-care, how you talk to and about yourself, impacts your children's internal dialogue.

We are our children's foundation. We are their first building blocks. If taking the time to have self-care feels hard because (fill in the blank, aka it takes time away from them, I feel guilty, I don't know how, I don't have support) I want you to say "How can I?" How CAN YOU make it work? Are you seeing a trend yet in how to respond to your own self limits? This isn't a luxury. This isn't easy. This is almost life or death. Our self-care is a direct correlation in how we experience our role as a mother, and even more importantly, how our children will learn to navigate their own lives. Give them a strong foundation. You CAN do it. And guess what? If you're meeting your basic needs, you're already doing a lot of your self-care.

Here are my top 10 self-care ideas for you. Some we've already discussed at length, and others we'll expand on in a later chapter.

1. **Find a meditation practice.** Mindfulness will change your life. My favorite app is Insight Timer.

2. **Have a healthy evening routine.** I know that wine and Bravo TV are appealing and sometimes a necessary evil, but work on creating an evening routine that helps you decompress and move through your emotions in a healthy way. Journal, meditate, have tea, do a breathing practice. Make it easy. It doesn't have to be an hour long; even just 10 minutes is a starting point. For mothers, evening routines are more important than morning routines.

3. **Find a morning routine.** If your kids are a bit older, aka not nursing every 2 minutes or co-sleeping, wake up at least 10 minutes before your kids. Breathe, ground yourself, meditate, smile, and set your intentions for the day. If you want to make it more than that, add onto it as the habit takes shape.

4. **Meal prep.** Find a way that's easy, just be sure you eat well. Hormonal health is vital.

5. **Move your body.** You don't need to do it all day every day and become a CrossFit junkie, just move. Even if it's some dancing. Move.

6. **Delegate.** Don't take on the busy badge. It's nothing to be proud of. Implement chores and, instead of getting angry at your spouse for not helping, directly ask for what you want and need. Delegate.

7. **Develop your mind, body, and soul.** If you're ready to expand even more, delve into podcasts, books, or hire a coach or mentor—Hi! I can help!

8. **Remove the shame, judgement, and comparison.** This helps no one. You are doing the best you can every day, and that's phenomenal. You are you, not anyone else. Get off of social media if you're comparing yourself. Remember that your judgements of others are a beautiful mirror to learn more about yourself. Motherhood is hard. Not a single one of us is going to be perfect. You will burn out trying to do it perfectly.

9. **Connect.** As mothers, we disconnect when we are exhausted, overwhelmed, and anxious. Connect with yourself, your children, and the important people in your life. Tomorrow may never come. Get on the floor and play. Laugh. Stop and give a hug. Put the phone down and look the person in the eyes. Go out in nature, device free. Go to church. Meditate. When you don't know what else to do, just love. Love your kids. Love yourself.

10. **Drink a lot of water.** When I make time to implement this type of self-care, I find more patience, less yelling, more energy, and less anxiety. Now that my kids are seven and five years old, I'm seeing the benefits I've described in them, which is incredibly validating for me. Hearing my son look at the monkey bars he's been tackling and saying, "I can do this!" instead of, "I'll never be able to do it." Or hearing that my daughter replied to unkindness with self-confidence, saying, "My body is perfect because it's how God made it." Or when my son was having an emotional meltdown and was in fight-or-flight mode, he knew how to deep belly breathe and meditate. It's because they have been doing this with me. My kids watch me make my self-care a priority, and they model *me*. The next time you feel guilty asking your significant other

for 20 minutes alone each day to meditate, or that you left the dishes in the sink so you could soak in a bath, remind yourself that it's not a luxury or something that is naughty. It's imperative for you and your children's well-being.

IMPROVE YOUR SELF-WORTH

I have a lot of childhood memories of my mom being a mom. My mom sat with me and French braided my hair every day. She drove me to and from nursery school and had an after-school snack ready for my brother and me when we got home. She sat with me to do crafts; she's an artist after all. I remember her taking us to the pool almost every day in the summer until I was in high school. She wrote notes and left them for me anywhere and everywhere, whether it was to spill her guts full of love, wish me a happy birthday, remind me that she loved me, or wish me a Happy St. Patrick's day. Her nostalgia was an undoubted devotion of love for being a mom. She played in the backyard with us, twirling her baton. On special mornings, she made my older brother and me German pancakes. Each year, she took us to a local shopping area called Peddler's Village to see the scarecrow decorations, and she often took us spur-of-the-moment to a candy store to get maple candies. These things and more are what made my mom an incredible, loving, devoted mother.

What don't I remember from my childhood? Dishes in the sink, laundry, or toys lying around anywhere. I don't remember if my mom went through my clothes seasonally to take out what didn't fit. I don't remember how often she cleaned the toilets. I don't remember any of that stuff.

Whether or not my mom did any of that perfectly has absolutely no bearing on whether or not she was a good mom. So why do we constantly pressure ourselves to complete all of these tasks with perfect standards to determine if we are good moms or not? *Why?*

Your worth is NOT in your sink.

Your worth is NOT on your kitchen floor.

Your worth is NOT in the pile of clothes.

Your worth is NOT in your decorating ability.

Your worth is NOT in your child's outfit choice.

Your worth is in YOU. *YOU* get to decide your worth. According to the Oxford dictionary, self-worth or self-esteem is "confidence in one's own worth or abilities; self-respect." (I know. Here I go again with definitions.)

We live in a cruel, big, loud world. We often hold ourselves to unattainable standards because of it. But you can rewrite these standards and make new ones. Rewrite what it means to be able to do something, especially being a mother.

To me, being a mother means being still and present, connecting, creating memories, and maintaining sight of my priorties and my children's priorities. My worth is not in being a perfect mom; it's in being a *real* mom. Remember that I (hypothetically) yelled at my kid for spilling yogurt. Even I—the energy, scheduling, and self-help guru—have moments of losing it. I'm a human being. It doesn't mean I'm a bad mom.

I also respect myself. I try to treat myself the way I treat other people I love. I would never, ever push my children past their limits if they were tired. I would never expect my husband or best friend to skip meals to get work done for me. I would never make my children scrub toilets instead of playing outside. I would never do these things because I respect them as humans, and I respect their needs.

How can you create more self-worth? I know you're not going to read these few pages and be a changed woman. If you're a woman who has been beating herself up over laundry, it's going to take time to rewire your thinking. Here are my tips.

- Use positive affirmations with I AM statements. Start your days by telling yourself how you want to feel. "I am a good mom. I'm connected with my kids. I'm patient. I'm happy." If you practice a morning routine, write your affirmations down each morning.
- Ask for help and receive it. Remember, you are not worthless if you hire someone to clean your house, ask your husband to fold the clothes or empty the dishwasher, or have someone watch your kids so you can go for a walk to get fresh air. Doing these things is making you a better mother.
- Consider therapy. I'm just gonna keep throwing this out there. It's beneficial to go to therapy to work through unprocessed trauma, negative thinking, and anxiety.
- Mother yourself. Anytime you are engaging in a task, ask yourself, "Would I make my kids do this if they were me?" If the answer is no, stop. If you would tell your kids to eat some food, rest their body, or go play outside, then you should be telling yourself the same thing. Also, when you talk to yourself ask yourself, "What would I tell my kid if they were talking to themself this way?" Adjust accordingly.

BE PRESENT

Ever since my children were born, I always had a camera in hand. I have strongly desired to document our days, unscripted. Doing this ended up becoming one of my lifelines.

My mind was on an endless hamster wheel of worry and to-dos, but the second I put a camera in front of my face, everything stopped. It felt like the energy that ran the wheel came down into my body like it was being sucked down by a straw. All of my focus and attention were on exactly what was in front of me, which was always my children.

I began watching the light, anticipating their next move in their innocent play. I would just be. I'd be right there with them in that exact moment. Because I created the habit of taking pictures daily, my mind was regularly looking for these moments—even when my camera wasn't in hand. My mind took notice of the smallest moments that filled my soul with joy—whether I was taking a picture of it or not. If a rainbow bounced on a wall from the beautiful sunlight pouring in, I stopped and saw it. If my daughter was playing "kitchen" and feeding her baby dolls, I stopped and saw it. If my son was taking his first steps, I saw it. If my kids were exploring a new area on a vacation, I saw it. I stopped and really took in every part of these moments.

Taking pictures makes me present. I take pictures almost every single day. Even if I don't have my camera in hand, I see the moment. I stop and feel the moment, finding myself in a state of presence where anxiety and overwhelm don't exist. Let me repeat myself so that can sink in for you. Anxiety and overwhelm are incapable of co-existing in the state of presence. Being present is being here, right now. You're not thinking about the past or the future, you're simply here.

My camera was my tool to help me to be present. You might find it helpful, too. Use your camera, photographer or not, to help you to focus in on what's most important. Another easy way to be more present is to set a timer every hour to remind you to stop and be present.

If your brain has been used to working overtime in anxiety and overwhelm, it's not going to be easy to find presence. If you have a lot of trouble getting present, try the 5-4-3-2-1 method. Look for:

- 5 things you see
- 4 things you hear
- 3 things you smell
- 2 things you can touch
- 1 thing you can taste

BE GRATEFUL

If you are taking on any type of personal development, you will hear about how powerful it is to have a gratitude practice. Overwhelmed and anxious mothers' mindsets are in a constant state of lack and survival. We are so focused on everything we have to do, everything that didn't get done, everything we believe we failed at, and everything we feel we did wrong. One of the most profound things you can do for yourself is create a gratitude practice.

A gratitude practice is simply the act of mindfully becoming more grateful. It's certainly necessary to be grateful for the big things in life like your health, kids, relationships, shelter, and having enough money to buy food to eat. But a gratitude practice that will completely shift your life is when you begin to see and appreciate the little moments, too. I call them microgratitudes. Think of a smaller moment you've had recently, such as hearing your baby's contagious giggling fits, getting to open your windows for the first time in the spring, or seeing the vibrant fall foliage. Stop for a moment and remember this. How did it feel for you?

When I physically feel gratitude, it's like a wave of chills with a little bit of a belly flip. I smile just thinking about it. You know that feeling you get when someone's playing with your hair or rubbing your back? It's a calm, secure, happy feeling that you never want to end. For me, this is what gratitude feels like. Tapping into this as much as you can will rewire your brain. Isn't that amazing? You get to rewire your brain simply by taking the time to enjoy the little things in life.

While having a gratitude practice won't entirely eliminate your anxiety, it will be a huge component of creating and keeping a strong foundation that is able to withstand the stress of life.

What can a gratitude practice look like?

- During your morning or evening routine, write three things you are grateful for that day.
- Have a gratitude accountability partner - someone who you share your daily gratitudes with and, if you don't, they make sure you do.

Creating a gratitude practice will immediately relieve you from your monkey mind. With consistent practice, you'll find that your brain is creating more space for grace. Feeling grace, my friend, is like relaxing in an inner tube down a lazy river. I highly recommend it.

I find it helpful to combine the practices of being in the present and gratitude. For example, after doing the 5-4-3-2-1 exercise, if you have the mental capacity, find something that makes you feel a sense of gratitude. Maybe it's the sunshine on your face, the sound of your kids playing, a cup of hot tea, a great yoga workout, or an unsolicited hug from your kiddo.

• • •

Hopefully now, you are drinking a lot of water, you're making good action steps in eating better, you are working on sleeping, removing toxins, adding in self-care, redefining your self-worth, and finding gratitude and presence. Your foundation is actively under construction and getting stronger with each day. So, what's the next layer?

LAYER ONE
SUMMARY AND MAIN TAKEAWAYS

- Be sure you are meeting your basic needs first and foremost.
- Eat healthy meals built with protein, micronutrients, carbs, and healthy fat.
- Work with a naturopath or nutritionist if necessary.
- Drink water. A lot of it.
- Make sleep a priority.
- Begin a ditch and switch practice to start removing toxins from your home.

- Remember self-care is not a luxury. It is self-discipline, and it's an integral part of parenting.
- Find a meditation practice.
- Develop an evening routine.
- Develop a morning routine, depending on the ages of your kids.
- Redefine your self-worth.
- Stay in the present.
- Find a gratitude practice.

BOUNDARIES AND RELATIONSHIPS

AS WE MOVE ON TO LAYER TWO, it's important to recognize and hold in your awareness that your foundation will never get to a point of no longer needing attention. We never completely graduate from Layer One. The basics of Layer One are the number one priority in anything you do. You will never master them and find yourself in a state of perfection.

The goal is progress—not perfection. It's having a day of indulgences, being aware of it, and knowing how to feed yourself to get back on track. It's recognizing that you have been short-fused with your family lately, which is likely tied to the fact that you haven't meditated in a week. It's recognizing that your evening routine doesn't seem to be fulfilling you anymore, and you may need to adjust it. It's always keeping this part of yourself in the forefront of your mind and dancing with the needs as they present themselves.

You will find yourself in phases where you are in complete flow and feel amazing. But other times, you will find yourself in phases where it feels like not much is working, and you need to start at square one. This is not only okay; it's an inevitable part of life. The awareness of it will guide you through the constant evolution of your needs with more grace.

With all of this understood, I can't tell you when you will be ready to begin tackling Layer Two. The great part about this is there is no right or wrong, and you will be working on all layers together, not in isolation. Follow your gut and desire.

In my experience, I worked on Layer One with intense focus, but because I found that many components of Layer Two were just as important for my well-being, I worked on both areas almost simultaneously for about two years before really delving into Layers Three and Four. Fun fact: As I write this book, I have circled all the way back to Layer One this year as my primary focus.

So, what are the components of Layer Two?

- Set healthy boundaries in work, expectations, and relationships.
- Mend your marriage (if applicable).
- Practice playful, present parenting.
- Rid yourself of comparison and competition.
- Find your tribe.
- Use the wheel of life.

There is a lot to cover. I feel that a lot of these components are as important as Layer One, and I fully believe that working on these areas is just as important as meeting our basic needs. However, you can't find success in these later areas without addressing the areas in Layer One.

You cannot have successful relationships with others if you do not have a healthy relationship with yourself. Always remember this rule. Many of us know "The Golden Rule" of do unto others as you would have them do unto you, but, with this rule, you need to do unto yourself as you would do unto others. You can remember it as "The Golden Mirror Rule."

SETTING BOUNDARIES

In the fall of 2016, several months after I started therapy, I sat on my therapist's couch crying amidst my annual fall overwhelm. For photographers, fall is like our tax season—busy! Like clockwork, I found myself wondering, *How did this happen again?* I was swamped in editing, e-mails, and weddings and family photography session inquiries on top of all of the regular day-to-day tasks that are required of a wife and mother of two children. As I sat in front of my therapist, her eyes laser focused on me in my overwhelm and anxiety, and she listened. She listened, quietly and intently, as if she was studying something new for the first time, and then she'd ask me questions that prompted me to think so hard it nearly made my insides hurt. This discomfort? This was change taking place.

I remember she asked me a simple question—a question that was so simple, it was nearly stunning that I never considered it before. She asked me, "What if you had working hours in which you can offer sessions. And then that's it. Once they're filled, there's nothing else to offer. If those dates and times don't work for your clients, oh well. Isn't that how most businesses operate? You don't call your dentist's office and tell them when you want to come in. They tell you when *they're* available, and you work by their availability. Right?" I looked at her nearly dumbfounded as if there was an actual lightbulb above my head that lit up. Boundaries: She was teaching me about boundaries.

We women spread ourselves painfully thin, taking on every single thing we can. Right when we think we are at a breaking point, we take on more. Many of us are people pleasers and always say yes.

At the peak of my anxiety and overwhelm, I found so much power is saying, "No." The first few times I used it, the first time I began setting boundaries, it was terrifying. People don't like boundaries, and there are always push backs and challenging responses. But the more I practiced it, the more I saw the power in protecting myself. The more I practiced it, the more I allowed others to handle their own feelings and take ownership over them. For instance, if someone reached out in mid-October to schedule a family session, and I had no room left, I found power in saying, "I have no more availability."

It's hard saying no. I get this so, so much. When I said no to clients or opportunities, I'd be terrified. My ego would ramp up, making me ruminate over if I'd lose business, clients would be upset with me, it would hurt my reputation, or I'd miss future opportunities. Because of these fears, I had a really difficult time finding my power and the value in saying no. I kept at this concept with awareness and intention to create necessary boundaries in life. Two concepts put all of this into perspective for me and gave me the permission I needed to set imperative boundaries in my life. They are:

Make decisions out of love, not fear.

Saying yes to one thing is saying no to something else.

MAKING DECISIONS OUT OF LOVE

This concept means that when you choose to do something, you do it because you WANT to, not because you're afraid of what the repercussions will be if you choose not to. This is also a great time to really look at delegation and how to set boundaries, which can be one and the same. What is it that you can let go of? Let's gain more clarity out of examples.

Cleaning your house. Are you cleaning it because it makes you feel good, because you love a clean house, or because it connects you with your environment? Or are you cleaning it because if you don't, you're afraid you'll be labeled dirty, you are comparing your home to your friend's clean house, you want to be Pinterest worthy, or you want your spouse to think you're productive in a day?

If you are happily cleaning, wonderful! If you are doing this out of fear, it's time to delegate. How? Divvy up chores among all who live in the house. If finances permit, hire a cleaning person. Or let go of the need for it to be perfectly clean.

Working overtime. This could be taking on too much work, staying late at the office, or putting your all into your home-based business. Are you working overtime to finish a project that pumps you up and is giving you life, finding huge momentum in your business that feeds your soul, connecting with clients and feeling fulfilled in the work you're doing? Or are you working overtime because you're afraid your boss will be mad, because you are afraid of how your clients will respond if you say no, because you are worried your business will die if you aren't working on it non-stop, or out of fear of potential judgement of others if you're not "hustling"?

If you are working OT out of love, great! If you're working late out of fear, reconsider doing it. If you can, delegate the task instead.

Could you hire a virtual or a real-life assistant? What can you get off your plate and give to someone else if you have so much going on you feel like you can't not work overtime? Delegate. Set boundaries!

If you are doing something out of fear, have a conversation about what's expected of you and what you're willing to give. Another reminder: You need to be clear on what you want before you can communicate it. This example is also a bit of a trick question. Sometimes, putting in extra work from a place of love is good, but I don't believe it's ever healthy to be working overtime all of the time. We'll talk more about how to manage our energy through the masculine and feminine and our monthly cycle as women in Layer Three.

A social date. We've all been there. You make a date with a friend. You're following the advice earlier in this book about finding your tribe, but every single part of you wants to stay home. In Layer Three, we'll dig deeper into when it's a great time to schedule social dates, which will be a part of how you can set your boundaries with this. For now, ask yourself: Are you going out with your friends because when you're with them you feel good? Because they give you insight that you need to become more grounded? Because it's the reprieve you've needed and wanted all week? Or are you going because you read in a book that you need to find your tribe? Because you're worried they'll be mad at you if you cancel? Because you're afraid to be alone? We don't need to WANT to be social all the time. Sometimes it's better for our well-being to go inward. I'll tell you now as a cheat, schedule your social dates between approximately days 7 and 21 of your 28-day cycle. We'll delve deeper in Layer Three.

Answering emails/texts. When I was in the thick of my anxiety and overwhelm, I was answering emails and texts as soon as they came in. My kids would be playing, and I'd have my face buried in my phone. I'd randomly run to my computer to answer emails. I was worried I'd forget to reply to someone. I was scared if I didn't reply to emails right away, people would think I was a bad business person, and I'd lose a job. I was working out of fear. I don't think there's any reason to be answering texts or emails at a specific time all of the time. I have a rule: The only emails I answer almost right away are initial wedding inquiries. That's it. If I'm with my family when I receive an email alert about an initial wedding inquiry, I ask their permission to excuse myself to reply to the inquiry. Sometimes they're not okay with it, and I wait. Boundaries are set by others, too.

I also am now notorious for not replying to texts. Why? Because they come in at all hours of the day, seven days a week, and while my phone is around all the time, I just don't want to be answering texts. I triage texts and reply to necessary ones quickly. Others, I will often batch-reply once a week. Yes, I have a very high number in my little red alert circle. Many say, "That drives me nuts. I can't stand that." Me? Answering texts and emails all day is what drives me nuts and what I can't stand. This is my boundary. Find yours with this. Also, delegate. If you are a business owner getting a lot of emails, consider hiring a virtual assistant.

In summary: Find what matters. Do what you're doing out of love, and let the rest go. Set your boundaries.

SAYING YES TO ONE THING IS SAYING NO TO SOMETHING ELSE

Figuring out the whole "choose out of love not fear" thing takes a lot of trial and error, attention, and awareness. It's going to take work. It's never perfected, and it will always be evolving. Take it from me. I'm taking inventory on all of my decisions, functioning in my many roles, and regularly checking to see if I'm choosing out of love or fear. For instance, I love cleaning my house, but not all of the time. My work schedule changes, and my cleaning needs change. When I'm not loving cleaning, I hire someone to clean. Done.

As you become aware of choosing out of love or fear, the second step is recognizing that when you say yes to one thing, you're saying no to something else. This concept fuels a lot of my big decisions—both work decisions and day-to-day activities. This is a huge component in managing our energy, which will be discussed at length in Layer Three.

My biggest ah-ha moment with this was realizing that when I say yes to any work coming in, every single yes is a no to something else. Often, I get a full body yes to do work, visit with friends, or go away for a night. But sometimes, the thought of saying yes results in a full body no. No, I want to be home with my kids that day or no, I want to spend the night quietly or no, I'd rather take a day trip with my family. Before I understood this concept, I was saying yes to every opportunity, leaving no yeses left for my kids or my husband. It was in this moment that I realized I was losing precious time with them, my husband, my family, and myself by saying yes to other things too often. It's a moment where my eyes close in a tight grimace of pain, and I realize the consequences of my actions. I've realized I get to choose again, though. And I do. This is how I have found alignment in doing the work I want to do and spending time with my kids and family the way I want to.

Every single thing that I choose to do, I ask myself, *If I do this, what am I choosing not to do?* For example, I will not work on my son's October birthday or birthday weekend. Watching our town's Halloween parade is a cherished tradition. It always falls on his birthday, and I decided that no wedding could ever be more important than being with my family on this day. If I say yes to work, I say no to these memories.

My kids take swimming lessons, and they can choose a second activity to do each year. I will not schedule work for those evenings. If I say yes to work, I say no to being with them during their extra-curricular activities. I would be absent from this time in their lives, and for what? While I absolutely adore all of my clients, I love my family more than them, and that's okay.

Another way to use this in your day-to-day life is for cooking and eating. If cooking is draining you and doesn't feel good, you are saying yes to cooking and saying no to more relaxing time, time with your kids, or sitting down and talking to your spouse. In this case, maybe consider a cooking subscription that makes meals quick and easy or budgeting to get takeout. Saying yes to takeout, though, could be saying no to something else, like new clothes or a weekend family trip.

In this yes and no game, we need to take constant inventory. Everything is interconnected, so it requires routine checks and balances. In the moment, when you ask yourself, "If I say yes to this, what am I saying no to?" you'll be blown away by the clarity it brings. The more you practice this, you'll find yourself gaining decisiveness and confidence. Start little and keep going.

MEND YOUR MARRIAGE

I believe that what I have experienced in my marriage can likely apply to almost any relationship. By making your own adjustments. I believe the love and support that I have in my marriage can and should be the foundation of any and all relationships. It is my firm belief that every single one of us deserves love, support, understanding, and to find a partner in life who is going to give this to us, and to whom we can give. So, as I always say, chew the fruit and spit out the seeds. If something I share doesn't apply to you, let it go, and take what does. In fact, you can just go ahead and do this to the entire book. Nothing we read or listen to will ever apply to us in its entirety. We need to take what does, and let the rest go.

As I brainstormed and collected all of the ideas for this book, this section has stumped me the most. I suppose because it's an area that can be so specific that it's hard to write anything that can apply to a large group of people as a whole. Marriage and relationships have so many layers, and adding in anxiety and overwhelm is going to make things even more complex. The two variables that I personally feel play the most important parts are a full understanding of your own role in your relationship and communicating well. Having these two pieces will provide a strong foundation, no matter what other complex variables may play into your relationship.

Before becoming a mother, my life roles were very familiar to me. I felt very comfortable in them. I was a daughter, friend, student, and wife. Sometimes things felt hard in these roles, but overall, I had a really good handle on them, as I outlined in the early chapters of this book. When you add mother on top of these roles, something very overwhelming happens. I can't fully articulate it because it's not just on a level of "here are all of the things I need to do," but on additional levels including our mental and emotional wherewithal. It's a huge, jarring shift, and it takes time to really adjust to this new role. Your relationships with your friends change; you'll find a distance with your non-mom friends and new connections with mom friends. Your relationship with your own mother changes; you are no longer the child as you've entered into motherhood but it becomes very complicated and emotional to figure out how to need your mom when you're a mom yourself. In fact, I believe this in and of itself could be a book and perhaps is one that also needs to be written. Along with all of this, your role as a wife also changes.

As I had mentioned in the beginning, many women struggle with forgetting who they "once were." I hear men say, "She's not the woman I married." And he's right. You're not. You are a brand spanking new version of yourself. You may cry more and worry more. Because so many of us enter motherhood without the proper tools, we also detach and distance ourselves from others to try to protect ourselves from these new, unknown, uncomfortable feelings.

This is where I see a breakdown happen in a marriage. Mama, I know how hard it is to feel misunderstood. I know how hard it is to feel like your emotions and experiences are belittled with words like "you're overreacting," or "it's not that big of a deal," or "you worry too much." As a response, many of us shut off. We become resentful and disconnected, and it's because even *we* don't fully understand these new feelings. How can we possibly explain them to our significant others?

I believe it's crucial for mothers who suffer from anxiety or overwhelm to clarify what we're feeling, what we're doing, and what we need from our significant others. Likewise, they should be doing the same.

Get out a journal, and let your pen flow. Something remarkable happens with the brain when you put actual pen to paper. It's why journaling is commonly recommended in the personal development world. Let this journal be your private space to really dump everything you're thinking and feeling. It's not about making sense, but rather finding clarity once it's all put on paper. Let your brain and heart have the space to unload the stress, worry, and overwhelm. Find the clarity around what you think is expected of you, and what you expect of yourself. You and your significant other did not go into these new parenting roles with experience. It's a job that holds the highest weight of importance with absolutely no experience requirements. No wonder new parents feel like fish out of water, right?

As you journal, I bet you will be journaling from the perspective of a mom, feeling the weight of the world on her shoulders, on her own without enough support from others. Is this going to be a blanket truth? Absolutely not. In fact, I'm married to an insanely supportive man, but even he hasn't always known how to fully support me until I explained it to him. I can't explain it to him until I'm aware of what I actually need from him.

Let's get clear on roles for a minute, because I think having this understanding is really important. It's something that has come up a lot in conversations with my friends when we've discussed our moments of overwhelm in our roles as mothers in relation with our husbands. What I am going to discuss here is specifically a heterosexual relationship, though, parts of this might relate to any relationship because I believe that we take on different roles in parenting no matter our gender.

Let's keep this short and to the point. Biologically speaking, we have hunters and gatherers. The men hunt. The women gather. The men leave the house to get the food and do the work. The women keep the home and raise the kids. It's literally a part of biology. Let's fast forward to the 1950s. Things kinda looked the same, didn't they? The woman would stay home, keep the house, raise the kids, and have dinner on the table at 5 pm for her husband. Now, let's fast forward to the 1990s. Both of the parents were out of the house working, but the mothers were still responsible to keep the house, raise the kids, and have dinner on the table at 5 pm. Now let's fast forward to 2020. The mothers are still doing these things, working, maybe not, but trailblazing, men have an equal part in keeping the house and raising the kids. Quite frankly, it's going pretty well.

Let's come back to biology for a second. Society is making massive strides in evolving the roles of mother and father. But I believe women are becoming frustrated with our men, because they are not doing all that we expect them to without us having to ask. It's creating frustration and resentment. I've felt it, and I still do. We have to remember that biology is a part of our makeup, and while we have evolved socially, our brains won't evolve as quickly. This shift is going to take work and time. I actually don't have any idea if this is an evidence based finding, perhaps it is. It's simply my own personal finding.

If this applies to your relationship, I strongly suggest you take the time to figure out what it is you expect of yourself in the role of a mother and a wife, what you believe society expects of you, and what you believe your spouse expects of you. This is something great to journal about. Then become clear on what you actually *want* in these roles, and encourage your spouse to do the same thing. We absolutely cannot create strong relationships and defined roles if we don't even know what we want out of them. It's important to become crystal clear on this.

Once you've reached this point, now it's time to communicate. *All of the time.* We've heard it a million times: Relationships take work. They are not going to magically stay healthy. In the thick of parenting, it's more important than ever to communicate. If you need to schedule meetings with each other, then schedule meetings. No, not dates, we'll get to that, but meetings. Set aside an hour or so a week to check in with one another. Perhaps take this journaling prompt, take time to do it apart, and then share it together. Humans are innately preoccupied with ourselves and what we want and need, which is the crux to why relationships fall apart. We don't know what the other person needs. The only way that we can know is through communication.

When you communicate with your spouse, go into conversations with the intent to listen—not with the intent to respond. I believe we have become so accustomed to defending ourselves and trying to prove our beliefs, that we forgot how to truly hear each other. I want to give you a counseling trick that I think we all need to learn and apply to every darn conversation we have. It's called reflective listening.

When your spouse is talking to you, I want you to listen. I know, I know! We are so eager to respond and share our own beliefs that it's hard to even do this, but instead, trust you'll get your turn to speak, but in the moment they are talking, it's your turn to listen. The beauty in this is that often, when we actually hear what the other is telling us is, it may actually shift our own thoughts and beliefs and CONNECT us—instead of driving a wedge between us.

In reflective listening, we take the time to hear what the other person is saying, and in order to validate this, we paraphrase back what we just heard. So, instead of responding with our own opinions, we are validating the other person. Confirm you understood what they said, and then they can do the same for you. It creates bonds, connections, and the feelings of being heard and understood. You can almost see a person's shoulders drop in relief when you use reflective listening. I'm going to share a conversation below to actually show what reflective listening looks like.

Before this, let me explain what "I statements" are. Often, when we approach someone in a conflict type of conversation, we are very defensive in what we are saying and often we're pointing the blame at the other person through sentence structure. We say things like, "When you do _____, it pisses me off!." Instead, if we structure our sentences to take ownership and accountability for how we're feeling, it often allows the other person to hear us better—rather than flipping the defensive switch for them. The way the sentences are structured are, "I feel _____, when you _____, because _____."

Side note: Ladies, I want to give you advice that my husband gave me. I am always ready to talk at the drop of a hat. If he didn't take out the trash and it pissed me off, I want to talk about it RIGHT NOW. This is not going to be effective. A man's brain thinks in a very linear fashion. His side of the conversation won't be receptive, and in turn, it won't be a productive conversation. It's very important to tell our men, "Hey, I want to talk to you about something," and then schedule a time to talk about it. This allows their brains the fighting chance to fully attend to the conversation.

Okay, so now you two are sitting down at your scheduled meeting to discuss your roles. Let's look at two different conversations: defensive listening (I don't know if this is a real term, and if it's not, I own it now. Just saying.) and reflective listening.

Wife to Husband, using no I statements and defensive listening

Wife: "Lately, I've been feeling incredibly overwhelmed with everything I have to do from buying teacher gifts, to scheduling doctor appointments, birthday parties, homework, dishes, and trying to build my own business. On top of that, some days I feel like I can't function because my anxiety is so high, I feel like I can't breathe. You come home and just sit down. I need a break! You don't understand what it's like for me!"

Husband: "YOU don't know what it's like for ME! I work all day to put food on the table for this family. I need a break, too!"

You know how the rest of this conversation goes, I'm sure. Now let's take a look at this conversation with "I statements" and reflective listening.

Wife to Husband, using I statements and reflective listening

Wife: "Thank you so much for sitting with me to talk about all of this. Your support means so much and makes me feel like I'm not alone in how I'm feeling. I feel so overwhelmed lately with everything I have to do as a mom from birthday parties, to helping with homework, doctors' appointments, and laundry. Meanwhile, I'm also trying to run my business. In the middle of all of this, my anxiety has been out of control. I know that when you come home, you need a break, too, because you're working just as hard during the day. I feel really exhausted and overwhelmed when you come home and sit down because, while I know you need the break, it makes me feel like you don't understand how much I need one, too, or that me taking a break isn't as important."

Husband: "It sounds like you have a lot on your shoulders right now with all that's expected of you being a mom and working, too.

You know I work just as hard and need a break, but it sounds like you're feeling your need for a break isn't really being acknowledged. Is that right?"

See how these two conversations feel completely different? To me, one feels combative and one feels bonding. Another point to take in here, also from my husband's wisdom, is for the ladies. He recommends that ladies be very clear on our expectations and our needs. He holds a belief that many men don't understand the severity of some situations or the weight of some of their actions or inactions, so when things in the relationship spiral or possibly lead to divorce, many men can feel blindsided, per Dustin's observation. And let's be honest here. This has nothing to do with men and women, or husband or wife. This has to do with one or both people in a relationship having unmet needs and being sure they are expressed clearly. Period.

For me? The trash not being taken out is a huge trigger. Think about how this can be experienced differently by both sides. My husband sees a wife eye roll when there's a full trashcan and maybe hears a snide comment about it not being taken out. He sees this as being a nag or "here she goes again with the trash." Whereas when I see that full trashcan, it makes me feel like he doesn't care. It makes me feel completely disregarded as a human being by one full trashcan. For him to not have the self-discipline to take the trash out is one of the most offensive things he can "do to me" and essentially negates every single thing I've done in my role as wife and mother. Yes, this is actually how it makes me feel. These are really big feelings. These are the kinds of feelings, that, if not shared in their entirety, become toxic to a relationship. How on earth could he possibly know that the full trashcan could lead to a divorce or a completely broken relationship if I don't give him the privilege of knowing how I actually feel? All he thinks is that I'm nagging him.

This is not a made-up example. This is my real life, and I know I'm not alone in it. I had this exact conversation with my husband. I shared every big, ugly feeling with him, using reflective listening and I-statements so that we could really hear each other and understand. When we have our conversations, in his reflective listening, I'm able to hear if he's actually heard my feelings. This is how I know if we effectively communicated or not. If in his paraphrasing it's clear that he didn't get what I was saying, we are able to hash it out right then and there in real time. It's incredibly powerful to use this in any and all of your conversations. And you know what? My husband now regularly empties the trash. Every time he does, I thank him for meeting my emotional needs as my husband.

If you and your significant other are having conversations more like the first one, maybe times 10, you probably read the second conversation and started laughing thinking, "Are you f*cking kidding me?! We will NEVER have a conversation that sounds like this." It's absolutely a concept that's far out there, I know. You're not going to read this book, close it, and have a changed relationship with your significant other. To change the way you communicate, you need to communicate these different concepts, practice them regularly, and slowly shift how you're communicating with one another. Remember, relationships take consistent work. This is not meant to be easy or effortless, so if we read about this in the mindset of "that's ridiculous" or "that will never work," then you will be proven exactly right. We'll talk about mindset in Layer Three, but we may as well begin practicing it now.

MEN, STOP TRYING TO FIX EVERYTHING

Through the height of my anxiety and overwhelm, I truly can't tell you how many times I called my husband crying, completely broken from my demands as a mother and the demons that kept me from being able to continue. He'd be on the other line, desperately trying to make it better. I'd eventually thank him for taking my call but would hang up feeling even more alone. I couldn't quite figure out why I felt this way when my husband was there for me every step of the way.

If I said it once, I said it a million times, *we* need to know what we want and need. If we don't know this, how could anybody else possibly know this? I needed to figure out why I continued to feel unsupported in these moments of complete breakdowns. Getting angry with Dustin for not supporting me would be unfair because I didn't even know what he needed to do to support me. In an effort to figure this out, you guessed it, we communicated.

Here is what we concluded: Men, stop trying to *fix* everything! My husband had amazing insight in realizing that in his role, he feels responsible to provide for his family and make sure every basic need is met. We can go back to the hunters and gatherers, the male vs. female brain, masculine vs. feminine energy, or maybe it's just a personality thing. Who knows, but it's something that he and I concluded about our own relationship. What we realized was that when I was in a distraught state, my husband was hell bent on fixing it.

If the washer breaks, he fixes it. If a kid has a boo-boo, he fixes it. If we are low on money, he fixes it. If the internet isn't working, he fixes it. If we don't have enough food, he fixes it. If I'm crying, he fixes it. So, when I call him while he's in the middle of his workday and he hears me sobbing on the other end of the line, his brain works over-time to figure out how to fix it. He would meet my anxiety and overwhelm with, "Do your breathing, go for a walk, stop working for the day, take a nap, it's okay, don't worry…" or my favorite, "Let's think about this logically." Please don't ever say this to someone suffering from anxiety. I knew and still know every single thing I need to do when I'm anxious or overwhelmed. Certainly the reminders can be helpful because our brain literally can't think straight when it's in a state of anxiety, but you know what I really need in these moments? Reflective listening. I need someone to validate my feelings.

In anxiety, there is a tremendous amount of self-judgement and shame. You feel broken as a human being—like something is wrong with you. When your loved one is giving you advice to "fix" things, it validates that you're broken. But when your loved one looks at you and says, "Wow, that sucks. You have so much going on right now. I would feel really anxious, too," it feels like a safety net. What I really hear in this statement is, "You are not broken. Anybody who is in your situation would respond this way." This is how you fix it. And this is exactly what I shared with my husband, and I remind him of this regularly. Again, communication never reaches an end. I will even sometimes call him (much less often now) and start the conversation with, "I'm okay and don't need anything fixed. I just need someone to hear me," and then he knows exactly what I need.

This has been my biggest lesson in anxiety. It's one of the biggest pieces of advice I can give someone who has a loved one suffering from anxiety. Please don't try and fix it for them. That minimizes their feelings, it confirms their belief of being broken, and it can make them feel even more isolated. The most important thing for a person with anxiety to do is be crystal clear in how you're feeling so that you can communicate it. When I need validation, I ask for it. And if I truly need help fixing, I ask for it.

KEEP DATING EACH OTHER

The days are long, but the years are short. That's my company's motto, but really it's my life motto. I think it applies appropriately to marriage. You're both in new roles as a mom and dad, literally overnight. You're figuring it out as you go, your kids very quickly become the epicenter of life, for good reason, and all of a sudden you find yourself in parallel lives. You glide alongside each other, keeping your head above water, forgetting that you're even next to one another. We can find ourselves in the place of "I'll do it tomorrow," with so many things. One of the first things to get pushed to the bottom of the list is the relationship. Days turn into weeks, which turn into months, which turn into years. Eventually, the space between you and your spouse is so big that the effort to rebuild the bridge between you requires more strength and resources than either of you have. That's when people walk away.

Millions of variables affect a relationship. Sometimes it's in everyone's best interest for some couples to part ways. Only you know this answer. But what I can say from my own experience, and what I have seen in my work, is that relationships need prioritization to survive, especially when anxiety and overwhelm play a role. It doesn't have to be complicated. For example, I often hear, "We haven't been on a date because we don't have childcare." We are limiting ourselves with this. Lean on your tribe, take a day off of work, and have a day date, or have a date at home when the kids are asleep. Don't overcomplicate it.

When we become parents, we can get so lost in our roles, especially mothers. Our babies are our world. It's like a switch goes off, and nothing else matters. The love we feel for our child is more profound than any other love we felt before, yes, even for our spouses.

I think this becomes confusing; we have to redefine our love for our spouses in order to understand it. The only guarantee in life is change; we can't stop it from happening. The love in our relationships is going to continue to evolve whether we are putting effort into the relationship or not, so if there is no effort, you can guess how the relationship will evolve. No effort, no relationship. When we are putting all of our focus and energy into the love we have for our children, we are losing the bond we have with our spouse. For those of us feeling massive anxiety and overwhelm in motherhood, how can we possibly pay any attention to our significant others when we are simply trying to keep ourselves and our kids alive? I get it. This is where Layer One plus communication with your spouse is going to play the most important role in keeping the relationship alive.

Because our love has shifted so greatly and so unexpectedly when taking on the roles of mom and dad, facing this feels scary. It's also very confusing. Mama, have you looked at your husband holding your brand new baby and thought, "I've never been more attracted to this man in my life." And 20 minutes later, when he leaves the bottles on the counter and puts the wrong outfit on the baby you think, "He's useless." Not to be dramatic, but seriously! So many extreme emotions ping-pong back and forth in our hearts for our men. Let's face it: We're way too flipping exhausted to spend any time on that. This is where it snowballs. This is where we say, "tomorrow." This is where we say, "When the baby is a little older, we can go out." Then we say, "When the baby is fully weaned, we'll go out." Then we say, "Once they're sleeping through the night." Those are the days, which turn into weeks, which turn into months, which turn into years. Suddenly, you find yourself sitting next to your husband realizing that you're strangers. You both are living your own lives next to each other and haven't been playing as a team for who knows how long. Just as the overwhelm and anxiety can snowball into something massive, the lack of attention to our relationships can snowball into a huge change that we don't see until it's almost too late.

Your relationship is going to evolve no matter what. Growing together takes work. Here are ways you can continue to grow and evolve in your relationship from the beginning. Try to do at least one of these a week. Even if anxiety is taking over your life, add this stuff in. I did, and I'm so glad. Doing these things offered moments in between the falls where I could focus on something other than my racing mind and my to-do list. Choose to see this as a reprieve instead of a chore; remember, mindset is everything.

If you share this idea with your spouse and he shoots you down, clearly communicate why this is important to you and that the weight of it matters. It's okay to share the big, scary, uncensored feelings. We need to hear them to understand the significance of the situation. And most importantly, have fun!

- Have a device-free, TV-free night. Just talk.
- Cook dinner together.
- Share your high and low of the day.
- Leave love notes.
- Share one thing you appreciated from the other person.
- Schedule a date each month, home or out, any time of day.
- Slow dance in the living room.
- Choose a house project to do together, and work on it once a week for 30 to 60 minutes.

- Take a family walk around the neighborhood.
- Find a TV show to watch together once a week.
- Take a cooking class.
- Take a dancing class.
- Put date ideas in a jar and choose one once a week.
- Play a card game or boardgame together.
- Fold laundry together with no electronics.
- Make bedtime a family routine.
- Take a shower together.

PRACTICE PRESENT AND PLAYFUL PARENTING

Well, my beautiful reader, I have to say that Layer Two is a huge can of worms. I sit with each section thinking, "How on earth can I write about this in a succinct way without falling down the rabbit hole?" Essentially every single one of these sections, from marriage, to boundaries, to parenting could fill their own book. However, I know that each of these sections are imperative to address to manage anxiety and eliminate overwhelm. Parenting? Out of every layer, this is the biggest can of worms. I want to be sure to give you clear and concise information, knowing that, of course, we are just grazing the surface.

It's important to acknowledge that parenting is equivalent to lifting up the rug under which you've been brushing everything for your entire life. All of those skeletons and dirty laundry, some of which we don't even know we have, are under this huge rug. When we become parents, it's lifted. You're standing there, looking down, holding your baby on your hip, eyes bulging out of your head, your mouth dropped to the floor, your stomach churning with the realization that every part of your life, every wound, is now open and vulnerable. You might find that some childhood memories begin to make more sense. You might understand feelings you didn't understand before, such as the reason you don't feel enough. How you choose to parent highlights your approval or disapproval of how your parents chose to raise you.

And the biggest thing? As women, our relationships with our mothers turn upside down when we become moms. We are no longer the daughter, but the mother, and your mom is no longer the mother, but the grandmother.

Overnight, expectations shift without complete awareness. Unhealed wounds come to light, and it's as if someone is spilling salt into those aching wounds. It feels as though all we can do is respond to the pain with confusion, tears, and anger. Is this everyone's experience? No. Of course not. Nothing in this book is applicable in whole, but I know that this is a likelihood and a reality for many women.

While this section isn't going to delve into your childhood traumas and relationship with your parents, I bring this up because it's an essential component in your parenting journey. I strongly encourage you to find how to heal what is coming up for you. You might be healed over a cup of coffee and frank talk with your mom. Or you might need deeper work like therapy. Acknowledging the part of you that needs healing is the most important step. Having the awareness that this is a part of your reality will be the step that helps create the momentum in healing.

Healing is important because it's going to directly impact the relationship you have with your children. Find your healing to create more clarity and alignment in your parenting journey.

In addition to my intense healing process, I implement two components into my daily parenting. These components are not earth shattering, but they have allowed me to find the joy in my parenting instead of stress and overwhelm. They are present parenting and playful parenting. They essentially go hand in hand, but let's talk about them separately.

PRESENT PARENTING

Being present for your children by giving them your full attention creates the foundation for what will become their self-esteem later in life.

My photography allowed me to practice this from the beginning, without me even realizing it. A part of me believes that without this component, I would have fallen into a much darker hole. In my most trying days, having my camera to my face allowed me to be fully present. When I am creatively connected to my being and to the world in front of me, my brain is completely silent. If we're being honest, while much of our energy is in our bodies, anxiety and overwhelm absolutely stems from our brains. When the anxiety and overwhelm were turned off for me, I was grounded and in the present moment.

Being present is being in the here and now. It's reading this book—and not thinking about what you have to do later tonight. It's eating dinner with your family—and not thinking about a conversation you had earlier today. It's looking at the afternoon sun coming into your home from the window—and not thinking that you were near a full anxiety attack, even if it's only for a moment. It's stopping everything you're doing to see your children playing an imaginary game—and then feeling a rush of gratitude. It's stopping to build a puzzle with them, rocking them to sleep and singing their favorite lullaby, waking in the middle of the night to nurse them and feel the stillness of the night. This is being present. Here are a few ideas to find presence in your parenting.

Meditate. We've been over this. It's going to help you in every aspect of your life, especially parenting by helping you find patience, joy, gratitude, and presence. Don't ever underestimate the power of meditation.

Do 5-4-3-2-1. Count down, using your five senses: 5 things you see, 4 things you hear, 3 things you feel, 2 things you smell, and 1 thing you taste. You can make it about everything in general, or you can specifically focus it on your children, for example:

- 5 things you physically see in your child: long hair, luscious eye lashes, a smile, innocence, crumbs on their faces
- 4 things you hear your child doing: laughing, heavy walking feet, playing with Legos, asking for a snack
- 3 things you can feel: their small bodies, soft hair, little hands
- 2 things you can smell: their clean hair, fresh diaper (This was one of my favorite smells when my kids were babies.)
- 1 thing you can taste: the lunch you shared with your children

Doing this practice at least once a day immediately pulls you into the present moment and exactly where you are. Try it!

Daily journaling. Taking time each day to write down one or a couple things that you observed about your kiddos will help rewire your brain to notice these things as they're happening and in turn, to become more present.

Ultimately, finding your own ways to practice presence in your parenting is going to open your world in understanding your children, and in turn create less frustration and impatience as well as finding the joy in motherhood. So many of us are in our monkey minds, running on the hamster wheel, lost in our brains, and moving through the motions of each day with an empty tank. As you begin to implement the components of Layer One and start practicing your presence, you are going to reconnect with your joy, especially in motherhood. Things will become more clear, and each day will be one that you cherish— instead of a day that you're relieved is finally over. This sounds magical, doesn't it? It's not magic though. It takes work and intention.

PLAYFUL PARENTING

With the presence in my parenting, I often watch my children in adoration at their ability to use their imaginations and find their own profound presence as kids. I watch how their bodies effortlessly run laps in our yard, climb trees, scoot and bike for hours, crawl along the floors, build with Legos, create forts out of cardboard, and design games of creative role playing. I watch them and wonder why this is something we let go of as adults. The easy answer is because now we have bills to pay, mouths to feed, and chores to do. We don't have time to play. Or do we? I have chosen to intentionally take on more play in my role as my kids' mother. The results have been profound.

First of all, I absolutely don't play like my kids or at the same frequency. In fact, I think the biggest thing I've realized is that five minutes of play is enough to create the connection and fulfill the emotional needs on both sides. I think we scare ourselves into thinking it's a much longer commitment when our kids ask if we'll play hide and seek. We cringe and think, "It's too hard. I have too much to do." But really, taking two rounds of standing behind a wall they don't think to look by is enough to create an epic few minutes of playtime with your kids. Don't overcomplicate it.

Playful parenting is actually a strategy designed by Lawrence J. Cohen, PhD. It's the understanding that play is natural for children and, in meeting them where they are, it can assist us in finding presence (imagine that!) in moving more easily through life's challenges. It's also quite powerful to use play in place of aggression or authority.

For a simple example, let's say your kids have to clean up all of the Legos and separate the colors. This may or may not be a real life example that happened to me yesterday. Initially I found myself nagging the kids with authority, "If you don't clean these Legos up, I will, and you'll never play with those Legos again." (Friends, I'm not writing this book because I'm perfect. I'm human, and I'm learning and practicing this stuff, too. It's progress, not perfection.) When my kids responded with grumbles and "this is too hard," I decided to put a play spin on it. I turned it into a game. I set the containers in a row and challenged my kids to toss the Legos into the correct bin. I also layered it with, "I'm going upstairs to shower. Let's see if you can get it done by the time I'm out." And guess what? They did. They didn't respond to nagging, authority, or threats, but they responded to play.

Mama, I know it feels really hard to find the time and mental bandwidth to engage in some play with your kids, but I ask that you try it. Put the phone away, get rid of the distractions, 5-4-3-2-1, and commit to five minutes of play with your kids. And tell them this! Sharing your expectations and communicating is always something we should be doing, and never something that isn't needed. Tell them, "Yes, I'll play hide and seek! Let's set a timer for 10 minutes and when it's up, I need to do some laundry. Do you want to help?" Practicing presence and play isn't going to feel easy. If you're a mother sitting in anxiety and overwhelm, this will feel even harder. It's going to feel like you're swimming up river. Take baby steps. Set the timer for five minutes instead of 10. Meditate for three minutes instead of five. Taking these small action steps will repave a new path for your mind and spirit. This will rewire your entire parenting experience. It's not going to change overnight, but trust that, in time, it will change.

We get one opportunity to parent our kids, and it goes so fast. The days are long, but the years are short.

RID YOURSELF OF COMPARISON AND COMPETITION

Comparison is the thief of joy. Competition among mothers is fierce. Mothering in the era of social media is like parenting in a war zone.

I believe competition in motherhood is actually a competition within ourselves. We hide this internal competition in the mask of competing among other women. If you judge other women, please do yourself a huge favor and use your judgements as a mirror. Our judgements are always about ourselves and our own insecurities. We can use these revelations to foster our well-being and grow as humans, or we can simmer in our own stuff. It's a choice.

Likewise, one of the most valuable lessons I've ever taken in life is remembering that others' judgements about me are not really about me. It's a lot easier to blow off those judgements when we hold up the mirror for the judger. The way to do this is to be kind and project love. Easier said than done, but, by the end of reading this book, you'll be much more equipped to do this.

What do I mean when I say that we are in competition with ourselves and not others? A big part of this is a psychological concept called internal and external locus of control. Let's talk about each in turn.

Internal locus of control is the idea that we attribute judgements to our own selves—good or bad. It's our belief that we are the reason anything happens to us, and it's our belief that we have control. People who struggle with an internal locus of control believe that they are responsible for anything bad that happens in their lives, no matter the circumstance. They also believe that anything that happens in their lives is their fault. An example of this is a mother who blames herself that her child has a fever. Those who have a healthy internal locus of control use it as empowerment believing that they can do anything they put their mind to. An example is excelling in a job position because of hard work.

External locus of control is the concept of attributing judgement to the outside world. People who struggle with external locus of control believe that everything happens *to* them. They believe that they have no control over what happens in their lives. These people might live under a gray cloud with the belief that everything bad happens to them. An example of this would be someone who got into a car accident blaming it on the other driver or the bend in the road. Those who have a healthy external locus of control believe that nothing really affects them from the outside, which is fully tied to their healthy internal locus of control. An example of this would be someone who has a beautiful house recognizing that they earned it through hard work.

These examples are how we interpret locus of controls for our own lives, but we also apply this concept in how we judge others. Here is an example of how we use locus of control to understand other people. Let's say a woman is at a restaurant, and her waiter is slow serving her. If she assumes that the waiter is slow because he's bad at his job or is a miserable person, this is applying an internal locus of control to the waiter, assuming this is just who he is as a person. However, if the woman considers that the waiter may have had a bad day or being slow was the result of how his tables were seated, she is applying an external locus of control. She is assuming the slow service is a result of something outside of the waiter's control. It's my belief that how we apply the concept of locus of control is how we process our judgements of both others and ourselves.

I believe that mothers view our own experiences, particularly negative experiences, of motherhood with an internal locus of control. We also take our perception of other mothers, particularly their wins or positive experiences, with internal locus of control as well. This is detrimental, especially in the world we live in, full of highlight reels. We mothers are so quick to find proof that we aren't making the mark. We have a lack mindset (more on that later) that only allows us to see our perceived failures—what isn't going right. With our unhealthy internal locus of control, we take complete ownership over these perceived faults. Yet, when we see other moms' wins, we also assume that this is an internal locus of control—in other words, we give them complete ownership over their wins. Of course, we see ourselves as failures. We view our own experience of motherhood with a much more critical lens than the lens we are using to view other women's experiences in motherhood. The real irony is that neither lens is displaying the truth, and we get lost in our own projections of unmet expectations.

On days when I'm short tempered, I feel like I can't do it all, I can't even get a shower or the house is a mess, I immediately make this my fault. I never give myself the credit that external circumstance may affect my day-to-day to give myself grace and in turn help me shift my mindset. Instead, I assume all responsibility for the state of the house, others' well-being, and attitude.

We are being unfair to ourselves by applying an internal locus of control to other mothers' wins from our perspective because we don't see behind closed doors. When you see a mother being patient with her child at the grocery store, you assume this is who she is all of the time. You don't consider that she's biting her tongue because she's out in public. When you see a mother with her hair and makeup done, you assume this is how she always looks. You don't consider that this might be the first time she's done her hair and makeup in a year. When you see a mother post on social media a photo of cookies that she baked with her children, you never consider that she might have been yelling and screaming at the kids the entire time.

We mothers put a tremendous amount of pressure on ourselves to take full responsibility for all internal and external factors in our lives. It's no wonder we self-implode. It's humanly impossible to be responsible for every*thing* and every*one*.

Here's why when you think you might be comparing yourself to another mother, you're actually in competition with yourself. When we choose to view our counterparts in a highlighted way, we are comparing ourselves to them, but then we find ourselves in competition among ourselves. We are never trying to compare with anyone else, truly. Sit and break this down. If the mama around the corner looks like she has her stuff together, the moment I'm trying to do what she's doing, it is not to impress *her*, it is not to one up *her*. In fact, I forget about her 30 seconds after I saw her. I see her through my lens of expectations, and I use that as fuel to fight against myself. I put myself down, I try and one up myself and be a better version of who I was yesterday as a mother, but with toxic motivation. Then begins the self-destructive cycle of internal motherhood competition. How can you remove yourself from this cycle?

TURN OFF THE NOISE

What is the noise? For me, it's the noise in my head. I'm gonna assume that you are nodding your head—unless you're one of those rare people who don't have an internal monologue and to you, I bow. Turning off the noise is the hardest part in motherhood because we are so, so lonely. Becoming a mother often eclipses girls' nights, date nights, shopping days, talks on the phone with friends, and being as social as we'd liked. Whether you leave the house for work or not, being social has, for many of us, completely disappeared in motherhood. Motherhood brings a type of isolation that many of us are completely unprepared for, because no one really has an honest conversation about what it looks and feels like.

As I write this, in this very moment, the state of Pennsylvania is on lock down due to the coronavirus pandemic. Being in this state of waking up, skipping makeup, wearing yoga pants because "why bother," canceling ladies' nights, having to stay inside most of the time, and essentially being alone every day? This resembles motherhood, especially the first few months of motherhood. This quarantine is a humble reminder of what that felt like.

I believe that we try to fill this void of loneliness with technology and social media. As a society, we don't fully remember how to connect as humans. We text instead of call, we share pictures and statuses on social media, and we scroll through our newsfeeds instead of looking at our kids. It's counterproductive. What we are craving and looking for in our phones is exactly what is depleting us of what we crave. But the problem is that I don't think we fully understand how to identify what it is we're craving, let alone know how to access it. And I believe it's because we are ashamed and terrified to admit how lonely we feel in motherhood.

The reason we're full of shame is because of the intense dissonance that comes with loneliness. Even in my loneliest days as a new mother, my heart was exploding with joy while being with my children. How could I possibly feel so isolated and unfulfilled in some part of me when another part of me was filled with gratitude and joy in being a mother? And I'm a mom who didn't struggle getting pregnant. I can't imagine the intensity of this dissonance for mothers who had difficulty getting pregnant or becoming a mother. This is where it gets really hard and really shameful; we are afraid to really say how lonely we are because we're afraid it's going to steal from the love we feel for our children. Mama, it won't. We all have emotional needs that must be met, and it doesn't make you any less of an absolutely amazing mother. In fact, meeting those needs is what's going to make you an even better mom. Meeting those needs will help you to be able to experience motherhood with more peace and fulfillment—and to eliminate the dissonance that drowns us.

We are drowning ourselves with our phones. This is the worst way that we compare. This is where we set unachievable and unsustainable goals. It's where we set bars so high we lose steam and give up before we're close to reaching them. It's where we trick ourselves into thinking we're finding connection or reprieve, but really our brains are finding the toxic evidence to validate our beliefs that we are bad mothers. It's where our brain points out how Lindsay just completed her "century ride" on her Peloton, but you haven't even done a squat in two years. It's where you see Sarah's "Pinterest perfect" Christmas decorations, but you look up to see your cluttered, dusty living room and think, *I don't even know where our Christmas decorations are.* It's where you see Heather making her fourth home cooked meal with her kids this week, but you just threw a frozen pizza in the oven—again.

Do you feel connected? Or do you feel even more isolated? Do you feel good about yourself? Or do you feel even less self-worth as a mother? TURN OFF THE NOISE.

When you are in a vulnerable state of parenting, when you feel less than, ashamed, exhausted, and overwhelmed, social media will be gasoline to the fire that you're already fanning with your ego. Why are you torturing yourself? How do you turn off the noise? Delete your social media apps.

I know, your stomach just did a summersault. My business thrives on social media. I wouldn't have one without it. This is where I find an excuse. I'm afraid to get rid of it. Or what if it's your only connection to the outside world. But is it? Is this really true?

I challenge you to delete your social media apps on your phone for one entire week. Just one week. See how it feels to be unplugged. You might feel uncomfortable, but you'll have the room to acknowledge that and allow those feelings to move through you instead of unknowingly pushing them down, where they ruminate. Use your newfound free time to journal, play with your kids, read a book, or work on a goal.

Without social media at your fingertips for a few days, how can you stay connected with people? How do you create the connection that you're missing?

FIND YOUR TRIBE

When Hannah was born, because I was so nervous about succeeding in breastfeeding, I joined a breastfeeding support group run by the hospital. That group of brand new moms became my new mom tribe. A group of us immediately connected. Our weekly group meetings, our informal picnics, and playdates fulfilled my emotional need of connectedness. These became a part of our every day. With these women, I found commonalities, I found vulnerabilities being met with other vulnerabilities, I found laughter and tears. Our children grew together, and we worked through challenges, hardships, milestones, and joys together. It was the least lonely I have ever felt.

As time carried on and my business grew, it was harder to allow myself time for a tribe. "I'm too busy," was a constant belief and statement that fell out of my mouth with no regard for my own well-being. It was a survival mechanism. I was feeding my anxiety like the ravenous tiger it was by staying home and hoping that it would lessen its appetite, only to realize that it was growing bigger over time and requiring more fuel. While I remained in touch with a couple of these ladies and always had at least one close mom friend, I had put myself back into isolation after having my son. My sense of tribe was gone. I kept connections, I continued to go to a beloved exercise class, but I always felt like I was moving parallel to the women around me. I was still there, but I cut the ties that truly bonded me with any of them, and it made me feel lost. It left me living in my connections online in my photography forums, looking for connection through likes and comments with each picture I posted. The problem is that so many of us do this. We find it easier to live this way. We fill our silence and numb our pain with the noise.

When my mom was my age, divorced, with three kids, she was lonely, too. She often says, "I don't know what I would have done without my townhouse friends." They were her tribe. They weren't inside their homes hiding behind screens, seeing what the others were doing through the pictures they posted that day, and half-heartedly waving to one another as they drove through the neighborhood. They connected in person. They had parties, playdates, and get togethers. They took turns babysitting so each one of them could go out and have a break. Not today. We have lost our tribes.

To make our isolation even greater, we are living in a culture where it's very common to live away from family. Old-fashioned Sunday family dinners are a rarity. Hell, I didn't even have family come to the hospital when my son was born! It seems we have moved away from this as a society, and it's detrimental to our well-being, particularly as mothers who are bred to be social. How do we get this back?

I am easily one of the most introverted people I know. Yes, I have my Same Boat Huddle podcast, do regular live videos, and am wildly independent, but ask me to do something like go to my gym to cancel my membership, and I start sweating. Ask me to make new friends? No way. This is so incredibly hard for me. But I've realized how important it is to foster these relationships and connect on vulnerabilities. Not every relationship will work out or be perfect, but for each of the few that aren't perfect, you'll find one gem.

If you're an extrovert, you got this. You're a person who loves other people and can have a conversation with a wall. But if you're an introvert, you're probably thinking, *I can't*. I get it. Let me tell you how I created my most recent tribe.

I have two tribes. One tribe is virtual and scattered all over the world, yet they are some of the closest women to me. How on earth did this happen? It happened because I took a chance and invested in a brilliant coaching program lead by Heather Chauvin of Mom Is in Control. In February 2018, I was nearly two years past my anxiety attack, making great progress, almost two years into therapy, and ready to expand even further. I was ready for Level Three. In a group coaching program like this one, you are virtually connected with very like-minded women—women who are suffering from similar blocks and limiting beliefs, but women who hold similar values and cravings for life. In coaching groups like this one, we are connecting on a deeply vulnerable level—one that you will never get passing the mom at school pick-up with a wave or in your comments on Instagram. We connected through live video meetings and voice memos weekly and sometimes daily.

In the program, I really connected with a handful of the women, whom I open my biggest and scariest feelings too. The way I connect with these ladies, funny enough, is through a walkie-talkie app on our phones. It's an app where you can leave a voice memo for a friend or a group of friends and then they can listen to it at their convenience and reply. I have found that using this format has allowed us to hear our voices, we hear our tears, anger, joy and wins, and it's so much more personal than connecting through writing. We also connect through planned group calls on video. Whether it's scheduling a casual meet-up to see our faces and chat or to schedule meetings that include agendas like talking about books we're reading, meditating together, or journaling together. While it's amazing to think about how it was for my mom as a mom in the 80s and 90s, the world has changed and it's been amazing to use current technology to foster these relationships. These women hold me accountable to the things I say I want to do, challenge me when I am in a negative space instead of stewing in the negativity with me, and talk with me on a near daily basis. I haven't (yet!) met these women in person, but they have become some of my closest connections and friendships. They are my mental, emotional, and spiritual tribe. While they can't physically be here for me in a heartbeat if I need help with the kids, they are there in a heartbeat when I leave a message crying that I feel lost and confused, or if I leave a message with excitement about a win. These ladies are what a millennial tribe looks like. It's ironic that, while social media has a way of creating noise, it also has an amazing way of bringing people together. So, don't shy away from a virtual tribe through a personal development investment; they can end up being a lifeline.

Dustin and I live around one mile from his parents and about an hour from my parents and two of my brothers. We are very fortunate to have family close by, and we stayed close to keep family as a part of our tribe. Though family dynamics seem to have changed, overall, our family has helped us more times than I can count. I joke that I'd never have a business if it wasn't for my in-laws.

I recognize that not all tribes are created equal. I know many mamas who don't have a family support system. These women might have to make sacrifices that I haven't, or they might not have opportunities that I have had because of that support. I get it. But again, it's about looking at things with an abundant mindset, not a lack mindset. (Again, we'll go over this in Layer Three, but see how this keeps creeping in here?) Instead of focusing on what you don't have, think about what you do have and what you can create.

When Hannah started preschool, I would make small talk with some other moms, waiting for our kids to come running out the doors. I would think about how much I liked these ladies and wished that I had more confidence to say, "Hey, let's exchange numbers!"

Somewhere along the way, now that all of our kids are in first grade and our second kids are all in pre-k together, a friendship formed. Over the past year, I learned that four of us were connected to each other separately, holding separate friendships and moving through our busy lives beside each other. I realized I needed an in-person tribe. I needed women like me: women who loved their husbands and motherhood, but knew it was hard, believed in something bigger, and wouldn't think twice if they saw my crystals fall out of my bra or if I reeked of sage at pick-up. These were those ladies. I somehow had to connect us all together, which is when I thought of ladies' night.

Each Wednesday, after the kids are in bed, my husband goes out to his guys' night. It's held at the same house every Wednesday from 8 pm until whenever. Do they love their microbrews? Yes, absolutely, but they're not hanging out to get wasted. They're hanging out to *bond* and to blow off some steam. Over the past few years, I've watched their friendships grow in size and deepen in connection.

I thought, *Why can't I do the same thing?* Throwing caution to the wind, I sent a group text to my tribe of three women and said, "On Wednesday's my house is open from 7:30 to 9:30 pm. Door is open.

Walk in as you are." Since then, we don't meet every single week, but we do at least once a month. We sit around my kitchen island, drinking water or tea and talking about anything from big serious life stuff to hysterical life stuff, laughing until our sides hurt.

These ladies have become my second tribe, no less than my first. There's something magical in creating a consistent, reliable, dependable connection. And funny enough, with quarantine disrupting our in-person connection, we have taken to video calls and voice messages and have found our bond deepen even more in a time we aren't even allowed to be near one another. It takes effort and maybe even a little discomfort, but we've got to get uncomfortable and vulnerable to create those connections.

I know you're reading this thinking, *I'm too busy*. We are always saying we don't have time. We're in charge of bedtime. We need to prep for the next day. We have work we need to get done. Ladies! We *need* to recognize that maintaining our friendships is not a waste of time. Bonding with other women is essential to who we are. Studies conducted at Stanford and UCLA explain that our close connections to other females increases our oxytocin and serotonin, which are our bonding hormones. It's actually important for our health!

Can you imagine what it does to us if we don't have connections with other women? When we put work, house chores, and everything else before our own needs, it depletes us. Spending two hours each week with friends could completely shift who you are and how you feel. You're literally changing the chemicals in your brain. This isn't some self-help suggestion that I'm throwing at you; this is science. Make it a priority. If you can't meet in person, connect over video. Just connect.

USE THE WHEEL OF LIFE

In life, we have relationships with everything: ourselves, our minds, our bodies, our significant others, our children, our friends, our environment, our work, our money. *Everything.* To have healthy relationships, we must give them attention, right? If we stop paying attention to our significant others, the relationship suffers. If we stop paying attention to our spending, our bank balance suffers. If we stop giving attention to cleaning our home, its cleanliness suffers. Relationships take work.

In the beginning of my journey healing my anxiety, I discovered an incredibly useful tool: the Wheel of Life. It's simple and concrete, but for me, a visual person, this tool offered tremendous insight and feedback. It helped me to put my attention where it was needed. Because let's face it, we can't spread ourselves evenly across every area. Needs adjust and change, so it's important to have perspective. Where our thoughts go, our energy flows. For example, if your relationship with money is suffering, but you put all of your energy into your friends, things may become a little unbalanced.

If you are currently in a space of your life where you feel like you are completely out of alignment and all the areas of your life need attention, I recommend that you use this wheel weekly. Maybe even daily. Check in to see what needs your attention the most, and then check in again a week later. As your relationship with all of the areas of your life begin to move higher on the scale and become more evened out, then you can pull back on the frequency of using this. I love to use it quarterly to help assist in creating goals.

Here's how to use the Wheel of Life. Put an X in each section to indicate how well you are maintaining that relationship. If you feel

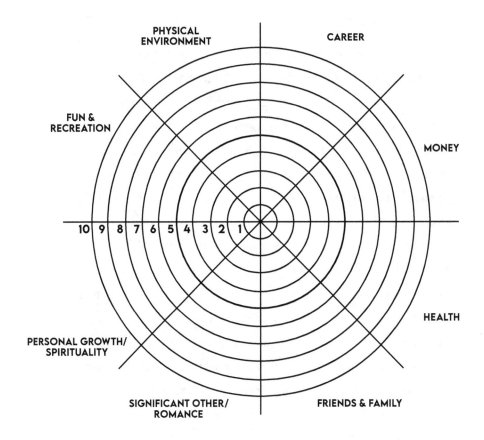

your relationship with your significant other is really strong, put an X on the 9 or 10 circle. If you feel your relationship with money is lacking, put an X on the 1 or 2 circle. Go around the wheel to assign a score to each section.

After I've done that, I identify the three areas with the lowest scores. Let's say they are money, environment, and health. For each of those areas, I define a goal that I'd like to reach in the next three months. For each of those goals, I list three or four measurable action steps I can take to help improve those areas. It'll look like this.

A. **Money.** Goal: To increase our savings account by $3,000.

1. Communicate this goal with my husband by the end of this week.

2. Set up our accounts to shift $500 into our savings every other Friday on payday.

3. Review our bank statements for 30 minutes every Friday morning to be sure spending is on track with saving.

B. **Environment.** Goal: To organize the basement.

1. Communicate the goal with my husband so we can work on it together.

2. Schedule a set amount of time each week to be in the basement.

3. Find one bag a week to throw out or donate.

C. **Health.** Goal: Find a regular workout routine.

1. Find two to three exercises that I enjoy and feel good doing at least three times a week.

2. Share my commitment to someone who can help keep me accountable.

3. Set up a reward if I work out 12 times in a month.

You might wonder if my focus on the three lowest sections will cause the other sections to suffer. With these goals outlined, while it's impossible to ignore the other areas on the life wheel, ideally since they are rated high, I can maintain those "scores" while I work on increasing the lower three areas.

How do you keep on track with goals? Here are the ways I stay on track with my goals.

- I find an accountability partner, such as my husband or a friend from my tribe.

- I review these goals at the end of every week on Sundays when I plan for my week to come. Essentially, designing these goals and then closing a book is not going to make these goals happen. You want to keep them in front of your face so that you remember they're there and ready to be accomplished.

- Ultimately, use this wheel in whatever way feels good. It's a simple tool that you can use to create life-changing awareness and change if you choose.

LAYER TWO
SUMMARY AND MAIN TAKEAWAYS

- Identify your expectations in your roles and communicate them.
- Keep dating your spouse.
- Find your presence in parenting.
- Don't forget to play!
- Be mindful of whether you're applying internal or external locus of control to yourself and/or others.
- Manage comparison and competition by eliminating social media or setting boundaries around how often you use it.
- Connect with other women either virtually through a coaching program or asking for a woman's number who you see around from time to time and want to get to know more. Find your tribe!
- Use the Wheel of Life to measure how you're feeling, bring awareness to what needs the most attention, and create actionable goals.

MANAGING YOUR ENERGY

ALL OF THESE LAYERS ARE TIED TOGETHER, and they intermingle, which I'm sure you've seen with all of my notes in Layers One and Two of how "we'll talk about that more later." Layer Three, without question, will not be successful unless you have implemented the pieces in Layers One and Two. However, Layer Three has been one of the most pivotal layers for me in my ability to manage my anxiety and overwhelm and to shift clear out of surviving and straight into thriving. We still have one more layer beyond this, so imagine the growth and expansion you can experience!

For women, it is incredibly important to understand the components of this layer, to implement them, and to live them. This is where things really begin to click into place. When you live these practices, you'll find yourself saying, "Oh, I get it!" and "I'm truly living the life I've always dreamed of." You'll feel in control, you'll feel balanced (or what I like to call aligned), and you'll feel in flow—like things are happening with more ease. I know, you're thinking, *Okay, enough introduction! Tell me how to do this!*

Here are the components we are going to cover:

- Shift your mindset.
- Understand masculine vs feminine energy.
- Harness your 28-day cycle and the moon cycle.
- Understand and read energy in your body.
- Distinguish between intuition vs. anxiety.

SHIFT YOUR MINDSET

This word has already come up a lot in this book. What does it mean exactly? Certainly, it's not a foreign term to anyone, but taking the time to fully understand your mindset and how it might limit you is absolutely crucial to designing a life with less anxiety and overwhelm.

According to *Psychology Today*, mindset orients the way we handle a situation. Your mindset can help you see opportunities to improve, or your mindset can keep you from seeing and seeking opportunities—limiting you. I think the easiest way to conceptualize mindset is to understand the difference between an abundant (or growth) mindset and a lack (or fixed) mindset. In psychology, this relates to the therapeutic approach of cognitive behavioral therapy. Let's break this down.

ABUNDANT MINDSET

An abundant mindset is essentially seeing life as the glass half full; it's being the optimist. It's a choice to view life this way. Seeing things abundantly is choosing to see that you have enough. It's finding gratitude. It's a belief that the sky is the limit in your own growth and opportunities. It's being happy for others' success. It's seeing failure as feedback to continue growing. An abundant mindset is the feeling of freedom.

LACK MINDSET

A lack mindset is the belief that you are who you are and will never change. It's the belief that if anxiety runs in your family, you'll always have it. It's comparing yourself to others and finding what you wish you had. It's avoiding taking any risks because of fear of failure. It's being indecisive, judgmental, and ungrateful. A lack mindset is the feeling of being trapped.

Understanding these two mindsets is the first step in finding awareness and then being able to shift your perspective and your life. In my anxiety journey, I found that holding onto an abundant mindset completely shifts my perspective of what anxiety really is. When I first began to experience anxiety, my inner dialogue would say things like: "This is going to kill me. I can't live like this. This is keeping me from living a good life. I can't function with this." And the list goes on. Honestly, I could write several pages of the lack that consumed me in my anxiety. However, once I shifted my perspective, I was able to view my anxiety much differently, having an inner dialogue of, "These are labor pains to birth a new me. I'm growing into an even better me. My body is so intuitive. This is how it's communicating with me. Anxiety is a small part of me—not all of me."

When you read these different sets of inner dialogues, which one feels better? The second set, obviously. The amazing part is that in either of these inner dialogues, the anxiety isn't actually any different. It's showing up consistently, in the same way each time, but your mindset shifts how you experience it. How amazing is that? We actually have that much control over our own experiences!

When working with my clients, I devote an entire module of my course to help women identify their limiting beliefs and reframe them into affirmations. This is essentially turning a lack mindset into an abundant mindset. I explain in my community, on my Same Boat Huddle podcast, and in my course that what we think shapes how we act, which shapes our beliefs. This is the essence of cognitive behavioral therapy.

At the peak of my anxiety, it wouldn't be unusual for me to wake up and immediately think, *I feel so anxious.* Just this statement alone can prompt anxiety, can't it? Thinking this would influence how I moved throughout the day—figuratively and literally. Because this was my thought, I'd focus on any symptoms of anxiety, like a churning stomach, which would then lead me to not eat, resulting in the feedback loop of my hormones continuing to be out of balance. My thoughts of being anxious would keep me from taking a walk because I'd be scared that my body would break down underneath the stress of moving too much. And, as a result of a day full of thoughts like this, it would support my belief that I was suffering from anxiety, which would lead right back into my thoughts of being anxious. This is the loop of our cognition affecting our behavior affecting our beliefs, which then influence our cognition. It's a vicious cycle, isn't it?

Viewing this thought loop that I just described as a vicious cycle is a lack mindset. Tricky, huh? In identifying our limiting beliefs, we can then adjust our thought around this, triggering a different cycle of behavior and thinking. So instead of thinking *I feel so anxious,* I could wake up and think, *Even though I feel anxious, I also feel happy and excited to spend the day with my kids.* This thought will guide me into the presence of playing with my kids, going outside with them, and enjoying my day with them. Yes, the anxiety may still be there, but it's not all-consuming because I shifted my mindset to focus on something else. By the end of the day, while anxiety was still a part of it, the actions or behaviors I had that day support the belief, "My anxiety can't control all of me."

Do not underestimate the power of what a single thought can do to adjust your entire being and how you experience your life. If you choose a thought like what I shared above, but you also think, *This is a crock of bologna, I'm anxious AF.* Great, that's okay. It takes time to rewire; it takes consistent, itty, bitty action steps that will eventually result in big changes. It's about *choice.* You can either stick with the *anxious AF* thought or think, *I see you, anxious AF, and raise you the thought that I'm gonna have a good day anyway."* Faith it 'til you make it. Choose.

The first step in adjusting your mindset is to test your ability to reframe limiting beliefs. What does this mean? Many people have go-to beliefs about themselves and their lives. We get "stuck" with these thoughts playing on loop in our heads. They are called "limiting beliefs" because they limit us—they're like a glass ceiling over you. Try to raise yourself up and grow, and you crash right into that limiting belief. But you aren't powerless against these beliefs. With time and practice, you can reframe them—think of new ways to think about them. Then each time you think the limiting belief, counter it by thinking the reframed one. Use the following limiting beliefs as journal prompts if you want to gain more insight and clarity around your own mindsets:

- I don't have enough time. But I can adjust my schedule to free up some time.
- I'm too tired. But if I drank a glass of water and ate a healthy snack, I would feel better.
- This is too hard. But I always try my best.
- I'm not a good mom. But I am the best mom that I can be.
- I didn't do enough today. But look at all that I did accomplish!
- I feel like a failure. But I'm being too hard on myself.
- _____ is a better mom than me. But I'm the best mom for my kids.
- I'm too anxious. But this anxiety is not all that I am.
- I don't know how to _____ (eat well, exercise, clean, organize, declutter, do that much). But I'm learning!
- I can only mom if I have caffeine. I love my coffee, but I can absolutely live without it.
- I can't wait for a glass of wine. I deserve it at the end of this day. But I will feel better if I drink water instead.
- My kids are driving me crazy. But I have more patience than I even know.
- If I have to wake up one more time tonight, I'm going to lose it. But I take good care of myself so I can take good care of my family.
- My husband never helps. But he probably does more than I actually see, and for that I'm grateful.
- No one understands me. But I can try harder to explain myself to them.

What are your own limiting beliefs? How can you reframe them?

UNDERSTAND MASCULINE VS. FEMININE ENERGY

Now that you understand mindset and how your thoughts can guide your actions, it's imperative to understand how to implement these actions. Many components build on top of one another to create an epic technique in managing energy called Aligned Energetic Scheduling, which I teach in my mentoring course. But to manage energy and design a day full of actions to support your new mindset, it's key to understand the concept of masculine and feminine energy.

The concept of masculine and feminine energy was completely foreign to me. Even when I learned about it, I was so stuck in my masculine energy that it blocked me from being able to tap into my feminine energy.

One night I had a scheduled phone call with my nutritionist, who is also certified in a system called Chakredy and energetic support. We focused a lot on her coaching me through surrender. This theme of surrender was huge for me because it's the idea of allowing myself to let go of some of the control. A lot of my anxiety stemmed around control, or lack there of, of my time and my children's health. We both knew that if I could release some of this need for control, or surrender, it could assist in helping some anxiety dissipate. I remember her words; she always talked to me with such tenderness, but with confidence and authority at the same time. Tears ran down my face as I asked her, "How? How do I surrender?" She lovingly urged me to get out of my head. It's where I lived, and I tried to think my way into or out of everything.

"It's like sitting back into a couch and letting your body rest into the cushions. It's not a matter of thinking how to do it. It's letting your body do it. You have to get out of your head." She said again.

I listened, feeling the frustration bubble up inside of me. I was an overachiever, and I couldn't figure out how to do this one thing. It reminded me of fourth grade when we were learning long division, and I just couldn't figure out how to do it. I sat at my desk with tears of anger running down my face, my teacher saying, "It's like getting to a brick wall. It's frustrating, but keep trying, and you'll break it down."

I held onto these thoughts and words of wisdom from my teacher as I continued to sit in my frustration and thought of how to surrender.

This is masculine energy.

Around the same time that I was beginning to understand and conceptualize what the heck it meant to surrender, I remember my therapist asked me, "Do you know if you hold more masculine or feminine energy?" I thought it was a funny question at first. She continued to explain that it's not about being male or female, but that every person holds both energies. The thought intrigued me, but I left it there in my therapist's office.

Thinking back, it's amazing to me how many times this came to my attention, but I didn't choose to fully embrace this concept until early in 2019. This, Mama, is proof that you will pick up what you need in the moment. If there is another concept or tool that can benefit you, it will keep showing up for you. Trust the process.

In 2019, I took a business coaching program. A large portion of understanding how to build a business was built on this concept of masculine and feminine energy. For me, this is when it clicked, and not just for building and growing my business, but rather, in how to completely change the way I was living my life and managing my energy throughout the day. This concept is, in my opinion, a key component in how to survive motherhood and how to thrive in it and find the joy.

MASCULINE ENERGY

If this concept is completely new to you, you may be starting this section with excitement or curiosity to learn it. You might be surprised to learn that you've been living in masculine energy your entire life. Wild, right? Our entire culture is designed and wired with masculine energy. Because of this, it takes intense focus, awareness, and intention to figure out how to pull in feminine energy to become more aligned and in control of how we're feeling.

Masculine energy is characterized by structure, to-do lists, achievements, direction, boundaries, focus, discipline, logic, goals, and drive. When I picture masculine energy, I picture a man in a business suit sitting square and still at a desk. That's not bad, is it? Those are really great traits to have. How can masculine energy help us mother?

- Maintaining a schedule
- Holding this schedule with boundaries
- Having a to-do list
- "Scoring" yourself at the end of the day by how much you got done
- Being in charge and in control
- Sticking to the plan and schedule

Reading this you're probably thinking, *How is this a bad thing?* It's not. However, if I am so strict with my schedule that I'm completely inflexible when it needs to change, I'll short circuit, it's bad. Or if I measure my worth based on how much I can check off of my to-do list, and I push myself to the point of depletion, it's bad. If I am so strict with my boundaries and discipline that I am screaming and yelling with aggression, it's bad. And this is where I think many of us end up. This is called the "wounded masculine." We also end up in this place when we are not balancing masculine energy with any feminine energy.

FEMININE ENERGY

Feminine energy is characterized by creativity, being in flow, compassion, empathy, nurturing, flexibility, vulnerability, trust, and feelings. When I picture feminine energy, I picture a woman dancing in a field of flowers wearing a flowy dress. How can feminine energy help us as a mother?

- Comforting a crying child
- Listening to the needs of the family
- Going with the flow of the day
- Taking a bubble bath
- Making meals when people are hungry instead of based on time
- Parenting through listening
- Nurturing without discipline or need for control

All of this feels pretty good, too, right? However, if we are avoiding housework and sitting around all day with no schedule, this is bad. If we are in loss of control completely, and there is manipulation, this is bad. If we are feeling depressed because of the lack of structure and routine, this is bad. If we feel "needy" and "over emotional," this is bad. This is called the "wounded feminine" and this happens because we are not balancing feminine energy with any masculine energy.

BALANCING THE TWO ENERGIES

The masculine and feminine energies are two different energies. It absolutely feels difficult to bring in both of them when we are so used to being rigid and goal-oriented. In my coaching course, Create Your Best Life, I teach a scheduling concept that I created called Aligned Energetic Scheduling. One of the biggest components is gaining the understanding of masculine and feminine energy and applying it to our day to day. The concept of these two energies will guide you as you say yes to this and say no to that. Using this concept will allow you to complete more than you can imagine. It's a concept that will get things done yet connect you with your family. It's a concept that will allow you to find yourself in a space of what feels like balance. Let's break down how so you can start practicing.

SCHEDULE WITH THE MASCULINE

Get everything out of your head. On a piece of paper, write all of the things you need to do. I do this weekly. I can't stress how important it is to get into a rhythm of weekly scheduling. Start with getting all of your nagging to-dos out of your head, such as washing the sheets, making phone calls, cleaning the bathroom, cooking, scheduling an appointment, supervising kids' activities, and accomplishing

the list of things you need to do for work. Having this organized in a
list on a piece of paper means it's not ping-ponging and taking up
valuable space and energy inside of you.

Schedule your self-care. In your planner, list all of the things
that you need for self-care. If you need ideas, see "Increase Your
Self-Care" in Layer One. Scheduling in "you" is a priority. This is
non-negotiable, is absolutely necessary for survival, and is especially
important for personal thriving.

Determine how you want to feel as a mother. Remember this
question from the introduction of this book? It's time to put this into
play here. What feeling word did you write down? Now, list any actions
that make you feel that feeling. For instance, my feeling is "connected."
If this emotional need for me isn't met, I unravel. It's where I begin to
get upset, angry, depleted, and feel a lack of purpose. It's my black hole.
Over time, I have learned, and will continue to learn, different ways
that this need is met for me. It will continue to evolve as my children
get older. Right now, ways that I can feel this are: family dinners,
family walks, family movie nights, unplugged time playing with my
kids, photographing my kids, picking them up from school, having
weekends at home with them, and taking them to their weekly activities. So what do I do with all of these things? SCHEDULE THEM IN.
Knowing that all of these activities make me feel connected means that
if I don't do them, my emotional needs won't be met. It's as simple as
that. Understanding this component guides me in setting those very
precise boundaries with when I work, they guide me in getting off of
my phone, and help me be fully aware if we are moving through our
weeks completely disconnected. Using this scheduling concept is the

easiest and most straight forward way to measure if your primary emotional need as a mother is being met. And if it's not, this scheduling concept will help you figure out how you can change that. So schedule these things into your week, too!

Put everything else into the schedule. This can look however you want it to look for you. I use an hour-by-hour weekly planner and put in everything that's necessary into the daily slots e.g. my self-care, the activities to meet my emotional need, appointments, and activities. I list my to-do items inside the weekly schedule, but not strictly scheduled in to be completed at a particular day or time. Stay consistent and tweak your scheduling to feel good for you.

IMPLEMENT WITH THE FEMININE

Do a morning review. Each morning, spend about three minutes looking at your day ahead. What do you need to accomplish? What are your non-negotiables? This is an amazing way to offer clarity and direction into your day so you don't start like a chicken with your head cut off and not remember what you need to do next. Having an awareness of what it is that you have scheduled today is from masculine energy, the structure, and schedule. Taking a few minutes to review your day ahead is a step in being able to have an awareness so that you can be flexible in your execution, which is feminine energy.

Consider how you want to feel. This is where you really pull in the feminine energy of things. You have a beautiful schedule and plan laid-out for the week, but you don't know how you're going to feel day to day. As you move through your schedule, adjust it based on how you want to feel the emotional needs of you and your family. For instance, the laundry needs to be done and that's next on your list, but your child asks you to cuddle. Ask yourself, "How do I want to feel?" My friend, this is where it gets really, really hard because we have learned to put our worth in the laundry pile. We have learned that if the laundry isn't done or dishes are in the sink when we go to bed, we have failed at motherhood. This is coming from the wounded masculine. HOW DO YOU WANT TO *FEEL?* Here is the amazing part in following this feminine implementation. Let's say you want to cuddle your child because that will fulfill your emotional need to connect, but you "push through" (wounded masculine) to get the laundry done. You will feel depleted of your energy being physically tired and exhausted, maybe even prompting some anxiety and you'll feel unfulfilled as a mother. BUT if you take those seven minutes to sit and cuddle your child, your emotional need is met, you physically feel more energetic, and then you fold the laundry. Both things are accomplished and you FEEL GOOD.

Use your schedule as a guide. There are always going to be components of the schedule you can't skip. But overall, use this schedule to guide you; implement it as described on page 225 and find the *flow.* This is where you tap into that feminine energy of flexibility instead of staying rigid and inflexible.

Take inventory. At the end of every day, take five minutes to circle the things you haven't completed. Did you skip all of your self-care? Did you skip the activity that fulfills your emotional need as a mother? If this keeps happening, ask yourself why. If you are feeling depleted, sad, depressed, anxious, or unfulfilled at the end of the day, look at how your day went. Do you need to add in more flow? More structure? Do you need more self-care?

I have used this scheduling technique for more than two years now, and it's derived by a technique taught to me by my coach Heather Chauvin of Mom Is in Control. Understanding how to schedule in this way completely shifted my life. I teach all of the other components I've added to it to make it Aligned Energetic Scheduling, it digs into our limiting beliefs, how to accomplish our big dreams, and how to manage our energy through other components—one of the most important being our 28 day cycle as a woman.

HARNESS YOUR 28-DAY CYCLE

Another concept, like masculine and feminine energy, that has come into my field is understanding the woman's 28-day cycle. Women are taught to be ashamed of our periods. If we show emotion that resembles anger or authority, we are told we are being "hormonal" or asked if we're on our period. In my study of the woman's cycle, I am astonished at how much power we can hold in understanding this part of ourselves. It almost disgusts me that we are not taught about this in our youth and how many years I've lost because I didn't have this information. Wait, did you catch that? Lack mindset. Let's reframe.

While I am just learning about the woman's cycle and all of its power in my mid-thirties, it excites me to be in a position where I can share with other women and even more importantly, be a part of the trailblazers who are paving the way for how the younger generation of women will experience life. It's empowering. It excites me to know that I have the opportunity to raise my daughter to know the power of her body and how she can use it to guide her.

The reason we aren't aware of the woman's cycle is because our society functions on a man's 24-hour cycle. Yes, our society fully embraces the masculine energy (which any gender can hold) and the 24-hour cycle that is specific to the male body. A woman moves through the same cycle—but in 28 days. Yup, imagine that. Talk about trying to fit a round peg into a square hole.

As Alisa Vitti describes in her book *In the Flo*, the man's 24-hour cycle wakes their bodies with elevated levels of cortisol and testosterone, prompting them to hit the ground running and ripping through all of their to-do lists and tasks of the day. They have the energy and focus to get it done. By the late afternoon and evening, their levels begin to drop; this is when they are ready to shoot the shit with the guys at the end of the workday and go to happy hour. Finally, by the late evening, they land on the couch, unwinding and eventually falling asleep. Our 9-5 workday is designed to perfectly support this cycle.

The woman's cycle mimic's the man's cycle, but over 28 days. No wonder some weeks feel harder than others, right? Understanding the phases of our cycle are imperative for us to have a better grasp on what to expect of ourselves week to week and adjust our schedules, projects, and self-care accordingly.

Understanding our cycle as women is so much more than what I have written in this section; however, these components of each phase will absolutely help guide you in being able to manage your anxiety and overwhelm. If you keep track of your cycle and how you're feeling each week (even each day) to find your patterns, your cycle will ultimately become an essential barometer in your scheduling and actions toward reaching bigger goals.

If you do not experience a period, whether it's due to menopause, no uterus, PCOS, hormonal imbalance, nursing, pregnancy or anything else, know that you can follow the moon phase, which is directly connected to our cycle. And for anyone who thinks that sounds crazy or "woo-woo," consider that the moon pulls an entire body of water in and out all day.

Also, for any of you who are feeling the tug or fascination to learn about this in more depth, I strongly recommend the books *In the Flo* by Alisa Vitti and *Do Less* by Kate Northrup.

Let's take a succinct look at what each phase brings.

MENSTRUATION PHASE (DAYS 1-7)/NEW MOON

What it feels like: This is when we are inward. You might feel like you have no energy, no motivation, wish to not talk to people, no desire to do work, and no inspiration, which can trigger concern and worry that you no longer want to do your passion or "the things." You are tired.

What to do: Your body is shedding, and life feels a little dark. You need to re-energize and rest. It's okay to move social plans off of the calendar. If you have the ability, move projects, presentations, and meetings. Schedule time to nap, rest, journal, meditate, and be still. If you are exercising, choose slow movements like walking or yoga.

FOLLICULAR PHASE (DAYS 7-13)/WAXING MOON

What it feels like: This is when you begin to feel like *you* again and have the urge to bloom. We begin to move out of our inward feelings.

This is where we begin to have ideas sprout and our imagination runs wild with what we can do with our lives. You're beginning to feel more energetic and excited to do things.

What to do: Use this time to really brainstorm your ideas. Collect them, and give them room and space to live somewhere. Create timelines as you're dreaming, and journal through this growth. Begin connecting with others who may be part of the brainstorming process and those who could help you foster your ideas. Begin moving a little bigger and harder in your exercise.

OVULATION PHASE 14-20/FULL MOON

What it feels like: BIG energy. This is when we feel on top of the world. It's the complete opposite of the New Moon feeling, so when we get to the new moon, it's such a stark contrast that it feels confusing, and we feel lost. Know that this is all a part of our cycle! This is the time to do big things. We want to take action, put ourselves out there, apply for jobs, start a business, network, socialize, and do it all.

What to do: Take advantage of this time! It's a great time to do interviews, start a big project you've been thinking about, or put yourself out there on social media. It's a very exciting and exhilarating time of our cycle when we feel like we have so much energy and ambition to do everything. Feed this feeling! It's also a great time to do big exercises. You can run a marathon or do a crazy HIIT workout where you push yourself harder. Also, go easy on the carbs, because we have enough energy during this part of our cycle.

LUTEAL PHASE 21-28/WANING MOON

What it feels like: You feel good but shift into feeling quiet and maybe even a little sad, and you begin to want to slow down. You want to go to bed earlier and cozy up under the weighted blanket. You'd rather stay in snuggled than go out. This is the time in our cycle where we go from big energy and "out there" in the ovulation phase to, within a day or two, beginning to feel like we want to be a bit more quiet. Often, this shift can leave many women feeling confused and translate it into, "I don't know what I want out of life anymore." Be aware of this and remember, it's just a phase. We start to go inward in preparing for the menstruation phase. This is a great time to wrap things up in a way that feels like nesting. It's my favorite time to clean!

What to do: Look at your projects and things coming up. Get them to a point that things are wrapped up and either completed or can hold for a week or so as you begin to move through your inward time. Move appointments around, review your schedule, and shift it as needed to support your energy. This is also a great time to move a bit slower again with walks and yoga.

Because we live in a world that functions on the 24-hour schedule, it takes intention and awareness on our part to understand ourselves, our needs, and our phases so that we can fully support ourselves. This is where implementing our schedules with feminine energy, holding boundaries, and advocating our needs are going to collide to create spellbinding fireworks in your life.

Obviously, we don't live in a world where we can say, "Sorry the house is a mess. I'm in my menstruation phase, and I'm going to wait two weeks to clean again." That's not sanitary. But you can honor your energy by doing less intense cleaning, maybe simply wiping the counters of the bathroom and doing a quick sweep of the floor. And then when you hit your higher energy phases, do your deep cleaning. Again, for me it's luteal.

As a wedding photographer, I can't say to someone, "Sorry, I am starting my period the day of your wedding, so it's not in the best interest of my energy to be your photographer. Best of luck!" Um, no. Doesn't fly. What I can do, though, is know that my period will be coming up, be sure that I'm preserving my energy leading up to the wedding by taking naps, getting to bed on time, limiting or eliminating alcohol, fueling my body the day of, and being sure my schedule is clear the following day so that I can sleep in, take a bath, and replenish. Whereas, when I'm shooting a wedding during my ovulation phase, I am like the energizer bunny. I can go out on a date the night before, wake up on the day of the wedding, work out, shoot the wedding, and the next day wake up early and have a full Sunday with my family. It's simply about honoring our energy, listening to what our body is asking, and doing that.

How do you listen to your energy? Know your chakras.

UNDERSTAND ENERGY AND CHAKRAS

Understanding our energy and what chakras are can trigger an insecurity. Again, if you are in the United States, especially the east coast where I am from, it's not exactly the most accepted way of thinking. Particularly being raised Catholic, allowing myself to be open enough to understand this way of thinking has been hard, but in my personal and spiritual work, I have learned to give myself permission to believe in both of these things. I also hold a master's degree in psychology, I'm a science and research geek, and, while chakras and energy can fall into the "woo-woo" category, it's science.

If you feel a little apprehensive about accepting the idea that we are made entirely of energy, rub your bare feet on a carpet and then touch another person or object. Static electricity can't happen without energy. Or what about when you meet a person and you don't like them, but you don't know why. You know exactly what I'm talking about! You know when you meet a person, and you walk away saying something like, "I don't know what it is about them; they just have a bad vibe." Cause they do. There are actual vibrations coming off of them. This is energy. Or what about a time that you were faced with a big decision; maybe it was buying your wedding dress, choosing a new house or a name for your baby, or knowing your spouse was the one. This is all energy. It's a knowing in our bodies. The flow and good feeling we have when faced with these decisions is all energy! Just the same as when we have that gut feeling that something isn't right, this is also energy.

In managing anxiety and overwhelm, reading your energy will be that additional layer to guide you in creating boundaries, making decisions, and knowing whether to cuddle your kid or do the laundry. Mentoring women to read this in their own bodies is some of the most exciting work I do. I get to watch women come to me completely defeated, anxious, and lost and, within a few months, they are glowing, know exactly what they want from life, and how to get it. They do this by taking complete hold on understanding all of their power. One of the biggest components, is reading the energy in our bodies, using our chakras as our guide.

Chakras are seven energy centers throughout the body. They are correlated with different organs as well as the physical, mental, emotional, and spiritual layers of our aura. Chakras derive from an Indian belief and, while chakras can certainly seem like a fad in today's world, they have a very dense history that goes back hundreds of years. Like other sections of this book, if this is something that piques your interest, follow the bread crumbs. It's your intuition guiding you into what your energy wants to know. A great starter book is *A Little Bit of Chakras* by Amy Leigh and Chad Mercree.

When our energy is aligned, it flows freely through all of these centers. When the centers are blocked, we experience different symptoms of the energy not being able to flow.

The seven chakras are:

- Root
- Sacral
- Solar plexus
- Heart
- Throat
- Third eye
- Crown

ROOT CHAKRA

FIRST

Color: Deep red (Each chakra has a color associated with it. You can wear the color, eat food of that color, etc.)

Location: Base of spine, tailbone area

When in balance: We feel supported, safe, and secure in our lives. We have stillness, stability, and abundance.

When out of balance:

Physical: hemorrhoids, bowel issues, sciatica, and knee and lower back pain

Emotional/mental/spiritual: over identification with material possessions, hoarding supplies, ungrounded or feeling spacey, excessive or irrational fears and anxiety

How to unblock/realign: Go for a walk outside, lie in the grass, do anything connected to the earth, eat root vegetables.

Affirmation: "I am grounded and present in my life."

Crystals: Tumbled hematite and black tourmaline

Essential oils: Frankincense and cypress

SACRAL CHAKRA

SECOND

Color: Orange

Location: Above pelvic bone, below belly button

When in balance: This area houses our creativity, sensuality, sexuality, and procreation. This is where joy for life is held and how we experience life.

When out of balance:

Physical: uterine, bladder and prostate problems

Emotional/mental/spiritual: addiction to sex, lack of libido, overly emotional, lack of emotional response, lack of creativity

How to unblock/realign: Wear the color, do something creative (maybe different than your normal modality if you are having a writer's block), or do something pleasurable (does not have to be sexual).

Affirmation: "I feel pleasure to my core and allow myself to gain vital life force from it."

Crystal: Carnelian

Essential oils: Ylang ylang and clary sage

SOLAR PLEXUS

THIRD

Color: Yellow

Location: Above belly button

When in balance: Strong sense of self, self-confidence, personal POWER, free will, authenticity

When out of balance:

Physical: Symptoms connected to your pancreas, such as blood sugar issues, liver, gallbladder, ulcers, or digestive issues

Emotional/mental/spiritual: Fearfulness, anxiety, depression, out of alignment, lack of confidence, insecurity, depletion of energy

How to unblock/realign: Looking at pale yellow can help relax, and looking at bright yellow will help build. Positive thinking, tackling limiting beliefs. This chakra is how we SHOW UP in the world. How are you showing up?

Affirmation: "I am confident, and I stand in my power."

Crystals: Citrine, tiger's eye, and yellow jasper

Essential oils: Geranium, ginger (digestive), and grapefruit (gallbladder)

HEART CHAKRA

FOURTH

Color: Green

Location: Center of chest

When in balance: You feel loved, cared for, and a strong sense of self-love. This space holds love, breath, balance, relationships, unity, compassion, and connection.

When out of balance:

Physical: Immunity related to your thymus gland. It's important to boost the immune system through meditation and exercise. Ailments may be heart disease and asthma.

Emotional: Fear of not being loved enough and not being able to fully receive love from others, including yourself.

How to unblock/realign: Immerse yourself in love. Pet dogs! Spend quality time with kids (older, not babies or toddlers), do deep breathing and EFT tapping. (We'll talk more about this in Layer Four.)

Affirmation: "I open my heart to the immense love in my life."

Crystals: Rose quartz and moss agate

Essential oils: Rose, jasmine, ylang yang, joy, geranium, Joy and Sensation (Young Living blends)

THROAT CHAKRA

FIFTH

Color: Blue

Location: Throat

When in balance: This space holds speech, communication, and creative expression. When open, you're able to let things go, especially our own past choices, and express views in a healthy way.

When out of balance:

Physical: connected with your thyroid, ears, and speech. Any ailments in these areas (sore throat, thyroid issues, ear aches, etc.)

Emotional/mental/spiritual: Personal expression is limited. Shame over past, present, and the future. Difficulty living in the present.

How to unblock/realign: Headstands and singing!

Affirmation: "I express myself with ease and grace."

Crystals: Sodalite and blue lace agate

Essential oils: Chamomile and valor

THIRD EYE CHAKRA
SIXTH

Color: Indigo or purple

Location: Between the brows

When in balance: This is an area for spiritual awakening, psychic abilities, intuition, dreams, and common sense. When it's very open, you may be more sensitive to light.

When out of balance:

Physical: Headaches, vision problems, insomnia, nausea, sinus infections

Emotional: Judgmental, anxiety, mental fog, feeling overwhelm

How to unblock/realign: Meditate, drink water, eat less sugar and dairy, work on limiting beliefs, draw, color, take photographs, and allow yourself to daydream.

Affirmation: "My intuition guides me for my highest good."

Crystals: Amethyst

Essential oils: Cypress, frankincense, and vetiver

CROWN CHAKRA
SEVENTH

Color: White or purple

Location: Just above head

When in balance: You are fully present and have the power of now. This is the area of enlightenment, pure awareness, not fearing death, inspiration, and creativity.

When out of balance:

Physical: Light and sound sensitivity, headaches, weak memory, and poor coordination

Emotional: Loneliness, insignificance, meaningless, and disconnected from higher power

How to unblock/realign: Gratitude practice, inspiration, affirmation, and spiritual connection

Affirmation: "I easily connect with the universal life force."

Crystals: Clear quartz and howlite

Essential oils: Frankincense and cedarwood

• • •

Now that you have all of the basics of understanding each chakra, how do you actually apply this to your life and use it to guide you in feeling energetically aligned and in flow? Much like how you can't go to a gym and bench press 250 pounds on your first day, it takes time, intention, and daily work to build your energy and find strength. Here are the exercises I recommend to build this muscle.

JOURNAL PAST EXPERIENCES

Journaling about past experiences is an exercise you can do. To find even more awareness, clarity, and experience ah-ha moments, I recommend doing this regularly. Think of a time that you were faced with a life-altering moment, often a decision that had to be made.

Some examples might be when you decided a new job wasn't right for you, decided to leave your job, decided you were ready to have a baby, found your dream house, or even knew what you wanted for dinner. Think of anything that sticks out in your mind. Close your eyes, and experience this moment in your body. Take five cycles of slow breathing, and focus on your body, starting at the top of your head down to your toes. Feel everything that is happening in your body. Open your eyes and journal about the experience—and about your experience remembering it in detail. Did you have flickering light behind your eye lids? Was your stomach tight? Did you have tingles running down your back?

Next, try to connect the sensations you were feeling with the different energy centers, and interpret if it was a block (imbalance) or a flow (balance). An example might be if the memory made you feel nauseated, your solar plexus chakra might be blocked. Or if the memory made you feel safe and secure, your root chakra might be in flow. Did you follow what your body was guiding you to do? If you did, then how did you feel? If you didn't, what happened?

Continue to take on this journaling practice regularly. The more you give time to your past experiences, the more insight you'll gain about how your body experiences different types of energy when communicating.

PRACTICE IN THE PRESENT

This exercise is exactly what it sounds like. Essentially, it's doing the same exercise as past experiences but in the present moment. This is a beautiful example of how we need to work in layers, but not compartmentalized layers. We need the foundation of understanding how to find our presence, all covered in Layer One, and this will assist in your ability to have mindfulness when reading the energy in your body.

This practice goes hand in hand with implementing a schedule through feminine energy. Reading your body's energy will guide you through your structured schedule and offer you the flexibility and confidence to know that what your body is asking is the right decision. For instance, let's stick with the example deciding whether to cuddle your kiddo or do the laundry. You're standing in the living room, making your way over to the laundry, when your sweet baby asks, "Mommy, will you cuddle me?" Stop right here, and feel it in your body.

Okay, I get a pang in my chest and chills down the back of my spine. I imagine going over toward the laundry, and my stomach flips. It doesn't feel good. If I were to actually follow through with this decision, I would become depleted in my energy because the flow through my chakras is blocked. Considering I felt a pang in my chest, it's likely there is a block in my heart chakra.

However, if I choose to sit and cuddle my baby, I feel my chest expand. It's like a rush of energy comes through me; likely because I'm honoring my energy, doing what it's asking of me instead of what my to-do list is asking of me. In turn, I feel an influx of energy, get my fill and connection with my kid, and then have the energy to also get the laundry done because my energy is in flow.

Do not overcomplicate this! This isn't about judgement, shame, or winning. That's masculine energy! This is about observing and learning. Let's say you pick the laundry over your kid because you fully believe that is what your energy is asking, but then observing it, you realize, "Hey, I think I was supposed to spend a few minutes with my kid." Observe that, take note, and recognize that you just learned something. Tackle it with your abundant mindset; you didn't fail. You took action and got feedback. See how beautifully this all ties together?!

Having the knowledge and understanding in reading your own energy is the key to unlocking yourself from the cage of anxiety and overwhelm. It's like freedom. It shines a new light on seeing life through a completely different lens. You will find yourself with more confidence, decisiveness, permission, and connection. It's not something you will perfect. But the goal is progress—not perfection.

If you don't get it right the first time, your body will keep talking to you. Ultimately, I believe this is where a lot of our ailments come from. Disease causes disease, however you want to define this word.

My body talked to me when my back wasn't working the right way. My body was asking me to slow down, but I didn't. I then began suffering from adrenal fatigue, resulting in the inability to physically work out without having an anxiety attack. Anxiety came almost every day. I experienced such intense nausea I was nearly anorexic, getting just enough calories in my Pirate's Booty and wine each evening when my anxiety was low enough that I could eat something. I caught gastro-intestinal bugs every single month right at the time I was getting my period, prompting me to go to my physician in conjunction with my pivotal anxiety attack, leading to test after test showing me that I was healthy.

Your body is incredibly intuitive, just like mine. If you don't understand what it's asking, it will continue to talk louder. Many women feel trapped by their bodies; we feel betrayed, as if it's not showing up for us. But is it the other way around? I didn't feed myself nutritiously, I didn't engage in any self-care, I spoke very poorly of my body in my negative self-talk loops, and I ignored all of my body's needs. Who was betraying whom?

INTUITION VS. ANXIETY

One of the biggest questions I get from my clients and community is how to tell the difference between intuition and anxiety. Now that you understand masculine and feminine energy and how to read energy in your body, you have the tools to distinguish between intuition and anxiety. I know, Mama. It can be really hard when we're in the thick of it.

I view intuition as feminine energy and anxiety as masculine energy. If we want to get really specific, I view it as the fight between a divine feminine power and a wounded masculine power. Intuition is a grounded energy that is trusting, confident, loyal, empathetic, and sensitive. It's like a soft-spoken powerhouse. Anxiety is chaotic energy that feels as if it's controlling us like a puppet with strings. It's all about control, fear, and aggression. When broken down this way, they feel very different, don't they? So why is it so hard to decipher between the two?

It's because we get stuck in our heads. We allow our own energy to get mixed up inside of these other energies, and we can't discern what is what. It's like being in deep, dark water and not knowing what direction to swim. If I go this way, will I go deeper or will I find myself swimming to the light? It's full of fear and panic.

The stronger your intuitive muscle gets with the exercises I offered in the previous section, the more clear your intuition will become. It's a muscle. Again, you won't read this section, close this book, and be an expert in telling the difference between the two. Hell, I still have to work at it! But the more you practice and use this muscle, the easier it becomes.

Your intuition is tied into the sections of setting boundaries, saying yes to something is saying no to something else, choosing out of love not fear, feminine energy, and reading the energy in your body. All of this combined is what it is to read your intuition. You've already gained all of the tools to be able to do this, now it's simply a matter of trusting yourself.

Many of us think we need numbers, statistics, concrete proof, and proven outcomes to support our decisions, and without this, we don't trust ourselves. We have to let this go. This is not trust. Your trust and your knowing are sitting right inside of you. This is the free fall exercise; it's closing your eyes and falling backward with no guarantee that your friends are going to catch you, knowing that they could drop you, but trusting you will be caught. When your friends catch you, that is your intuition. When you try to control outcomes, micromanage situations, and make choices out of fear, that is your anxiety.

Just as your intuition-reading muscle grows, the power of your anxiety will begin to dissipate. This is when it becomes easier to read between the two. In the meantime, continue the practice of reading the energy in your body! Constantly studying this with curiosity free of shame and judgment is where you are going to find the most information about your own body. No book or technique can teach you more about your intuition than your own awareness and intention. You are your own teacher in this. Trust yourself.

Confidence isn't born by choice. Confidence is born by taking action even when you're scared. Confidence comes when you choose to pay attention, when you choose the action that you want to take. Action will breed your confidence in yourself and your own intuition because with each step forward, you will gain more feedback, not failure. But you must decide what action to take. Inaction *is* a decision.

Let's address intuition vs. anxiety in real life decisions. I hope reading the above few paragraphs has created several ah-ha moments for you, but applying this into real life can look and feel completely different. I find that the struggle between leaning into these two things comes up for women very often with work. Whether it's to start a direct sales business or close it up, to move across the country with their family or let go of that work opportunity to stay put, to leave a secure job to pursue bigger passions, or to have another baby and continue growing a family or to close the doors and start the next chapter.

Our anxiety interferes with our intuition. But some of the loudest noise that interrupts us is others' expectations—our parents, our families, and the society's "shoulds," such as:

You should go to college.

You should get a job out of college and stay in it until retirement.

You should have 2.5 kids by the time you're 30.

You should be more than "just a mom."

You should be married when you're 25.

You shouldn't rely on a man.

You shouldn't get divorced.

You should be divorced, independent, and fabulous.

You shouldn't quit your job.

You should be home with your kids more.

You shouldn't have another kid.

You should give your child a sibling.

You shouldn't worry so much.

You should vaccinate.

You shouldn't vaccinate.

You should be more feminine.

You should be more assertive.

You should live close to your parents.

You shouldn't rely on family to do your "job" as a mother.

You should get eyelash extensions.

You should have a cleaner house.

You should lose 10 pounds.

Talk about overwhelm! Just reading this list brings on anxiety, doesn't it? How on earth can we tap into our own intuition with all of that contradictory noise buzzing in our ears?!

Yup, you guessed it, turn off the noise.

One of the most valuable lessons I've learned so far in life, one that has offered me complete freedom from everyone else's judgements and pressures, is that none of what anyone else is saying has anything to do with me. These are they're OWN judgements, their own projections, and their own triggers. Our parents (the baby boomers) were raised by a generation who experienced the Great

Depression. They were raised to be scared to lose their jobs, so of course their advice is that you shouldn't quit yours. My grandmother's generation, the one who experienced the Great Depression, consisted of women who didn't work and stayed home to child rear and take care of the house. Things change! So why on earth should another person's judgements and insecurities guide me through my life decisions? They shouldn't. It's as simple as that, and it's as complicated as that.

This thought process and the freedom of letting go of others' expectations didn't happen overnight. It happened through those tiny action steps I took and continue to take every day that build my trust in myself. The steps that have shown me that I know what's best for me, and that I get to own every single thing I choose to do.

Had I listened to others' judgements and criticism to stay in my school counseling position, I'd be completely burnt out, unhealthy, stressed, probably in a strained marriage, and missing my children's childhoods. I chose to connect with my intuition, without even knowing it, and took a leap of faith to walk away from a career I worked eight years to get. Now look where I am. I'm thriving in my own body, mind, and soul. I'm embracing and cherishing every minute of my kids' childhoods. I have a strong and healthy marriage. I've manifested a life that used to be just a dream. All because I trusted my own intuition.

It's scary and takes practice, but you'll get it as long as you keep trying. Let's apply this to your life. You are now equipped to complete this exercise because you have moved through the information in Layers One through Three.

Think of a big life decision you're faced with right now, such as deciding to move across the country, choosing to put in a pool, or determining whether or not to send your child to kindergarten this year or the next. Whatever it is, grab it and sit with it.

Go to a quiet space where you won't be interrupted. Maybe this is in the shower, maybe it's on the toilet, sitting in the car in the driveway after running an errand alone, or in bed at 11 pm when the rest of your family is asleep. Let's be real about where a mom can get a quiet uninterrupted space, shall we? Next imagine one of your options in full detail and following through with it step by step. If it's moving across the country, imagine finding your new home, telling your family, packing, flying or driving, arriving at your new home, and actually living there. Write down what it feels like in your body. What came up for you? Start from your head down to your feet, what sensations did you feel? Don't judge them, just list them.

Now, I want you to imagine making the other choice. Using our example, imagine deciding to stay home, continuing in the job you're in, telling your boss you're not going to take the opportunity to move across the country, and so on. Again, write down all of the sensations in your body from head to toe.

Remember the exercise you did to learn how to read the energy in your body? Here it is again! Which decision felt in flow, and which one felt blocked? This is how we read our intuition. You feel intuition in your body, and you feel anxiety in your head. Intuition feels like a quiet knowing, something you can't quite explain. You're listening to your intuition when you say things like, "I know it seems like it doesn't make sense, but I just know that this is what I'm supposed to do."

You're listening to your anxiety when you say things like, "If you go, it's going to cost ____ amount of money, and what if we don't acclimate? What if I miss my family? Everyone is going to think I'm crazy, and I don't want them thinking that. What if they're right?" Move out of your mind and into your body and you will find your answer. And then trust. I know we want the crystal ball, showing us we are going to make the right decision. Intuition is feminine energy, which means it's not about the end goal or achievements. It's about the journey—not the destination.

Trust.

Congratulations, you just successfully read about three layers to find alignment in your physical, mental, and emotional wellness. With constant practice and implementation, I believe that you have the tools to unlock yourself from the societal omissions of motherhood, the veils and facades that lead us into a life changing role and feeling plummeted by the unknowns and changes in all context of our bodies. You will have all the secrets and tools to design a life that feels good. You will know how to move through the challenging, not-so-good moments with grace instead of the pressures of perfection imposed on us. And if you're a mama reading this who has already found herself in a state of overwhelm and anxiety, you will be free. You have what you need within you to rewrite your story. But what about Layer Four?

This layer isn't imperative, but boy will you expand if you choose to open this layer up. Correlating with our crown, or Maslow's self-actualization, it's a layer not everyone will get to, or maybe some of you will pick at as your interest guides you. So, while I feel Layers One through Three have everything you need to live your life in motherhood with control, balance and ease, Layer Four is what is going to light you up and bring in even more abundance. It's one of my favorite layers. Give yourself a shake, loosen your brow, relax your tongue off of the roof of your mouth, smile, and enjoy the final layer.

LAYER THREE
SUMMARY AND MAIN TAKEAWAYS

- Be aware of your mindset and if you are thinking abundantly or in lack.
- Abundant mindset is a glass-half-full way of thinking.
- Lack mindset is a glass-half-empty way of thinking.
- Your thoughts create your actions, which confirm your beliefs.
- Choose your thoughts wisely to shift your actions and ultimately your beliefs.
- Find a balance in using masculine energy to design your weekly schedule and feminine energy to implement it.
- The 28-day female or lunar cycle can guide you in how to show up each day by knowing what your energy levels will be.

- The menstrual phase is inward energy, the follicular phase is when you get your energy back and you're excited to do things, ovulation is when you're most productive, and luteal is when you want to go inward again. Adjust your schedule according to where you are in your cycle.
- If you don't menstruate, use the lunar cycle instead.
- The chakras will help connect you with your body and energy, ultimately connecting you with your intuition.
- Intuition is fueled by feminine energy, and anxiety is fueled by masculine energy.
- The more you connect with your intuition, the easier you'll find reading the differences between the two. Practice regularly to build this muscle.

LAYER 4

EXPANSION

BY NOW YOU'VE PROBABLY NOTICED how the layers are working, from the foundation, bottom up. Another way to view them is in the perspective of our chakras. We are supporting ourselves from the bottom up. We meet our basic needs (the root). Then we address and create healthy relationships with ourselves, our family, and our friends (the sacral, solar plexus, and heart). And then we learn how to read our energy and intuition (third eye). The way all of these components, perspectives, theories, therapeutic approaches, and ideas intermingle, collaborate, and coexist gives me goosebumps. The alignment in all of these pieces is so divine and validating in how it comes together and makes sense. I hope that after reaching this part of the book you're reading with new perspective, awareness, and power in who you are and the life you are choosing to live—the life you are creating for you and your family. Take a moment to really acknowledge this shift because it's *big*.

Layer Four is about expanding into your higher self. Looking at the chakras, this is about the crown. Is this step crucial in tackling anxiety and overwhelm in motherhood? Nope. It's not crucial in any context of life, but if and when you're ready for this expansion, it amplifies all of the work you've done and opens you up into an even more profound and abundant way of living. Buckle up.

This is what we'll be talking about:

- Frequencies
- Law of attraction
- EFT tapping
- Reiki
- Oracle cards
- Crystals

FREQUENCIES

Do you know the feeling of being "on cloud 9?" Now that you've been feeling and identifying energy in your body, this may come easy to you. It's called cloud 9 because we feel like we're floating, right? We are so happy and joyous that we feel like our feet can lift right off of the ground.

Now, think about how you feel when "your blood is boiling." It's this saying for a reason, isn't it? It's a feeling of anger pulsing through your veins, making you feel physically unwell and weighed down.

These two feelings—being on cloud 9 and feeling like your blood is boiling—are extremes. One is pretty much the best you can ever feel, and the other is pretty much the worst. Of course, there's a wide spectrum of feelings in between these extremes.

Introducing the frequency scale, which came into my field around two years ago. Really sitting with it and considering what it encompasses begins to make a lot of sense. And, like everything else I've discussed in this book, it's connected to everything I've already

OMEGA

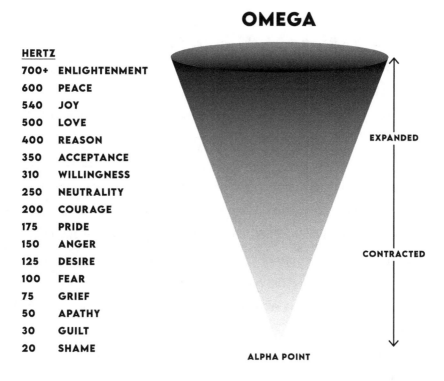

HERTZ	
700+	ENLIGHTENMENT
600	PEACE
540	JOY
500	LOVE
400	REASON
350	ACCEPTANCE
310	WILLINGNESS
250	NEUTRALITY
200	COURAGE
175	PRIDE
150	ANGER
125	DESIRE
100	FEAR
75	GRIEF
50	APATHY
30	GUILT
20	SHAME

EXPANDED

CONTRACTED

ALPHA POINT

shared. There is a tighter circle to these tools than the six degrees of Kevin Bacon. (If you're too young to understand, I'm sorry you missed out.) Everything is tied to everything, which creates a lot of validity in the tools shared here.

The frequency scale is a visual representation of emotions, their relation to each other, and their frequencies measured in hertz. Higher frequency in measurement equals higher vibration. And at this point, I think we are all familiar with "high vibes." You can see low frequency, contracted emotions like shame, guilt, and apathy at the bottom of the scale. And you can see high-frequency, expanded emotions such as enlightenment, peace, and joy at the top of the scale. The emotion that you are feeling is the frequency you are vibrating at.

We are balls of energy, and the energy in our bodies vibrates all of the time. This is why we use the phrase, "They had a good/bad vibe." It's a literal meaning; we are always vibrating at a frequency. Mind blowing, I know!

Even more mind blowing is the fact that your energy vibrations attract similar energy to you. And it repels opposite frequencies. Have you ever noticed that when you feel joyful, great things seem to come to you as if by magic? And when you feel sad, not-so-great things happen? You are attracting those things to you with your vibrations.

So, just like our thoughts create our actions and our beliefs, aka our thoughts create our reality, our frequency also creates our reality. You are literally attracting everything that is happening to you.

Why is it so important to understand this concept? Because, if you're constantly sitting at the low-frequency level of anxiety and overwhelm, you can't then create the life of your dreams. It's scientifically impossible. You'll lose steam and stay in your anxiety and overwhelm. Who wants that?

The beauty in this is that you already know how to raise your vibration. Everything in Layers One through Three will help keep your vibe high. One of my favorite ways to raise my frequency is to simply move, especially dancing. It's fun, and it's easy. Keep eating and moving, keep your energy flowing through your chakras, think abundantly, use affirmations in place of limiting beliefs, and watch your life take shape into the one you have always imagined.

Having an understanding of frequency is incredibly helpful in finding and holding your own awareness around your energy so that you can move yourself up on the scale. You can also use this information to help guide your boundaries for people, spaces, and work. Protecting your energy should be a priority. To delve deeper into this topic, I recommend the book *Frequency: The Power of Personal Vibration* by Penney Peirce.

THE LAW OF ATTRACTION

Now that you understand vibrational frequency and how you attract similar frequencies, the next step is to use the Law of Attraction. Understanding the Law of Attraction is the key to life.

Many books cover this topic, and, if it's something that interests you, I recommend you dive in. Any book by Abraham Hicks (Esther and Jerry Hicks) will open the door to a whole new world of understanding and another favorite is *The Secret Daily Teachings* by Rhonda Byrne. On thelawofattraction.com they summarize the Law of Attraction in this simple and understandable way:

"Simply put, the Law of Attraction is the ability to attract into our lives whatever we are focusing on . . . It is the Law of Attraction which uses the power of the mind to translate whatever is in our thoughts and materialize them into reality. In basic terms, all thoughts turn into things eventually. *If you focus on negative doom and gloom you will remain under that cloud. If you focus on positive thoughts and have goals that you aim to achieve you will find a way to achieve them with massive action."*

This really plays in mind with everything we've discussed already hasn't it? Your mindset creates your outcome, and your vibrational frequency attracts people and things with similar vibrational frequencies.

The Law of Attraction helps you to attract what you want. So it makes sense that to use the Law of Attraction, you first have to understand what it is that you want. If you don't know what you want in your life, how can you attract it to you?

Are you feeling overwhelm and anxiety? Isn't it incredibly freeing to think about the fact that this Universal Law can hand power over to you to figure out how to create the life you've always wanted? Let's break down how to apply this law in four simple steps that I've curated in teaching this to other women.

STEP 1: VISUALIZE

To create the life that you have always dreamed of, you have to know exactly what it is that you want! And you need to visualize it. Get comfy, get quiet, close your eyes, and imagine the life that you want. What does your life look like? How does it make you feel? Be specific. Imagine it. Daydream about it. If you want, write it down.

STEP 2: PUT IT OUT THERE

To attract and create the things you want in your life, you need to say them out loud. This feels scary and goes against how we've been raised. We are told to make wishes and blow out candles but to never share what it is that we've wished for or else it won't come true. *False.* The Universe doesn't know what you want if you aren't saying it out loud. How do you put it out there? Share it with your spouse, a friend, your blog, your vision board, or an accountability partner. Yes, the vision board is based on the Law of Attraction.

STEP 3: THINK ABUNDANTLY

I told ya everything was connected! This is where you get to continue to use your abundant mindset to create a life you've always dreamed of. Whether it's a perfectly clean house, your dream car, a fit body, or an anxiety-free life, this is how we do it. If you are putting out there that you want your dream house, remember that when moments and opportunities fall through or it looks like it's not going to happen, don't drop your vibrational frequency with a lack mindset! This is where you could get pulled into low vibes and lose your opportunity to manifest. In turn, you could be feeding your low vibration with the belief that it doesn't work and before you know it, you're living under a dark cloud. Remember, the glass is always half full. God-Universe works in the most synchronized divine timing I've ever experienced. Trust it.

STEP 4: SURRENDER

Surrendering is the hardest part. This is where the trust comes in—trusting that divine timing allows us to co-create with the Universe. This is what happens after you take the action steps that you can control, the point when you know that ultimately we have control of nothing. An example of this is after you get finances in order to apply for a mortgage, hire a Realtor, find a house, and put in an offer. Then you wait and surrender to learn if you got the house. I can't tell you how many times things didn't happen in the way I had hoped only to find out that it was for a perfect reason. Trust it.

The Law of Attraction is a really fun thing to learn and practice. Create a vision board, and dream big. It will give you clarity on what you want out of life, encourage you to articulate it, and give you a vision for how to set goals and take actions toward them. Embracing the Law of Attraction is a win if you are ready to expand even further. Enjoy the process.

EMOTIONAL FREEDOM TECHNIQUE (EFT)

EFT tapping is gaining popularity all over the world as research studies support it with significant evidence that it works. Emotional freedom technique is also referred to as tapping and is exactly as it sounds. You can Free yourself from Emotions by Tapping on particular points on your body while talking about your emotions. You tap points following a sequence, and then you repeat that sequence seven to nine times, which are sometimes called "rounds." EFT is a technique that is easily learned and easily adapted to whatever emotion or issue is bothering you. People use it with great success to decrease anxiety and overwhelm and also to lose weight, stop smoking, and improve relationships.

Tapping has everything to do with the energy in our bodies. If you aren't convinced yet that our bodies are big balls of energy, I'm not sure what will change your mind, but it's science and pretty darn awesome.

Although I have placed EFT in Layer Four, it is a primary tool I use to manage my anxiety and overwhelm. This amazing technique has been an important tool in managing my anxiety, and I also believe was a huge part in rewiring my brain from my post-traumatic stress disorder brought on by my daughter's sickness. Let's discuss what it is exactly, and then I'll share how I've used it.

One of the main sources of information for tapping is the Tapping Solution Foundation. They're my go-to in understanding tapping and being guided through some of the most amazing tapping sessions. You can download their app (The Tapping Solution) and use it regularly. I tapped into it recently (see what I did there?) when I needed to manage some anxiety around flying. I highly recommend this resource!

The Tapping Solution Foundation describes EFT as a practice in which you tap specific meridian points on your body while talking through traumatic memories or a wide range of emotions. The talking that you do while tapping is quite specific, as well as the order and locations in which you tap. To find the points and possible scripts, head over to the Tapping Solution Foundation website.

The meridian points are spots on your body that can be tapped to help move energy through your body. Our negative emotions and trauma get stuck at certain points of energy. By tapping, you remove these blocks, which restores the energetic balance in your body. The Tapping Solution Foundation shares that, according to Dr. Dawson Church, "Accupoint tapping sends signals directly to the stress centers of the mid-brain, not mediated by the frontal lobes (the thinking part, active in talk therapy)." Because EFT simultaneously accesses stress on physical and emotional levels, he adds, "EFT gives you the best of both worlds, body and mind, like getting a massage during a psychotherapy session."

Earlier, I touched the surface of the functions of the brain in explaining anxiety and post-traumatic stress disorder. Similarly, EFT accesses the amygdala, an almond-shaped part of your brain that holds onto our memories and traumas. It then prompts your body's negative reaction to fear by signaling the hypothalamus to turn on that switch, or the "fight or flight" response, that makes it so powerful. EFT helps to rewire this signal from your amygdala. For scientific studies and nerdy reading, visit thetappingsolutionfoundation.org to read all of the yummy research.

Using EFT, you tap nine of your meridians based off of acupuncture points. You do seven to nine rounds, tapping specific points as you speak through your trauma or emotion.

Tapping can be emotional because it's necessary to fully feel the trauma or emotion as you are tapping to rewire your brain and signals. However, as you tap and move through more rounds of tapping, you begin to shift your dialogue to accept and resolve the emotion. As mentioned, apps, videos, and professionals can support you through a tapping session.

EFT was introduced to me early on, but I only began using it regularly two or three years ago. When in fight or flight, it feels nearly impossible to know what to do to support yourself. Yes, even for a person who can write a book sharing ways to help manage anxiety! It's not a fault or a shortcoming, it's my brain doing its job. When you are in full-on anxiety, your brain shuts off all other functions, thinking that it needs to in order for you to survive. So, yes, that rational thinking part of your brain had last call and is shut down. Don't beat yourself up over forgetting your best tools when you're in the height of anxiety.

To support me in knowing what tools to use, I made a list of my go-to tools and stuck it in a place I could see. More importantly, I shared it with my husband. My husband is my "call a friend" in an anxiety attack. Give your list to your "call a friend." Dustin learned very quickly to ask me, "Did you tap?" This is his number one question because it works—fast.

Tapping uses a 1 to 10 scale for you to measure your response to your emotion or trauma. I use EFT in the middle of an anxiety attack, I can go from a level 10 anxiety down to a 7. If I continue tapping more rounds, I can bring myself down to a 4 or 5. It's really pretty amazing to experience.

As my anxiety became more manageable and needed EFT less, I decided to explore how EFT could support me in other ways.

One of the biggest ways I believe EFT helped me was in removing the trauma over my daughter getting the stomach bug. In late 2018, early 2019, my anxiety around the stomach bug took another spike. It was blindsiding and unwelcoming. I felt my anxiety rise past the level of manageable day after day for a couple months. I was becoming homebound with my uneasy stomach, and I felt my body succumb to complete exhaustion by mid-afternoon after its courageous fight to keep me standing all day through its perceived attack. I had reached a point of surrender—or perhaps fight. I threw my gloves off, and I was ready to fight dirty.

I wanted to take on my trauma in a new way and permit myself to rid my body of it for good. I no longer needed the trauma to keep any of us safe. I told my body I had a handle on things on my own, and the fight or flight could go. I chose to find a specific tapping video on fear of illness and added in some of my own rounds or changed some of the words to be specific to my trauma. I dedicated my daily time to doing the routine for nearly a month or more. If memory serves me correctly, this was the time that I ended up having some questionable stomach issues and chose to support my system with a certified energetic specialist in which I found relief. But I believe that I ended up moving so much trauma and emotion from my meridians that my system also felt a little blindsided.

When the fall of 2019 arrived, I braced myself for my PTSD symptoms to resurface like they always did with school starting and the flu season hitting. I was shocked to find myself not being triggered. At all. My daughter would come home and tell me about a kid who vomited in class, the stomach bug that took a whole family out, the kid next to her having a fever, or the student who shoved his fingers in my son's mouth. I waited for the anxiety to start, but it never did. The more I found myself not triggered by all of these things, the more I realized that I was free of my trauma. I will always stay diligent and aware to support my energy if anything resurfaces, but I contribute this freedom to the tapping I did in early 2019. To put it to the ultimate test, I am currently living through a pandemic, ordered to stay in my home "indefinitely" with a very real virus lurking outside my door, and I am not triggered. Am I cautious? Yes. Do I have moments of feeling scared? Absolutely. But I am not experiencing anxiety. This has been an incredible indicator of how far I've come and validation that these tools really do work.

One other way that I love to use tapping is to maintain my overwhelm during busy season. As I've mentioned, the fall is notoriously a very busy time of year for me with weddings, and I have always notoriously found myself in a state of such overwhelm, I could physically feel the tension in my body as if I was desperate to climb out of my own skin and run away. This overwhelm can creep in any time of the year because I'm a mother. I have a lot to do like every mother. I am slowly but surely making the shift to even out the playing field with Dustin and managing my energy through my scheduling technique, but I am still hard wired to give into the feeling of overwhelm.

The Tapping Solution has an outstanding guided EFT session for morning overwhelm. During times that I begin to feel overwhelmed in work and in life, I dedicate the seven minutes needed for this session into my morning routine, religiously. Here is proof it works.

In the fall of 2018, I launched my course Create Your Best Life, had weddings out the wazoo (that's an official term, right?), was taking an online course in understanding the Law of Attraction, moved on a weekend I had to shoot two weddings, sent my daughter to kindergarten, and was the main speaker at a local women's conference. I committed to doing the overwhelm tapping every single morning. I moved through that fall like it was the most elegant dance you'd ever seen. Oh, and not to mention, my new house didn't have a kitchen for seven months. And I still nailed life.

Fast forward to the fall 2019, I had weddings throughout the fall, but spread out. I took a break from family photography sessions, and I hired a photo editor to do most of my wedding editing. (Delegation!) I had a full-blown fall breakdown. What I mean by breakdown is some anxiety, going inward, and looking at my planner every day and hyperventilating in the overwhelm and thoughts of, *How am I going to do this? How am I going to get through this?* I still don't understand how or why this happened—especially compared with the year before. What was the difference? I analyzed my routines, my thoughts, who I was spending time with, everything. The only difference? I wasn't doing my EFT in the mornings.

Moral of the story? Tapping works. So, again, while this is an incredible tool to expand into abundance and find fun ways to use tapping in your everyday, it's also a vital tool that you can use to lessen anxiety and overwhelm. It's at the top of my list. I think it should be at the top of yours, too. Again, to find your own favorite tapping scripts, download the Tapping Solution app or search them on YouTube. Brad Yates is also a favorite on YouTube

REIKI

Continuing with energetic awareness, the next system I'd like to share with you is Reiki. The word Reiki is made of two Japanese words. Rei, which means "God's Wisdom or the Higher Power," and Ki, which is "life force energy." So Reiki is actually "spiritually guided life force energy." When a person is attuned to Reiki, they can connect with the energy and infuse it into another person by holding their hands over specific parts of the body, starting at the head and ending at the feet.

There are three levels of Reiki: levels I, II, and III. Levels I and II are generally people using it on themselves and for friends and family. Level III Reiki masters generally practice it professionally.

I am Level 1. (I can't progress to Level II because classes have been cancelled due to the pandemic.)

So why is Reiki so special and why am I telling you about it?

Reiki is a tool that is spiritual in its nature and is definitely a part of personal growth, and if you're open to receiving this healing, I fully believe that you will find yourself in a space where you can expand. Beautifully explained by reiki.org:

"Reiki is a Japanese technique for stress reduction and relaxation that also promotes healing. It is administered by 'laying on hands' and is based on the idea that an unseen 'life force energy' flows through us and is what causes us to be alive. If one's 'life force energy' is low, then we are more likely to get sick or feel stress, and if it is high, we are more capable of being happy and healthy."

Most mothers have three or four decades worth of memories and experiences. Some of us have childhood traumas. Even if those traumas don't need months of therapy to heal, the traumas still sit in our energetic bodies. We all have experiences that happened to us in youth, in college, at work, and through our interactions with our friends and society. We are complex, complicated creatures with a compounding of experiences that are sitting in our energy. Those negative energies block us from truly experiencing joy and happiness. Saying this, understanding this, doesn't mean that we have done something wrong. It means that we are human. But we also have an opportunity to remove these traumas and blocks to live the lives that we want to live—the lives that we deserve to live.

Reiki is a modality that is excellent for anything from healing these old traumas, relieving stress, healing from physical sickness, or healing from mental health problems whether long or short term.

To try Reiki, you need to find a Reiki master. If you want to practice some fun Law of Attraction, use it to find your master. A few years ago, I was finally ready to give Reiki a go. I Googled Reiki in my area. I had a difficult time finding someone, and when I finally did, she didn't return my call. My old lack mindset would have interpreted this with, "No one ever wants to connect with me. I guess I'm not supposed to get Reiki." But instead, with my abundant mindset, I saw it as a sign that this woman simply wasn't who I was supposed to work with. So, I put out into the Universe that I was ready for Reiki.

A couple weeks later, I got a message from a woman on Instagram. She was local, and I had seen her around, but we never connected. Her beautiful message was along the lines of, "I love everything you share and want to be friends with you! Can we meet for coffee?"

It was the most unexpected, beautifully extroverted message I had ever received. I happily met with her, and we found ourselves immediately knee deep in spiritual life conversations. The time flew by. As we left our coffee to get back to mom life, she called over to me and said, "I have a Reiki girl I think you'd love." A few weeks later, I experienced Reiki for the very first time, and it was such a beautiful, healing experience that I became hooked.

In Layers One through Three of this book, if applied, you are bound to experience motherhood with a smile and what feels like control and joy. I don't question it. I see it happen with every woman who works with me. But Layer Four? This is about expanding. This is peeling back even more layers and healing even more of us. With techniques like Reiki, it will catapult you into even more healing and having an innate and grounded sense of joy and freedom, no longer held down by the shackles of societal expectations, stress, anxiety, or overwhelm. It's like learning to fly.

ORACLE CARDS

Being raised Catholic, I was always scared to delve into any of this spiritual/woo-woo stuff, especially cards. We are raised to believe that it's not acceptable to know the future and to believe in things like psychics. In my personal growth and accepting who I am, I have found a lot of comfort in understanding how to hold space for both my Catholic upbringing and my spirituality. This is a heavy topic for many people, but the more you come into who you are, the more intuitively you will find your balance and comfort to mix these two things if both are a part of your life. Remember: Those who matter don't mind, and those who mind don't matter. Now, back to oracle cards.

It's very important to understand that oracle cards are not tarot cards. Tarot cards are designed to look into the future, in a way, and to help guide the reader to offer insight into what's ahead. While oracle cards can look very similar to tarot cards, they aren't so much telling you the future, but offering a piece of guidance for the current moment or possibly a future choice. To me, they are like a friend's great advice. Tarot cards are designed in a very specific order, whereas oracle cards are much more loose to the interpretation of the creator and can be used more freely by the owner of the deck.

I was first introduced to oracle cards in the early stages of my anxiety. Things like this have always piqued my interest. My childhood room was adorned with dream dictionaries, astrological books, and pictures of stars and moons. The fact that I'm doused in oils, wear crystals, and have cards in one hand and sage in the other should surprise no one. And yes, my rosary beads lie next to my crystals, but I digress.

My first deck of oracle cards became something of a best friend. Every morning, I would pull a card as a part of my routine. I would allow this card to guide my thoughts for the day, almost as if it was a mantra. If a card said that I was aligned and doing great things, it really shifted my mood for that day to be high vibe. If a card told me it was time to rest, that was the permission I needed to take a nap. If a card warned me to think deeply about work commitments, I was very intentional and thoughtful about any inquiries that came in that day.

At the time, my kids were very young, and I woke up like every other mom—in a fog and a haze, swinging my arms around just trying to find my way. Using these cards each morning gave me some direction—something to think about other than snacks and sippy cups. Without question, my oracle cards connect me to my inner self and my inner knowing. This is the big takeaway with cards.

I love using oracles cards for daily direction and to bond my connection with my intuition. On Instagram, I have a daily card drawing. (Check it out on my page @erinjoyceco.) I also love adding oracle card drawings into my closed Facebook Group, Same Boat Huddle. You can search the group on Facebook and request to join

Oracle cards aren't about controlling your environment or seeing what is happening *to* you. It's about guiding you to become more connected to the inner knowing that you have had inside you all along. They help you tap into that intuition and voice that is always there, but quiets down and gets lost in the midst of the chaos. If you're feeling lost in the day or decision, or if you don't know how to shift out of your current thoughts, pulling a card is a wonderful tool to give your thoughts and heart some direction, clarity, and validation. Plus, they're just super fun.

When choosing your first deck, follow your intuition. Don't get too much into your head about which is best for you. Just pick the deck that keeps calling your name and grab it. Many people prefer to find their first deck in person; they want to hold the deck to really feel it and see what they're more drawn to. I personally hit up good old Amazon. However, my intuition is quite strong, or my reading of it I should say, because we all have strong intuition, so I felt comfortable getting mine from there. My very first deck was *Wisdom of the Oracle* by Collette Baron-Reid, and it's still one of my favorite decks and one I recommend to many of my clients.

Today, I have at least a dozen decks. I like them all.

If you're not quite ready to delve into oracle cards, but you're intrigued, instead try mantra cards. Gabrielle Bernstein has a few decks with beautifully crafted quotes and mantras. These would be a perfect gateway into using a card ritual as a tool to help you shift your mindset, and offer clarity and direction in your daily life.

CRYSTALS

The final area I'll cover with you is crystals. I remember as a little girl, living in an area where there are caves and mines and mountains, it was common to walk into a gift shop and find stones. I was always attracted to them, arrowheads and amethysts in particular. Holding a crystal always made me feel grounded and safe.

Along with my oracle cards, I had a strong fascination with crystals. I began to hoard crystals very early on in my personal growth journey. They are pretty, but they are so much more. Crystal healing can be a bit daunting and slightly overwhelming. It's delving into a new world of healing, so take it slow and move at your own pace. I recommend this book—*Crystals for Beginners: The Guide to Get Started with the Healing Power of Crystals* by Karen Frazier if you are interested in learning more.

It's no wonder I always felt so grounded holding crystals; crystals are from the earth, and they each hold a different vibrational pattern. When crystals are used in healing, we use them with intentions, and we calibrate with these vibrations. Basically what this means, pulling in our new understanding of vibrational frequency, is that each crystal holds its own specific vibration. When you use crystals in your spiritual intentions, your vibration begins to meet the vibration of the crystal.

Obviously, me being a research nerd, I like to find the science to back this up. One of the first pieces of scientific evidence relating to the power of crystals is the work done by IBM scientist Marcel Vogel. He set up research to watch crystals grow under a microscope and noticed that their shape took the form of whatever he was thinking about. He hypothesized that these vibrations were the result of the constant assembling and disassembling of bonds between molecules. By testing the metaphysical power of quartz crystal, he proved that rocks could store thoughts similar to how tapes use magnetic energy to record sound. This research, to me, is also huge validation in the power of positive self-talk and an abundant mindset. It all fits together like a puzzle, doesn't it? To learn more about Marcel Vogel and his studies, head to marcelvogellegacy.com.

I recommend getting started with crystals by visiting a new age shop or Google "which crystals to get started with." Usually, rose quartz is a good starting crystal, but get one or two that really speak to you and that you're attracted to, similar to finding your oracle card deck. Heading back into the chakra section of the book, you can learn what crystals are associated with the different chakras and possibly even choose a crystal based on how you assess the energy in your body.

If following along with understanding the vibrations of the crystals or associating them with chakras feels too big or overwhelming, use your crystals as a tangible reminder. Often, I love to carry tourmaline with me when I shoot weddings. Vibrationally, tourmaline is known for protecting your energy and keeping you grounded. However, simply reaching into my pocket and feeling the stone is the tangible reminder I need to breathe in that moment and to ground myself. It's like a good luck charm, or a little friend. Every time you touch or see a crystal, it can serve as a subtle reminder to connect back with your intention.

Expanding in your energy, within your mind and body, is a journey that I hope you find yourself on at some point in your motherhood path, or simply your life in general. As I explained, it's not necessary, but I hope that after you read through the tip of the iceberg that is these few tools, you're convinced of the power that lies within you. So many tools and techniques can assist you in tapping into your own inner power and expanding that inner power into something magnificent. Enjoy the ride, and always remember that even if you're learning and growing in Layer Four, be sure to check back in with your other layers so that you are still addressing those areas. In other words, don't get arrogant in your growth. It's okay if you find yourself in a space of big growth and then need to circle back and spend time focusing on your health again. We are constantly evolving on every layer, and this is a part of our experience. When we embrace it, magic happens, even in the painful parts.

Our energy is always moving. One center can be open and flowing at one part of the day, and the next, it could be out of balance. This is how the layers work. We are constantly moving through all four of them, or maybe just the three of them. With our new tools and awareness, we will be guided to the areas we need to spend more time and attention on in order to create our best selves. Through these concepts, we can take back motherhood. Through these concepts, we can embrace the femininity in being a woman, bearing and raising children, but also finding our strength through balancing masculine energy. Through these concepts, we can be decisive and confident, understand and acknowledge exactly what our soul is craving, and understand how to make it happen.

LAYER FOUR
SUMMARY AND TAKEAWAYS

- Vibrational frequencies are the energy that runs through us, and our energy attracts similar energy.

- An easy way to raise frequency is through moving or dancing.

- The Law of Attraction is a Universal Law that explains how we can manifest anything in our lives with the power of thought. What we think is what we get.

- The Law of Attraction is connected closely to vibrational frequencies.

- I have coined the four steps in manifesting with the Law of Attraction: visualize, put it out there, think abundantly, and then surrender.

- EFT tapping is Emotional Freedom Technique, which uses tapping on specific meridian points while focusing on a trauma or negative emotion to rid anxiety.

- EFT tapping helps rewire the negative emotion or trauma stored in the amygdala, eventually rewiring the need for the fight-or-flight response to be triggered.

- Reiki is an energetic healing modality that can also help release blocks from energy.

- Oracle cards are a great way to help connect with your intuition, daily direction, or mantras.

- Oracle cards are more open to interpretation and use than tarot cards.

- Crystals also hold specific vibrations and can be used to help set and maintain intentions.

- Marcel Vogel found that crystals could change their forms in connection to what he was thinking about.

THE FINAL CHAPTER

AS THIS BOOK COMES TO ITS FINAL CHAPTER, I sit and ask my heart what it is that I really want you to take away. In a sentence? Motherhood is grossly underrated in its beauty, worth, and hardship, and your own experience in motherhood is rightfully yours and no one else's. You are fully permitted to feel every emotion in the spectrum as you navigate this part of your life. When you feel heavy shadows, hold on to knowing that there are no shadows without light. When you feel happy and joyful moments, hold on to knowing that there is no light without shadow. Embrace the heavy emotions in their entirety and in their own right, knowing that these emotions can't touch the big and joyous emotions and that they can absolutely co-exist.

You are no longer the woman you used to be before having children. In my constant steps forward, I have found that motherhood is full of grief, but grief isn't a bad thing. Grief is never absent of joy or transformation—a rebirth. We are never, ever the same person once we have grieved a loss. In motherhood, we must grieve the woman we used to be and not wish to be her again. You are wishing away the most glorious transformation you could ever have as a woman; you are a mother. You are a remarkable, feminine creature who holds power in the most divine way. The transformation is so big that you may want to go back to who you were, but please let her go. Please don't sit in a space of believing that you have lost yourself. You haven't, my beautiful soul. *You are not lost.* A caterpillar emerges into an entirely different being. If that butterfly sits still looking for her old self, she will miss the beauty of her wings. Fly, my darling. You are not lost.

Nearly 15 years ago, when I met my husband, I never anticipated that more than eight years later, I'd go from a happy, put together, anally organized, punctual woman into a woman who lost all organization, and was dropping balls and falling to the floor crying almost every single day. I didn't see it coming because there is no warning. Anxiety and overwhelm are not things you can see coming and prepare for. After the days slowly and achingly begin to mix together to create a week and then a month and then a year, in that hindsight we see how much we've changed—both for the better and the worse. We can find ourselves in a dark place with the feeling of being blindsided, but we may recognize that we had been slowly creeping into that part of ourselves over a stretch of time. Likewise, as we work on our own growth, remember, too, that your growth isn't going to happen overnight. You may not even see much of a change until after several months or even a year has passed. But it takes those still, thoughtful and intentional decisions to show up for yourself every day. And by showing up, I don't mean hustling. I don't mean for you to do all of the self-care needs and all of the personal growth things. Some days, showing up is going to mean not answering emails, skipping the laundry, and taking a nap. Sometimes it's going to mean honoring the season you need to sit in your grief and stillness so that you can be transformed. This is what it means to show up.

As you move through your journey, as you experience growth, momentum, and expansion, be in this exact moment because you will find your next challenge, and each challenge is another growth opportunity. So often, women ask me, "How do you keep going when you've had a setback?" Whether it's something as simple as having a kid get sick and disrupt your routine or something more profound, like a divorce or a new presentation of anxiety, it's not a setback. Ever. And this is all about mindset. When women are finding themselves losing momentum and falling into old habits and patterns, it not a setback, it's a choice. All of our experiences in life are just that; they are experiences. We *choose* how to respond to each of these experiences. And this, my beautiful friend, is the essence in continuing to grow. Know though, that this sentence is not to feed the connection in your brain that reads this as "hustle and push." This isn't about being perfect. It's not about living your life in a constant highlight reel. If we are not experiencing discomfort, we are not experiencing growth. Embrace the discomfort and know that there will be moments of challenge and labor pains as you expand into the next version of yourself. Remember to hold onto the abundant mindset, and it will allow you to find gratitude in all of your life's journeys and challenges. Approach every life experience with all of the tools shared in this book, and you will be guided through them like a dance.

This book isn't the secret to living the perfect life as a mother; it's living a real and honest life as a mother. It's learning to give yourself permission to experience the lows, but also the highs. It's learning where to take control and where to relinquish it. It's learning to unveil motherhood from the facade that it lived behind by revealing the truths, by stripping it down to see the rawness that fills motherhood and gives it life. The only way to truly experience motherhood in all of its depths and beauty is to *feel all of it*. We must embrace the dualities to experience all of it in its entire magnitude. So many of us have found ourselves closing our eyes in the darkness and refusing to see the bright light that fills the space behind us. It's always there, and you deserve to turn around and face it, letting the shadows fall behind you. Our experiences in life are all about our perspective and choice. We need to rise up from the societal myths of motherhood— that the only way to survive is through caffeine, wine, and messy buns. We need to give ourselves permission to be perfectly imperfect in our own right and not in comparison to the mom next door.

Being a mother is one of the most profound roles a woman can have. Motherhood is hard. It painfully, relentlessly opens wounds. But when we turn our backs to the shadows and face the light, there is the opportunity to experience motherhood in a way of empowerment and beauty. It's accepting ourselves as flawed humans and as powerful women.

A heartbeat, when shown on an EKG, is full of ups and downs, some high and some low. It's because we are living. We are alive. If that line is flat, we are dead. Don't wish for a flat line. Moving through the messy middle and feeling the intensity of each moment in life, whether it be defined as good or bad, is what makes us feel alive.

"You know it can get hard sometimes. It is the only thing that makes us feel alive." —Ed Sheeran

JOURNAL PROMPTS FOR SCHEDULING AND REFLECTION

USE THESE QUESTIONS HOWEVER YOU'D LIKE. Some could be during your daily check-in, your weekly planning, or your monthly planning. Answering these questions regularly and consistently will offer insight, clarity, and accountability.

The things I did today:

What went well:

What didn't feel good:

How I felt emotionally:

How I felt mentally:

How I felt physically:

Where am I in my cycle?

What phase is the moon?

Did I eat well?

Did I take my vitamins?

Did I drink enough water?

On a scale of 1-10 my anxiety was: _____ Why?

On a scale of 1-10 my overwhelm was: _____ Why?

One thing I'm grateful for:

What my child taught me today:

Tomorrow/this week/month I want to feel:

Tomorrow/this week/month I'm committed to:

In motherhood, I want to feel:

One thing I can do tomorrow/this week/month to bring this feeling is:

ACKNOWLEDGMENTS

FOR MY ENTIRE LIFE, SOME PART OF ME KNEW that I'd want to write a book someday, but I never imagined that I would have actually found the courage to follow through with it. And a huge reason I was able to was because of the people in my life and in my corner.

Dustin, thank you for always believing in me, especially when I have trouble believing in myself. Thank you for always being my number one cheerleader and loving me the way you do. Doing life with you is my very favorite thing. I love you so much.

To my beautiful baby girl, Hannah. You changed my life the moment I found out I was pregnant with you. You are growing into the most amazing young lady, showing me every single day what it looks like to be happy, social, and easy-going and seeing the bright side in everything. You are unapologetically you, and you teach me to do the same. You inspire me, every single day, in how you face the world. I thank God for you and everything you teach me. You will move mountains.

My cute John Paul. You saved me. God knew I needed you and your soul. You are a boy with the most incredible sense of life and its meaning along with a remarkable sense of humor. I've never in my entire life expected that one person could teach me as much as you have in six years. I can only imagine what else I will learn. Keep being you; you're changing the world.

Mom and John, thank you for being amazing role models. Mom, for being the most beautiful example and advocate for motherhood and instilling in me the quiet power and strength that motherhood carries. John, for showing me what it looks like for a man to love a woman and allowing me to believe that I deserved the same. For both of you raising me in a home with accountability, morals, and love, thank you.

To my incredible in-laws, John and Brenda, you helped pick me up countless times, showing up at a moment's notice when I needed you. Whether I physically couldn't care for the kids one day, watching the kids during all of my photo shoots, running errands, and being relentlessly loyal. Thank you.

Memom, for sending the cardinals every single time I needed one. Thank you. I love you and I miss you constantly, but you show me every day that you're here.

Shannon, you've been my best friend since forever, and the fact that you were with me on that fateful day was no coincidence. Thank you for being a calm in one of my hardest moments, for giving me permission to turn around and know that I'd be okay. I love you, Mama.

To my mama tribe, Nikki, Anna, and Antonelle, you breathe life, love, and laughter in my heart constantly. Thank you for being women who go deep with me. Nikki, for the random day you connected me with Momosa Publishing, this book's process started because of you. I love you, ladies.

Kristen, if there was ever such a thing as a soul sister, you are it.

You started as my mentor and over the years have become one of the deepest, soulful, and fulfilling friendships I've ever had. Thank you for always believing in me, helping me stand when I couldn't, and sharing life with me. You fill my cup, and I appreciate you more than I could ever say.

To my sweet friend Melissa, you are the most eclectic, funny, authentic, creative, and caring person I've ever not met in my entire life, yet you are one of my dearest friends. And we will meet in person one day really soon. Thank you for your regular check-ins, your support, your love, and sharing life with me.

Heather Chauvin, your podcast was in my ear daily. I took a huge big leap of faith working with you, and you showed me that I can fly. You continue to be one of the most amazing mentors I've ever had, and I'm constantly grateful to know you and have you as one of the women in my corner.

To my therapist, Kim, you welcomed me into your office when I was at my lowest point. Every week, you compassionately asked me the tough questions to help me change my thinking, validated every-thing I was feeling, and taught me to accept and heal myself. Thank you for your patience and concern, helping me remember the strength and courage I've always had.

To my Same Boat Huddle ladies and women who have been through my programs, you all play such a huge part in who I am—more than I think I could ever explain. Thank you for always ground-ing me, accepting me, letting me into your lives, and constantly displaying some of the most vulnerable courage I could ever see in a group of women. You're my heroes.

Of course, everyone at Momosa Publishing, especially Jennifer, you have exceeded any expectation I could have ever had in a publisher. You are the kindest, most encouraging woman, and I couldn't have asked for a better fit. Thank you for your positivity, support, and for always believing in me. Thank you for your phenomenal team, for their talent, creativity, and time. I appreciate all of you so much.

Kristie, the most fabulous graphic designer and cover designer, thank you for your creative mind, for understanding me, and bringing my vague ideas to life, always. I appreciate you so very much.

And lastly, to the women who unknowingly supported me every single day when I was in the throws of my deepest anxiety: Gabrielle Bernstein, Brené Brown, and Oprah Winfrey. You may never know it, but you held the rope for me in my slow climb.

ABOUT THE AUTHOR

ERIN JOYCE MILLER is a native to Pennsylvania, starting in Montgomery County, a suburb of Philadelphia and then moving to Doylestown, PA when she was 8 years old where she remained until she went off to college. She grew up in a Bucks County neighborhood with her mom, step-dad John, and three brothers, Michael, Sean and Paul.

For as far back as she can remember, she was a child who was obsessively intrigued with people, their thinking and processing of life events. Perhaps it was the result of being a child of divorce and growing up in a blended family, or maybe it's just who she's always been. Along with this intrigue, she was always writing whether it was in a journal or a short story on her dad's type writer and always had a camera in hand. She was a creative from the very beginning.

After high school, she went off to college at West Virginia University where she earned her BA in Psychology with a dual minor in Communications and Spanish. Upon graduation she obtained a position as a case manager for individuals with intellectual disabilities. While working full-time, she earned her Master's Degree in Counseling Psychology from Holy Family University with a dual concentration in elementary and secondary education. Upon receiving her Master's Degree in 2010, she obtained her position as a school counselor in Upper Bucks County.

Erin started dating Dustin in 2006 and married in 2009. They bought their first home in 2007 in Bethlehem, PA and then moved to Emmaus in 2011. Currently, they reside in Allentown, PA with their 7 year old daughter Hannah, 6 year old son John Paul, their 4 year old Red and White Irish Setter, Ronan, and 12 year old Siamese cat, Grayson.

In 2013, after having their daughter, Hannah, Erin resigned from her school counseling position to be home with their daughter. At this time is when her photography business, Erin Joyce Photography, organically grew, becoming a published photographer specializing in weddings and in home newborn lifestyle/documentary work. Whilst continuing her photography business, in 2018, Erin started her Facebook community, Same Boat Huddle, where she offers regular trainings and a community of support for other mothers who are dealing with anxiety and overwhelm. In 2018, she also birthed her podcast, Same Boat Huddle, where she focuses on sharing her real life thoughts, ideas, tools and interviews to help moms find more clarity and empowerment to live the life they crave. In 2018, she began offering mentoring services to work with women one on one who were ready to take the big courageous steps to change their lives and step away from the anxiety and overwhelm that entrapped them. In 2019,

Erin rebranded her business to Erin Joyce Co., the umbrella for both her mentoring and photography services and now being an author. She continues to build her mentoring business and is excited to see what the future holds.

When Erin isn't building her business, she's taking pictures of her family, spending as much time as possible with them at their lake house in the Finger Lakes, walking Ronan around their neighborhood or reading a book under a really warm blanket. She is a true lover of life, even in the times where feelings feel hard, and truly believes that every single person on this planet deserves to love life just the same. She has made it her life's work to help spread this light and guide others' on their journey.